THE CITY CHURCHES OF
SIR CHRISTOPHER WREN

St Antholin Budge Row, demolished 1874. Drawn by W. Niven, 1873.

The City Churches of Sir Christopher Wren

PAUL JEFFERY

hambledon
continuum

Continuum UK,
The Tower Building,
11 York Road,
London SE1 7NX

Continuum USA,
80 Maiden Lane,
Suite 704,
New York,
NY 10038

www.continuumbooks.com

First published 1996 in hardback, ISBN 1 8528 5142 2
This edition published in paperback in 2007, ISBN 1 8473 5014 9

British Library Cataloguing-in-Publication Data
A catalogue record for this book is available from the British Library.

Typeset by Carnegie Book Production, Lancaster
Printed and bound by MPG Books Ltd, Cornwall, Great Britain

Contents

PART II
A Gazetteer of Wren's Churches

Illustrations

Illustration Acknowledgements

The author and the publisher are grateful to the following for permission to reproduce illustrations:

All Souls College, Oxford: 10, 11, 16, 19, 21, 22, 36, 47, 49
Ashmolean Museum, Oxford: 1
Bank of England: 99
City of Westminster Archive: 37
Conway Library, Courtauld Institute of Art: 12, 13, 26, 34, 45, 138
Guildhall Library, Corporation of London: 2, 3, 4, 5, 6, 7, 8, 9, 50, 69, 154
A. F. Kersting: 96, 181
National Monuments Record: 18, 43, 44, 51, 52, 53, 54, 55, 56, 57, 58, 59, 60, 62, 74, 76, 77, 79, 82, 84, 86, 101, 112, 114, 117, 120, 122, 128, 130, 133, 134, 136, 140, 142, 151, 156, 164, 173, 174, 176, 178, 183, 185, 187
Pepys Library, Magdalene College, Cambridge: 14, 15
Public Record Office: 32
Richard Lea and English Heritage: 29, 142
Sir John Soane's Museum: 39, 40
Warburg Institute: 48

Acknowledgements

Material needed for the study of the rebuilding of the parish churches of the City of London following the Great Fire of London in 1666 is scattered among many institutions, public and private. I owe a great debt to their librarians and archivists, who have so willingly allowed me to consult their books, files, documents, drawings and other material. Whether as occasional enquirer, repeated visitor or habitual reader, these institutions have made me welcome and helped me enormously to find and use the original material. To their staff I give my warmest thanks.

I am grateful to the Rector and Churchwardens of St Bride Fleet Street, for permission to reproduce Hugh Chesterman's lines on Sir Christopher Wren, first published in *Punch* in 1928. This version was transcribed by J. Kirkland Robertson. Also to Richard Lea and English Heritage for permission to reproduce reconstructions of St Mary-at-Hill. The author and the publisher are grateful to the Marc Fitch Foundation for a grant towards the cost of the illustrations.

On a personal level I extend my thanks to Simon Bradley, Robert Crayford, Jessica Hodge, Stephen Humphrey and John Newman, who read the manuscript or commented on the material. Nor do I forget the many discussions that I have had a large number of other workers in this field. To them I record my thanks for sharing their thoughts and their work with me. Last, but by no means least, I record my debt to my wife, Sally, who has helped me enormously, by drawing attention to my extravagances and pouring cold water on my flights of fancy.

Introduction

The City of London is not short of visitors; St Paul's Cathedral and the Tower of London ensure that. Few of these visitors, however, give more than a cursory glance at its parish churches. Admittedly there is little to encourage them. Except for their steeples they are not particularly conspicuous, most are shut on Saturdays and some seem permanently closed. Excluding St Paul's Cathedral, there are now thirty-nine Anglican churches within and without the walls in the City of London, most but not all used for worship according to the Anglican rite. At the time of writing, most (but not all) are still in use as parish churches. Once there were over a hundred parish churches in London and its immediate precincts; of these eighty-six were destroyed in the Great Fire of 1666. This book is concerned with the fifty or so that replaced them, those with which the name of Sir Christopher Wren is associated. Of these, over twenty still survive. They may not all be masterpieces, but they are all well worth a visit.

Studies of the City churches began a long time before the Great Fire with John Stow's pioneering compilation, *A Survey of London* (1598; 2nd edn 1603). His work, revised and extended by a series of historians, including John Strype (1720), John Mottley ('Robert Seymour', 1734–35), William Maitland (1739) and others, provides much of our knowledge of the early history of the parish churches of London. Descriptions of the Wren churches by Hatton (1708), Malcolm (1803–8) and Godwin and Britton (1838–39) give a great deal of information, including much that would otherwise be unknown, concerning those churches demolished in the eighteenth and nineteenth centuries. W. Niven (1887) and George H. Birch (1896) continued the series of useful texts describing the churches and their fittings. In the twentieth century there have been many more. Credit is due, in particular, to the Royal Commission on Historical Monuments for meticulously recording the architecture and fittings of the City churches, as they existed in 1929.

Although neglected for many years, the churches attributed to Sir Christopher Wren have, since the mid nineteenth century, been repeatedly measured, drawn, photographed and described. Little attention has, however, so far been paid to exploring how they came to be designed and built after the Fire of 1666. For nearly 300 years these parish churches of the City have been accepted as the work of Sir Christopher Wren. Until the late twentieth century there has been no thought that others may deserve some of the credit for the unusual designs (as St Benet Fink), and some of the blame for jerry-building (as St Michael Bassishaw) or for crazy designs (St Dionis Backchurch, where the plan is devoid of right angles). Recognising that Wren could not personally have alone designed over fifty churches, what exactly did he do? Who else contributed, and what did they do? It is with these questions that this book is particularly concerned. But that is not all. Nikolaus Pevsner, writing in 1945 in *The Leaves of Southwell*, noted that: 'Personalities and genius are what have interested the West for the last hundred and fifty years more than anything else in the consideration of works of art.' This is no longer true: architectural history is nowadays far less dominated by the study of individuals, creative though they may have been. We now need to know more of the circumstances surrounding the creations. The questions 'what was done?' and 'who did it?' must be supplemented with 'how and in what manner was it performed?' and 'why in that particular way?' In the rebuilding of the parish churches it is now necessary to consider the extent and nature of the contributions of the commissioners, surveyors, rectors, churchwardens and others, and the importance of political, financial and social factors in the London of the time, factors which have been little studied and largely ignored.

The naming of the churches is by no means free from problems. Over the centuries all have been referred to by a variety of synonyms. St Mary-le-Bow, for example, has been known also as St Mary de Archis, St Mary of the Arches, St Mary de Arch, St Mary atte Bowe, Our Lady of the Arches and Our Lady of the Bow, with the earliest mention of the church as Ecclesia Sancta Mariae quae dicitur ad Arcus in 1091. Most of these names represent long-forgotten usage and we have no difficulty in settling on the familiar name, St Mary-le-Bow. With other churches the decisions are not so easily reached, particularly those for which two or more designations are still in common use. These include St Antholin Budge Row (St Antholin Watling Street), St Swithin London Stone (St Swithin Cannon Street) and St Vedast Foster Lane (St Vedast-alias-Foster). The names given in the London Diocesan Year Book are not necessarily the most familiar, nor is familiarity necessarily the best or most appropriate reason for the choice – one is tempted to ask 'familiar to whom?'. My solution has been governed by the need to ensure that the names do not pose problems for the reader. The need to be consistent is self-evident. Another problem is the vexed question of whether or not the saint's name in the dedication should be separated by a comma from the location or other identifier used with it. The present usage is inconsistent and illogical: if St Michael, Queenhithe why St James Garlickhithe? This arbitrary usage can be confusing, especially in listings of churches with yet more commas separating each. Regretfully I have decided, even where commas are generally used in names, to omit them entirely. Purists may not forgive me, but I am sure most readers will.

Abbreviations

ASC	All Souls College, Oxford
BL	British Library
Bute	Drawings of the Wren churches formerly in the collection of the Marquess of Bute
CLRO	City of London Record Office
Colvin, *Dictionary*	H. M. Colvin, *A Biographical Dictionary of British Architects, 1600–1840* (3rd edn, New Haven and London, 1995)
CWA	City of Westminster Archive
DNB	*Dictionary of National Biography*
GL	Guildhall Library
GLRO	Greater London Record Office
K. Top.	King's Topographic Collection, British Library
LPL	Lambeth Palace Library
MS	Manuscript
PRO	Public Record Office
RCHM	Royal Commission on the Historical Monuments of England
RIBA	Royal Institute of British Architects
SL	*Survey of London*
VCH	*Victoria County History of England*
WS	Wren Society

PART I

Wren and the Churches

Clever men like Christopher Wren
Only occur just now and then.
No one expects in perpetuity
Architects of his ingenuity;
No, never a cleverer dipped his pen
Than clever Sir Christopher – Christopher Wren.
With his chaste designs on classical lines
His elegant curves and neat inclines
For all day long he'd measure and limn
Till the ink gave out or the light grew dim;
      And if a plan
Seemed rather Baroque or 'Queen Anne'
      (As plans well may)
He'd take a look at his pattern book
And do it again in a different way.
Every day of the week was filled
With a church to mend or a church to build,
And never an hour went by but when
London needed Sir Christopher Wren.

'Bride's in Fleet Street lacks a spire',
'Mary le Bow a nave and choir',
'Please to send the plans complete
For a new St Stephen's Coleman Street';
'Pewterer's Hall is far too tall,
Kindly lower the N. W. wall.'
'Salisbury Square – decidedly bare
Can you put one of your churches there?'
'Dome of St Paul's is not yet done,
Dean's been waiting since half past one.'
London calling from ten to ten,
London calling Sir Christopher Wren.

Hugh Chesterman

I

Sir Christopher Wren

The Dean, Residentiaries, Archdeacons and Prebendaries remit their fees . . .'
So begins the cathedral bill for the funeral of Sir Christopher Wren.[1] The minor
canons, lay vicars and officers of the church, in addition to receiving their fees,
partook of eight quarts of red and three quarts of white port in celebration of
the life of the man who had raised above them what can well be described as
the most magnificent church ever to be erected in England to a comprehensive
plan in a single building campaign. In a pink shroud and a double coffin of elm
and lead, his mortal remains were laid close to the corner of the building that
had occupied so much of his time and thought for half a century, his resting-place
in the cathedral that he had watched rise to completion from the first stone laid
at this south-east corner.[2]

Wren was born in the little village of East Knoyle, to the west of Salisbury
in the county of Wiltshire, on 20 October 1632.[3] His father, also Christopher
Wren, was then Rector of East Knoyle. He later became Dean of Windsor as
his brother, Matthew Wren, had been before him. Matthew was appointed
Bishop of Hereford before translation to Norwich and then Ely. It is thus not
surprising that the young Christopher Wren was brought up in the tradition of
the mainstream, if somewhat conservative, church in England. He was educated
at Westminster under Dr Busby and spent a few years in London before going
to Wadham College, Oxford, most probably in 1649.

At Oxford the young Wren came under the influence of such eminent scholars
as Robert Boyle, physicist, Charles Scarbrugh, mathematician, Seth Ward,
astronomer and mathematician, John Wilkins, experimenter, and many others
who were later to form the nucleus of the Royal Society. His interests in natural
science, mathematics, physics and astronomy developed rapidly. At this time he
was little concerned with architecture but, even in his early days at Oxford, he
showed interest in models and drawings.

He took his BA in 1651 and MA in 1653, becoming a Fellow of All Souls
College later that year. He remained at Oxford until 1657, when he was
appointed Professor of Astronomy at Gresham College, London, an appointment

FIGURE 1.
Sir Christopher
Wren. Bust by
Edward Pearce,
c. 1673 (*Ashmolean
Museum*)

which was to last until 1661 when he returned to Oxford as Savilian Professor
of Astronomy (Fig. 1).

Wren's interest in architecture, if slow to begin, developed rapidly after 1663,
when he was consulted by the Commission appointed to repair St Paul's
Cathedral after years of neglect. It was also in 1663 that his uncle, then Bishop
of Ely, asked him to design a new chapel for Pembroke College, Cambridge.
It cannot be said that this, his first building, was particularly imaginative, but it
was a competent essay in classical architecture. The chapel was followed by the
design and construction of the Sheldonian Theatre, Oxford, based upon Roman
theatre designs. Such theatres were open to the sky, a feature which would not
suit the English climate, so Wren provided a remarkable roof to a novel design

which attracted much attention at the time. The theatre was followed by new building for Trinity College, Oxford, and by a visit to Paris in 1665. As far as is known, this was the only visit abroad made by Wren in the course of his long career.

In spite of a very limited experience in the design and construction of buildings, Wren was appointed Surveyor-General of the King's Works in succession to Sir John Denham in March 1669, probably at the insistence of Charles II. In addition to the many duties of this post, he found time to serve as Member of Parliament for Plympton in 1685–87 and for Weymouth in 1701–2. He was given his knighthood in November 1673.

In his parish churches, as in all his works, Wren's achievements are noted for their intellectual range and subtlety, coupled with their strength of imagination.[4] He was a scholar who, in all his studies, followed learning for its own sake. He avoided political commitment in the difficult times of the Commonwealth and was circumspect in all matters.

Wren was consulted concerning repairs and changes to St Paul's Cathedral again in 1666. Inspired by what he had seen in Paris, he envisaged crowning the existing crossing of St Paul's with a large dome, which would have been the first such structure to be constructed in London or indeed in England. His ideas for St Paul's were not, however, to materialise: the Great Fire of 1666, sweeping across the greater part of the City, destroyed a major part of the cathedral. First thoughts, that the cathedral could be restored, were rejected and the rest of the building was pulled down to make way for a completely new building. Seldom do such schemes come to fruition without argument and dissension, resulting in changes of both direction and plan. So it was with St Paul's, and it was not until 1675 that the new cathedral was started.

The cathedral has long evoked disagreement. There are those who see it as Wren's most glorious monument; others regard it as a lost opportunity. Whatever one's view, it remains a superb example of human achievement. Although on a smaller scale, the parish churches which are the subject of this book also are impressive. 'Fifty-one parochial churches erected according to the designs and under the care and conduct of Sir Christopher Wren.' In these words his son, Christopher, described his father's work in rebuilding the churches of London after the Great Fire of 1666.[5] So it has been accepted for three hundred years. Many of these churches have gone, others have been altered out of all recognition, but the fame of their author is assured and the exercise of his genius in the building of them fully acknowledged.

With increasing appreciation that one man, single-handed, could not possibly have attended to all the details of this enormous building programme, at the same time as building St Paul's Cathedral, supervising the Royal Works, undertaking numerous private commissions and attending to all the other duties incumbent upon His Majesty's Surveyor General, has come the realisation that others, subordinate to Wren and responsible to him, made significant contributions to the City churches. Wren was the mastermind, but his assistants contributed much to the negotiations, planning and decision-making involved, and to the design and construction of the churches. Wren's assistants were principally Robert Hooke, Edward Woodroffe, John Oliver, Nicholas Hawksmoor and William Dickinson.

This realisation in no way denigrates the role played by Wren nor the extent of his personal achievement. He himself designed some of the parish churches and for the rest it was his Office that managed the undertaking. He personally was responsible for the work of the architects, draughtsmen and surveyors and they responded to his direction. His style of management is not always clear, but its relaxed nature is apparent and his control of both men and money seemingly effortless. His relationships with the King, the Archbishop of Canterbury and the other Commissioners, to say nothing of the very large number of churchwardens and others in eighty-six separate parishes, all demonstrate his understanding and control of the situation. It was his tact, his diplomacy and his application that together ensured the success of the rebuilding programme.

The rebuilding of the City of London's parish churches after the Great Fire is so great a part of Wren's contribution to parish church building that it is easy to overlook those churches that he designed for the city of Westminster: St Clement Danes and St James Piccadilly certainly, St Anne Soho perhaps. Nor can St Andrew Holborn, within the City of London but without the walls, be neglected; rebuilt, like St Clement Danes, not as a result of fire damage but of decrepitude. There were also churches rebuilt by the parishes themselves; seemingly Wren had little to do with these, although the funding for them passed through his hands. Wren and his officers were, in addition, called to remedy the defects in them that later became apparent.

Even excluding the rebuilding of St Paul's Cathedral and the building, rebuilding or design of private chapels, the parish churches represent a distinct and comprehensive body of work by the Surveyor General of the King's Works, undertaken by the command of Parliament for the Church of England. Much of this book is concerned with this work.

2

Christian London: The Medieval Legacy and the Great Fire of 1666

It is not known when Christianity first came to Britain. The execution of St Alban, protomartyr, at Verulamium in the early fourth or possibly third century is an indication that by that time Christian ideas had already spread from the Continent.[1] The Christian element in the population may not have been large, and most of the inhabitants of these islands were probably still pagan. Christianity had infiltrated the Empire but had still to be officially adopted. In the fourth century the church of Christ in Britain, as in the rest of the Empire, became more organised as the spread of Christianity continued to the point, reached by the end of the Romano-British period in the fifth century, when the majority of the population was probably, if only nominally, Christian.[2]

There may have been churches in London in the later part of the Roman period, but none has so far been identified in excavation. The church of St Peter Cornhill stands within the site of a Roman basilica. On the basis of a tablet which in Stow's time was displayed in the building, and which stated that the church had been founded by the (legendary) King Lucius about AD 179, the parish vestry claimed precedence as the oldest in London. Such claims cannot be substantiated but equally cannot be dismissed.[3]

The barbarian invasions of Britain in the fifth and succeeding centuries, by pagan tribes originating from the north German plain,[4] are generally assumed to have put an end not only to much of the Romano-British civilisation but to the Christianity that had by then become established. The collapse of this civilisation and the reversion of England to the paganism that accompanied the Saxon invasion is likely to have included the destruction of many of the churches. This is not, however, a universally accepted view and there remains the possibility that the Christian tradition was uninterrupted in London, or at least interrupted for a much shorter period of time than has usually been thought.[5]

Archaeological investigation at a number of sites has, however, so far failed to uncover evidence for a continuity of Christian worship, or, in this period, of any extensive habitation within the City walls. Excavations further west have indicated that by the seventh century a new pattern of settlement was developing outside the Roman city walls and extending from the west bank of the River Fleet to the area now occupied by Trafalgar Square, sometimes referred to as Ludenwic or the Strand settlement.

The reconversion of England to Christianity, spreading from both Celtic Ireland and from Rome towards the end of the sixth century, eventually and finally put an end to paganism. Pope Gregory the Great, following the success of St Augustine's mission to England in AD 596, intended that the primary see of England should be in London. With this in mind, a new cathedral dedicated to St Paul was begun in the year 604 by Ethelbert, the Christian king of Kent. The building of churches within the City walls may have ensued but, following the pattern observed elsewhere, most of the inhabitants may have worshipped in the cathedral itself. In the mid Saxon period, the seventh to ninth centuries, there is as yet no evidence for the foundation of churches within the City walls. Claims have been made for St Alban Wood Street, but these were not confirmed in excavations on site. The undated early stone building which was revealed could as easily be of tenth or eleventh century date as earlier.[6] Despite extensive search, archaeological finds of this period from within the City are still meagre, suggesting that the area within the walls was largely uninhabited. Without a large enough garrison and an organised authority, the City had become indefensible.

Evidence for a recolonisation of the City does not begin in earnest until the ninth century and the reign of Alfred the Great, when London was once again fortified, this time against the Danes. The Danelaw, across the River Lea, was uncomfortably close. In the late Saxon period, the ninth to eleventh centuries, there is evidence for the existence of a number of churches, including All Hallows-by-the-Tower,[7] All Hallows Lombard Street, St Benet Fink, St Bride Fleet Street and St Mary-le-Bow, but by then there may have been many more for which the evidence has now been lost.

There is no building stone, of quality or otherwise, available close to London, so the houses of the City must originally have been framed largely of wood with infill of Roman brick and tile, or wattle and daub, and have had thatched roofs. Most of the churches are likely also to have been constructed of timber. With the passage of time this was replaced with more permanent materials such as clunch and ragstone, the materials closest to hand, cycled and recycled as the structures were enlarged and rebuilt. Kentish rag, or ragstone, is a sandy limestone or calcareous sandstone from the Lower Greensand geological formation, occurring near Maidstone in Kent. It is very variable in its quality and properties, ranging from hard and weather-resistant to soft and crumbly. The surface of the stone tends to harbour dirt and grime and, in London in particular, is usually black and unattractive. A similar stone, but from the Upper Greensand near Redhill in Surrey, is referred to as Reigate stone or firestone. It too was extensively used in medieval London. It tends to be soft, when first dug from the quarries or mines at the foot of the North Downs, but hardens on exposure. It can be cut and was used extensively for mouldings and carvings but, when used for exterior forms, it soon loses its edge. Stone was also brought from further afield, notably limestones from Caen in Normandy, from Oxfordshire and from Lincolnshire. These, together with worked flint from the chalk downs and bricks made from the extensive clay beds close to the capital, were also recycled.

The churches of the period were mostly small, a pattern which was not unique to London, being mirrored in other parts of England, notably Norwich and York. It seems to have been almost a national pattern, contrasting with the continental practice of the time of fewer but larger churches. It reflects the religious practices of the centuries following the Norman Conquest, the period in which most of the London churches were founded.

The precise origins of these London churches are now obscure. No written reference has been found to the establishment of any in the Saxon or early Norman periods. Archaeological evidence suggests that some of the later churches may have been built as private chapels in the grounds or houses of the more wealthy inhabitants, especially the nobles, bishops and abbots who had town houses. To these chapels of the wealthy can be added the chapels of foreign merchants who, in some cases, brought their favourite dedications with them. To the Flemings, for example, is attributed the origin of St Vedast Foster Lane.[8]

By the end of the thirteenth century the pattern of the parish churches of London had become established in a form that was to persist, more or less intact, for the next 300 years. The writings of Ralph de Diceto, Dean of St Paul's in 1181, and the records of the Taxation of Pope Nicholas IV of 1291, give names for many of the churches of the time.[9] Not all of these are the names by which the churches are now known, but it is not too difficult to identify most of them. The listing is, however, incomplete and does not contain a number that were, presumably, too poor to be taxed. In the 1170s William FitzStephen, a

FIGURE 2. St Martin Outwich, exterior from the north east, 1736. (*Guildhall Library*)

monk of Canterbury, clerk and biographer of St Thomas Becket, noted that London, including its suburbs, then possessed 126 parish churches as well as thirteen greater or conventual churches.[10] The total number may reflect the material wealth and piety of the individuals or guilds who gave and endowed them, but the number of available places within them must always have exceeded the needs of the churchgoing inhabitants – unless they too showed more than average piety in their observances.

Early maps show the parish churches distributed apparently at random both within the walled city and spread in an arc outside the walls. There are, however, certain patterns discernible. The City gates, for example, were all marked by a parish church where the faithful could make a suitable offering and give thanks for a safe journey, or ask for protection in a journey still to come. London Bridge, the entrance to the City from the south, was similarly marked by a chapel on the bridge and by the parish church of St Magnus the Martyr on the north bank. A number of churches were to be found at prominent cross roads or road junctions within the City and most of the churches had a frontage to the streets. A few that now seem to have been tucked away behind houses, such as St Michael Cornhill and All Hallows Lombard Street, were originally separated from the streets only by chapels or churchyards which have long since disappeared. Another feature, no doubt reflecting the pattern of settlement, is that the smaller parishes were those clustered in the central area around St Paul's and the markets of East and West Chepe (Cheapside), where the population was most dense in early times. The largest parishes were those which included open areas outside the City walls.

For more than half a millennium the old romanesque church buildings changed and evolved by alteration, enlargement and rebuilding, with the small boxes of the Saxon and early Norman periods gradually replaced by larger and more magnificent buildings in gothic style.[11] Some idea of their appearance can be gained from old prints of those churches which survived the Great Fire, such as St Martin Outwich (Figs 2 and 3), and by studying the few such churches remaining, particularly St Olave Hart Street.

FIGURE 3. St Martin Outwich, interior looking east, eighteenth century. (*Guildhall Library*)

Although there were a few losses in the late medieval period, notably the friary and other conventual churches which disappeared in the reign of Henry VIII, there were still 106 parish churches in the City and its precincts in 1666. Each of these had its own geographically separate parish, its own organisation and its own officers, who were responsible not only for the maintainance of the fabric of the church but also for what would now be termed local government at its lowest level. Each parish was responsible for scavenging the streets, relieving the poor and maintaining law and order. There was also some measure of care for the sick of the parish and foundling children. Almost all the parishes had churchyards or cemeteries for the interment of their own dead (and corpses from elsewhere at a premium), although some citizens were laid to rest beneath the floors of the churches themselves, a common but unsatisfactory practice, leading to uneven floors and the need for frequent levelling of the pews. There is also more than a suspicion that some churches collapsed as a result of disturbance to foundations caused by such burials. The services organised on a parish basis were thus partly ecclesiastical and partly administrative in the running and regulation of the City. To the Aldermen, the great number of parishes must have been inconvenient at the least. Although by 1666 further proliferation of parishes and parish churches had long ceased, no means existed for reducing the number, with parish pride and vested interest militating against it.

The day to day religious life of the capital was still, at the time of the Fire, far from settled. The controversial reforms of William Laud, introduced when he was Bishop of London, had not been forgotten. The puritanism of the Commonweath had given way to the more relaxed atmosphere of the Restoration, but scarcely six years had passed since the so-called intruders had been ousted from the pulpits of the City. Many clergy with sympathy for Dissenters remained. The accommodation in the Established Church of such men was still under debate, although agreement was to prove elusive. Catholicism, in contrast, was regarded as a bogey.

The Great Fire of 1666

London, like many other cities, has a long history of destructive fires and the Great Fire of 1666, great no doubt in the eyes and minds of those who witnessed it, takes its place with other great fires of earlier periods. Nor was it to be the last of the major fires in the City. In November 1765, for example, a fire in

Bishopsgate Street destroyed a large number of houses and other property in Cornhill, Leadenhall Street, Gracechurch Street and Threadneedle Street, with damage to the church of St Martin Outwich.[12]

The Fire of 1666 broke out in the premises of a man called Farriner or Farynor, the King's baker, of Pudding Lane in the early hours of Sunday, 2 September. Sparks from the burning timber were carried across a narrow lane by the strong east wind, setting light to hay piled in an inn yard. The inn caught fire and from there the flames spread rapidly. Fires in the City were by no means uncommon and at first the blaze was treated somewhat casually. Pepys, roused from his bed, watched it for a while but returned to bed and slept:

> 2nd September. Some of our maids sitting up late last night to get things ready against our feast today, Jane called us up, about 3 in the morning, to tell us of a great fire they saw in the city. So I rose, and slipped on my nightgown and went to the window, and I thought it to be on the back side of Markelane at the furthest; but being unused to such fires as followed, I thought it far enough off, and so went to bed again and to sleep. About 7 rose again to dress myself, and there looked out of the window and saw the fire not so much as it was and further off.

The Lord Mayor, Sir Thomas Bludworth, roused from his bed and on the scene by three o'clock in the morning, did not take it seriously. He is reported by Malcolm to have said 'Pish! a woman might piss it out'.[13] He soon had cause to change his tune. Before long the fire was out of control and there was little he could do but wring his hands in despair. 'Lord', he exclaimed to Pepys, 'what can I do? I am spent: people will not obey me.' History has dealt harshly with Bludworth; more decisive action on his part might have limited the fire to a limited area on the north side of London Bridge, but he had little authority to act and was afraid of overstepping what authority he had.

The hot summer had left London's timber-framed buildings as dry as a proverbial tinder-box; and the flames, fanned by a strong easterly wind, spread rapidly (Fig. 4). The first of the parish churches to burn was St Margaret Fish Street Hill, to be followed on that Sunday by St Magnus the Martyr, St Botolph Billingsgate, St Michael Crooked Lane, St Martin Orgar, St Lawrence Pountney, St Mary Bothaw, All Hallows-the-Less and All Hallows-the-Great.[14]

The fire crept slowly eastward, backing against the wind, while burning debris, scattered in the high wind, set light to buildings in the north and west. By midnight on Monday, 3 September, St George Botolph Lane, St Andrew

FIGURE 4. An imaginative prospect of London in the Great Fire by P. H. Schut, 1666. (*Guildhall Library*)

Hubbard and St Mary-at-Hill to the east had all been burnt, together with churches as far north as St Peter Cornhill, St Benet Fink and St Bartholomew-by-the-Exchange, and to the west as far as St Mary Somerset, St Mary Mounthaw, St Nicholas Cole Abbey, and both St Peter and St Benet Paul's Wharf. The greatest destruction occurred on Tuesday, 4 September, with the loss of St Dunstan and St Margaret Pattens in the east, St Paul's Cathedral on Ludgate Hill (Fig. 5) and more parish churches in the central, western and northern parts of the City. Also on Tuesday the fire reached Pye Corner, recorded in an old epigram to the effect that that 'The Fire of London began in Pudding Lane and ended at Pye Corner!',[15] although in fact it continued to make progress, blazing north of the City wall at Cripplegate for a further twenty-four hours.

There was nothing that the general populace could do except carry their goods away. There was no means of quenching the fire and the houses huddled along the River Thames, containing pitch and tar, oil and wine, were left to burn. The churches were filled with goods in the vain hope that they would be saved. Pepys evacuated his own house and the Navy Office, carrying with him gold to the value of £2350. He reported from his garden 'how horridly the sky looks . . . was enough to put us out of our wits'. He took a boat to Southwark and thence along the river to Westminster, commenting 'a sad sight to see how the river looks – no houses nor church near it'.

By Wednesday, 5 September, the east wind had abated somewhat, and with it the fire lessened, although there was further destruction to the north and west. The greater part of the City of London that lay within the walls and much to the west outside had, by then, been reduced to rubble. Only the north-eastern part of the City escaped. Here and there walls still stood, marking the position of those buildings that had been constructed of brick or stone. These walls too were heavily damaged, with mortar and stone badly calcined. Prominent among these were the churches, still identifiable, whose walls and towers, now roofless and bereft of their steeples, fittings, floors and bells, stood as gaunt reminders that the City had once flourished on a parochial basis. It was from these blackened and spalling ruins that at least some of the churches were to arise, phoenix fashion, with a new elegance and even prouder steeples.

FIGURE 5. The destruction of Ludgate in the Great Fire, with Old St Paul's and St Mary-le-Bow, by an unknown but probably contemporary artist.. (*Guildhall Library*)

Together with the new St Paul's, the new churches gave the City a distinctive skyline that was to last for nearly two and a half centuries.

Meanwhile the City was stunned. The inhabitants who had fled the fire, carrying and carting away what they could, returned to find that in many cases their homes were burnt, their property lost and their livelihoods destroyed.

3

Rebuilding the City:
The Acts of 1667 and 1670

Disastrous though the Great Fire of London undoubtedly was, and stunned as the inhabitants must have been, the City was soon to rise again. According to one account it was rebuilt within four years. This should not be taken too literally, but life in London was resumed remarkably quickly and its function as a working city seems hardly to have stopped. Credit for this goes in no small measure to the Fire Court, established by Act of Parliament.[1] This arm of the judiciary was set up to facilitate the rebuilding and the emphasis given to this is underlined by phrases in its decrees, probably used by the justices themselves in court: 'that the messuage may no longer lie in its own ruins' and 'may no longer remain buried in its own ashes'. The court aided those who were willing and able to rebuild, at the expense of those who were unwilling or unable. It endeavoured to find someone – freeholder, lessor, lessee, assignee, tenant for life or tenant in occupation – who wanted to and could rebuild, but gave preference to the person in occupation before the Fire. In many ways it dispensed rough justice, but it cut through red tape and across private interests where these did not serve the best interests of the City. Without the Fire Court to cancel agreements and substitute others, the flood of litigation would have delayed the rebuilding for decades. As a result, vacant plots were soon claimed and new building began at a furious rate.

The restoration of the parish churches was not, however, the first priority. With the building of new houses came the need to maintain law and order, to provide for the poor and needy, and to get the City government functioning again at all levels. This ensured that the organisation of the City parishes, the vestries which had collapsed as the churchwardens fled from the fire, soon recovered. However, parish incomes, derived mostly from property rents, had virtually vanished and even those parishes with the will to rebuild lacked the resources to do so. Parish records of late 1666, 1667 and to some extent 1668 are meagre in the extreme, and there can have been little for the vestries to discuss and few decisions to record. Moreover, not all the parish officers were prompt in returning. It was not until 1668 that much thought was given to salvaging the lead that had dripped from the burning roofs of the churches; and the solidified globules of bell-metal, recovered from some 200 or more bells, which, together with rusting iron, shattered brick, calcined stone and gaunt walls, were all that remained from the fabric of the churches.

Of the 106 parish churches in the City, eighty-six were either destroyed or damaged beyond repair.[2] Only a very small number were found to be capable of even a temporary repair. In addition to the eighty-six churches, a small number of others close to the limits of the Fire claimed to have suffered damage. How real or how extensive these claims were is difficult to establish, but for these vestries no public funding was available and such repairs as were necessary were undertaken by the parishes themselves.[3] Within the central area the devastation was complete.

Thoughts about the rebuilding of the City, directed especially towards an improvement of the cramped and crowded streets, narrow alley ways and overpopulated tenements, began almost before the embers of the fire were cold. On or about 11 September 1666, Sir Christopher Wren, or Dr Wren as he then was, produced to Charles II a plan of the City incorporating his ideas for improvement based upon a revised street layout (Fig. 6).[4] Emphasis was placed upon communications, with enlargement of the principal thoroughfares and significant improvements to the water front and to the Fleet river, which was to be made navigable as far as Holborn. The streets were to be laid out on a grid pattern, based upon thoroughfares driven in straight lines through the City. The broad quays and the introduction of *ronds points* at main street intersections may owe much to Wren's visit to Paris in 1665. The area burnt by the fire was to have nineteen new churches, replacing the eighty-six which had been destroyed, all to be placed on new and appropriate sites. Wren's plan is insufficiently detailed to reveal much of his intentions for these churches, but his drawing shows that he was in no way bound by pre-Fire ideas concerning church building. Some, certainly, would have been centrally planned. Few would have been on pre-Fire sites. Wren's plan for the City was not adopted. One of the earliest comments on it was from his son, Christopher Wren junior:

> The Practicality of the whole Scheme, without Loss to any Man, or Infringement of any Property, was at that Time demonstrated, and all material objections fully weigh'd and answer'd: the only, and, as it happened, insurmountable Difficulty

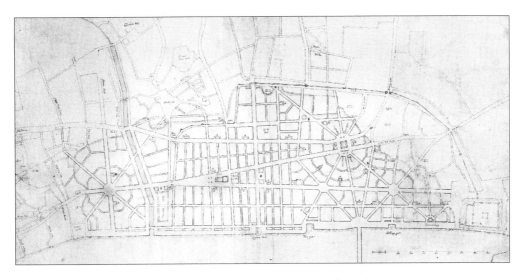

FIGURE 6. Christopher Wren's plan for rebuilding the City of London.
(*All Souls College, Oxford*)

remaining, was the obstinate Averseness of a great Part of the Citizens to alter their . . . old Ground and Foundations; as also the Distrust in many, and Unwillingness to give up their Properties, tho' for a Time only . . . till they might be dispens'd to them again.[5]

No evidence has so far come to light to support the suggestion that the practicality of Wren's scheme was ever seriously demonstrated or argued. Produced in a hurry, it was an idealistic view of how the problems might be tackled, never really considering either the practical difficulties in implementing it or the financial implications of what was being proposed.[6]

Wren was not the only man to be considering what could be done with the City. Two days later a plan was submitted by John Evelyn (Fig. 7),[7] and this was followed by yet more plans by Robert Hooke, Valentine Knight, Richard Newcourt and Peter Mills. Those by Robert Hooke and Peter Mills have not survived.

Evelyn's plan was geometrically more regular than Wren's. His public buildings were to be on prominent sites, many of them along the river front, others on a broad straight street extending from the Strand in the west to a new King Charles Gate in the City wall to the east. He recommended that the parish churches should be reduced in number and 'so placed and interspersed as may have some reference to the adornment of the profile of the city upon all its avenues', with 'modern architecture without and contrivance within, as may

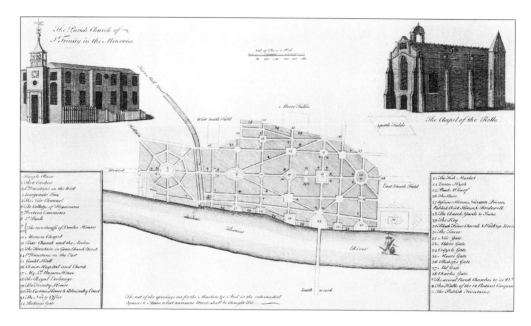

FIGURE 7. John Evelyn's plan for rebuilding the City of London. (*Guildhall Library*)

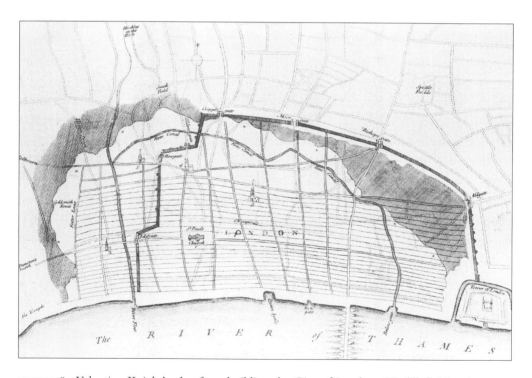

FIGURE 8. Valentine Knight's plan for rebuilding the City of London. (*Guildhall Library*)

best answer their pious designation'.[8] More explicit comment would have been helpful.

Valentine Knight's plan (Fig. 8) also envisaged streets at right angles giving greatly improved communications north and south.[9] His novelty was a canal built through the City linking the Thames at Billingsgate with the Fleet at Holborn. Newcourt's plans, in both the original and the revised forms (Fig. 9),[10] would have swept away almost all of what remained of the City, burnt and unburnt, and substituted a grid of broad streets, each at right angles to its neighbour, separating the residential areas into square blocks, with each block containing at its centre a new parish church and graveyard. Each church was to be 120 or 130 feet in length, including the tower and chancel, and fifty or sixty feet in width. There was to have been an open space in the centre of the City which would have included a new Guildhall not far from its old site, and also a palace for the Lord Mayor in his year of office. The existing London

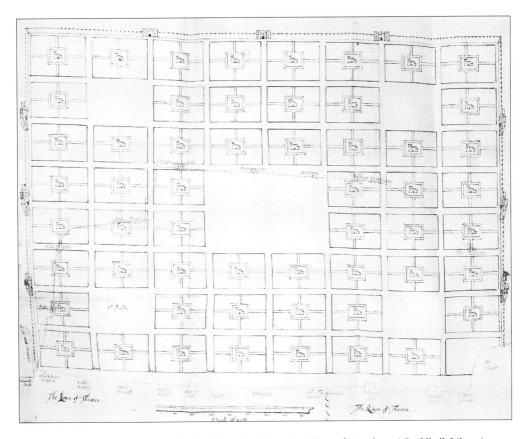

FIGURE 9. Richard Newcourt's plan for rebuilding the City of London. (*Guildhall Library*)

Wall was to disappear altogether and be replaced with a new wall around a much enlarged City.

All these plans had one thing in common – they were impractical at the time, not because they lacked good ideas, but because they could not be implemented within an acceptable time scale for rebuilding the City. Changes that cut across so many entrenched rights, especially property rights, could not be implemented without discussion and compromise, and in some cases without argument, legislation and inevitably litigation well beyond the compass of the Fire Court. These processes were all time-consuming and time was what the City did not have. The City had to be got running again, homes had to be provided for the returning population, markets had to be reopened, shops rebuilt and workshops brought into use once more. All were urgently needed to bring the City back to a semblance of normality. The plans for a new City attracted interest, but were quietly put aside and virtually forgotten, once their purpose had been served and their ideas absorbed. The comment by Ralph that the 'Fire of London furnished the most perfect occasion that can ever happen in any City to rebuild it with Pomp and Regularity', was just too idealistic for the scale involved.[11]

Although the plans were set aside, improvements were made, notably the widening of the main thoroughfares. These were enlarged by taking in, where necessary, strips of land from the adjacent properties. This land was paid for (at the rate of five shillings per square foot) by the Corporation of the City from a tax on coal. The need for this reform was widely accepted and there seems to have been little opposition to it. The streets were staked out to their new width by the City Surveyors, Robert Hooke, Peter Mills and John Oliver, and in due course compensation was paid to the owners of the land, whether private individuals, City Livery Companies, or churchwardens where parish land was taken.

Another widely accepted improvement was the removal of markets from their traditional street locations to new off-street sites. These made use of land previously occupied by churches which were not to be rebuilt and by their churchyards. The site of All Hallows Honey Lane was taken for the Honey Lane Market and that of St Mary Woolchurch Haw for the Stocks Market. The Monument, commemorating the rebuilding of the City after the Fire, was also erected on church land – land previously occupied by St Margaret Fish Street Hill, the first of the churches to be destroyed in the Great Fire, close to the baker's shop in Pudding Lane where it had begun.

These improvements were sanctioned by Acts of Parliament of 1667 and 1670,[12] generally referred to as the Rebuilding Acts. They provided, for the first time, that houses in the City should be built according to standards and regulations, themselves framed to ensure that never again would London experience such a fire as that of September 1666. Nothing else did more to change the character of London. No longer a city of wood, lath and plaster, densely packed with crowded and often mean houses, it was to become a city of brick and stone with fewer inhabitants. Although it was not realised at the time, the long march of the City towards becoming devoid of residents and occupied largely by an army of daytime workers had begun. The process of emptying London of its dwellers, so obviously a temporary process in time of plague and fire, was never to be fully reversed, and its effects were to be found in the subsequent history of its parish churches. Nearly 200 years more were to pass, however, before the decreasing population (and its increasing secularisation) became of immediate concern to the churchwardens of the City parishes and the headache of successive archdeacons and bishops.

The cost of effecting these improvements was met by a tax on coals coming into the Port of London. This was a relatively easy way of raising funds, destined partly for the rebuilding of St Paul's Cathedral, partly for the rebuilding of the parish churches and partly for improvements to the City. This tax, although unpopular as all taxes are, had two major virtues: it was generally accepted as being fair – everyone burnt coal, so everyone paid – and it was easy to collect. As far as central government was concerned, it was a London matter and the Corporation of the City administered everything. The Corporation collected the tax, allocated it according to the Act and accounted for its expenditure, at least in broad terms. It was the Chamber of London which provided the 'treasury' for the sums concerned. The rights of the Corporation of London to metage (the measuring of commodities, including coal) had been exercised since medieval times and these rights were confirmed in two charters of James I;[13] the mechanism for collecting the coal tax was therefore in place. No new machinery was required.

At that time coal was carried to London by sea. The coal tax levied by the Act of 1670 was collected not only from the citizens of the City of London but also from the inhabitants of a very wide area including all those parishes served from the Port of London, that is the whole of the Thames estuary. By the early years of the eighteenth century there were complaints from parishes on the outskirts of London, most with old and decrepit churches in need of rebuilding, that with their large populations they had contributed excessively to the coal tax fund, but had not then benefited from it. But in 1670 no such thoughts were voiced and there was little or no opposition to the use of the coal tax to finance the rebuilding of the ruined churches in the fire-devastated areas of the City. The envy of the surrounding parishes was a feature still to come.

Not only were the plans for a new street pattern put aside, Wren's proposal for replacing the eighty-six destroyed churches with a total of nineteen new ones was also rejected. This was too radical a solution to be accepted by the parishes, the clergy or the City. Instead the Act of 1667 indicated that thirty-nine should be rebuilt. The task of deciding which of the eighty-six should be selected for inclusion in this list was left to the Archbishop of Canterbury and the Bishop of London. The cost of rebuilding the thirty-nine churches was to be met by the sale of the sites of those churches not rebuilt, together with the sale of their churchyards. The existing plethora of authorities with rights of church ownership and exercise of patronage was to be replaced by the holding of all the churches by the Corporation. These provisions met with considerable opposition:

> That the Scite of all Churches, their Rights and Names, and all that belongs to them, should cease and be abolished, being in part consumed, is to add humane Rage against those places where the Divine displeasure hath left us hope of making them agayne fit for his service.[14]

The greatest opposition to the provisions in the Act of 1667 came in the form of squabbling over which of the eighty-six churches should be selected for rebuilding. The figure of thirty-nine in the Act of 1667 was less than half of the total destroyed and there were few parishes willing to contemplate extinction. In the central area there would have been a wholesale reduction in the number, although the larger parishes, such as St Bride Fleet Street, would have survived. The existence of a list of churches for rebuilding compiled by the Archbishop of Canterbury and the Bishop of London only invited representation from parishes determined to be on it. The list may have been no more than a draft; it was neither complete nor authoritative and seems not to have been published.[15] Its contents were probably well enough known. It pleased no one, least of all the Corporation of London. The proposal to rebuild St Mary Woolchurch Haw, for example, was contrary to the Corporation's proposal to use the site for the new Stocks Market. The compilers were in some doubt as to whether churches within the City, but without the walls, should be included: 'We leave . . . to ye Parliament to determine whether those two churches (being without ye Walls) are to be rebuilded over and besides the thirty-nine or whether they are intended to be included.'[16]

The suggestion recorded by Pepys that, in drawing up a list of churches for rebuilding, the establishment was looking after its own is no more than hearsay and does not stand up to examination:

> Mr Young . . . told me that those few churches that are to be new built are plainly not chosen with regard to the convenience of the City, they stand a great many in a cluster about Cornhill, but that all of them are either in the gift of the Lord Archbishop or Bishop of London or Lord Chancellor or gift of the City.[17]

It is true that in the Cornhill–Threadneedle Street area the provision of new churches was to be generous, but that seems to have derived from rivalry and parish pressure rather than patronage.

Even in the early post-Fire period it must have been obvious that some measure of reduction in the number of churches was inevitable. The total resources in money, men and materials required to restore or rebuild the eighty-six destroyed churches could not easily have been justified. Nevertheless, each parish had its ardent supporters and its own vested interests, sufficiently strong to cause Parliament to think again.

The outcome was the Rebuilding Act of 1670. This contains clauses relating to many aspects of the rebuilding of the City. With regard to the parochial churches, its provisions completely replaced those of the earlier Act. This time nothing was left to chance. It contained a detailed list of parish churches selected for rebuilding and those parishes that were to be united with them. The Act provided legal backing for an additional coal tax to finance the rebuilding and instituted a mechanism by which the rebuilding was to be managed. The scheme in which the patronage of the City churches was to be gathered to the Corporation was abandoned and new arrangements were made for presentation to the livings where parishes had been united.

The decision to rebuild only thirty-nine of the parish churches was abandoned with the comment 'the parish churches to be rebuilded . . . cannot conveniently by union or otherwise, be reduced to a less number than fifty-one'. Convenience in this case being what the parishes could be persuaded to accept. Agreement of the parishes to share churches, to worship together and to share an incumbent was one thing; surrendering their identity was quite another. All attempts to do this were abandoned and the pre-Fire structure of local government with over a hundred parish vestries, each with parish officials forming a chain of command leading to the Lord Mayor, was left in place. Each of the pre-Fire parishes was to remain as a separate legal entity with its own responsibilities for law and order, relief of the poor, street maintenance and cleaning. They were to continue to obtain funding by rates upon their own inhabitants, with access to law to compel compliance. The only joint expenditure was to be for the maintenance of the fabric of the church and its services, each parish paying its own separate contribution in a proportion agreed between them.

No document has apparently survived to indicate who was responsible for compiling this list of fifty-one parishes, how it was prepared or what principles were used to guide the choice of parish partners. Humphrey Henchman, Bishop of London, presumably had much to do with it. The parishes joined were all adjacent pairs and some effort seems to have been made to join smaller parishes with larger ones. Other than that, no pattern is discernible. There was no obvious union of parishes having the same patron and no attempt made to balance rich parishes with poor.

Parish records from later periods are full of details – mostly trivial – of disputes between the parishes united by the Act. They include arguments over the allocation of seats in church, how the sexton should be elected, how much should be paid to the organist, the degree of extravagance in redecorating the church, even over burial rights. Most of the arguments were related to money, many of them arising when one parish attempted to dictate to its partner. Gradually the parishes learnt how to sort out their differences without acrimony or resort to law, but it was a painful process destined to last for over a hundred years.

The plan to finance the rebuilding of the churches by selling off redundant sites was clearly unworkable. Both the derelict churches and their churchyards were in continued use for burials and the forced union of parishes did not immediately create large numbers of redundant sites. Instead, the Act of 1670 imposed a new tax upon coal coming into the Port of London, a part of which was set aside for the rebuilding of the parish churches.

Amongst other provisions, the Act established a Commission to be responsible for the rebuilding of the parish churches. The words 'Commission' and 'Commissioner' do not appear in the text, but were soon in common use.[18] The Commissioners responsible for the rebuilding of the parish churches were the Archbishop of Canterbury, the Bishop of London and the Lord Mayor of London then in office. Thus authority resided and was seen to reside with the ex officio heads of both the secular and religious bodies of the capital, the

Archbishop, as titular head of the thirteen 'peculiars' of the City,[19] being seen as an extra diocesan with City interests. Although perhaps high-powered in comparison with later Commissions, the choice of Commissioners to look after the centres for Christian worship incorporating secular administration was not unreasonable.

Even the way in which the churches were to be rebuilt was defined in the Act:

> That the . . . churches to be rebuilded within the said City of London . . . shall be built and erected according to such Models, and of such Dimensions, and in such Manner and Form in all Respects, as by the said Lord Archbishop of Canterbury, Lord Bishop of London, and Lord Mayor of London for the time being (with his Majesty's Approbation thereof) shall be directed and appointed.

It cannot have been envisaged that the Commissioners would concern themselves with the day to day construction of the individual churches, with details of their design, with the contracting of work and the technical and contractual problems that would inevitably arise in the course of the work. These were to all be the province of Wren, who was appointed by one of the first acts of the new Commissioners.

> [We] . . . doe hereby nominate constitute and appoint Dr Christopher Wren, Doctor of Lawes, Surveigher General of all his Majesty's Workes, to direct and order the dimensions, formes and Modells of the said Churches . . . to contract with . . . Artizans, builders and workmen as shall be employed . . . [to] take care for the orderly execution of the workes and accompts . . . and to receive from the Chamber of London such . . . summes of Mony as we . . . shall appoint for the constant and speedy payment . . .[20]

It was the limitations inherent in the Act, in spite of the great care taken with the framing of it, that ensured a continuing role for the Commissioners. Thus there was no indication of which churches should be accorded priority in their rebuilding, or indeed how such priority should be determined. Moreover, it soon became evident that financial problems would engulf the Commission if steps were not taken to match the building programme to the rate at which money became available from the tax receipts. Wren managed to resolve these and other problems, although how he did so is only recorded sporadically.

The difficulties encountered by the Commissioners are described later. They continued throughout the period, from 1 May 1670 to 29 September 1687, for which Parliament had granted the tax. The extension of authority to collect the tax on coal for the church-building programme for a further period, from

29 September 1687 to 29 September 1700,[21] allowed the Commission to complete the rebuilding of the fifty-one churches named in the Act of 1670; to repair some of the churches which, by then, were showing signs of hitherto latent fire damage; and to complete some of the towers and steeples. The renewal of the coal tax for its third and final period, from 29 September 1700 to 29 September 1716,[22] enabled more towers and steeples to be constructed. There is some evidence that, given further resources, the steeple-building programme would have continued until steeples had been added to the towers of all the City churches.

The decisions of the Commissioners were extensively influenced by Wren's views and advice. In ensuring that the building of the churches was not greatly out of gear with the income from the coal tax, he was doing no more than was expected of him. With his influence, arising partly from his stature, partly from his knowledge of the Office of Works and his acquired knowledge of building in general, and partly from his patent ability, it was Sir Christopher Wren who dominated the programme. His official role, which could be described by the modern title of executive officer to the Commission, was only one of his tasks.

What is not always obvious is the skill with which he led the Commissioners to reach the decisions that he wanted, the way in which he played one party off against another and the extent to which he exercised authority when that from the Commissioners was, for one reason or another, then lacking. His friendship with the King, his knowledge of government and his experience with both the City and Parliament were all used to good effect to carry on in the way he intended.

Although his skill as a diplomat occasionally appears from the available papers, his tracks are usually well-hidden. His early brushes with authority had taught him to be wary of committing himself to paper and of exposing his ideas to public criticism and debate. Nowhere is this more evident than in the rebuilding of the churches. Records often simply do not exist to tell us why particular decisions were made, or indeed who it was that made them. Yet what we know of the man suggests that final control of most aspects of the building programme was substantially, if not exclusively, in Wren's hands. This is very clearly illustrated in the period from 1686 to 1688, when Henry Compton, Bishop of London, was in dispute with James II.[23] Compton was removed from office by the Catholic King James, ostensibly as a result of his refusal to dismiss Dr John Sharpe, Rector of St Giles-in-the-Fields (who had preached a sermon which had incurred the King's displeasure), but in reality the royal dislike was directed towards Compton himself. The diocese was put into commission under the Bishops of Rochester, Peterborough and Durham. It is from this point that the orders of the Commissioners for building the City churches cease. We are left to guess how decisions were made. Possibly Wren consulted each of the Commissioners, including Compton at Fulham, but he may just have carried on, unwilling to record decisions on paper, but secure in the knowledge that he had the full support of the Commissioners, even though their attentions were largely diverted elsewhere.

It was only with the uncertainty of 1688 and ultimately with James's flight from London that work on the City churches came to a halt. Work was soon resumed and it must be concluded that the Commissioners too resumed their duties under the 1670 and 1685 Acts, although there are no further 'Orders' to Sir Christopher. By the end of the century, however, parish records indicate that a system of approval for his work was not only then in place but fully operative. How much of it simply rubber-stamped decisions that Wren had already made can only be guessed.

The problems with the Commissioners were not confined to the placing of the bishopric into commission. There had been difficulties earlier when Gilbert Sheldon, Archbishop of Canterbury, retired to his palace at Croydon where he died in 1678. From April 1675 onwards none of the existing orders are signed by him, suggesting that he was then playing no part in the church-rebuilding programme. His successor, William Sancroft, although a supporter of the Glorious Revolution of 1688/89, could not bring himself to take an oath of allegiance to William and Mary, for which he was suspended and removed from the primacy.[24] He had other things on his mind than the building of parish churches.

One particularly important part of Wren's work in the rebuilding of the parish churches was that of deploying the sums of money raised by the tax on coal and earmarked for this purpose. Quite apart from his responsibility for physically handling sums drawn from the Chamber of London,[25] he acted as what would now be called the finance or accounting officer. He had responsibility not only for the spending of the money in all its detail, in accordance with the approval granted by Parliament and passed to him by the Commissioners, but for its proper accounting in the form required by the public auditor. None of this work was shared with the Commissioners.

It was in the discharge of this duty that the detailed expenditure on each church, on the tabernacles, on salaries and other miscellaneous items was recorded in copies of the accounts transcribed by Hawksmoor, then still a junior in the Office of Works at St Paul's (from which the rebuilding of the parish churches was organised).[26] Copies of the church rebuilding accounts, now in the Bodleian Library, are incomplete.[27] Fortunately, another set of building accounts survived in the library of St Paul's Cathedral and have since been deposited by the Dean and Chapter on loan to the Guildhall Library.[28] This set contains a complete record of all the expenditure in building the parochial churches from 1670 to 1717, when the fund derived from the levy upon coals was exhausted. The documents on loan include other accounts of the Commissioners (e.g. the miscellaneous expenditure account), but these are not complete, ceasing long before 1717, the year their work ended.

4

Architects and Surveyors

The Commissioners appointed by the Rebuilding Act of 1670 – the Archbishop of Canterbury (Gilbert Sheldon), the Bishop of London (Humphrey Henchman) and the Lord Mayor of London then in office (Samuel Starling) – met for the first time on 13 June 1670.[1] The record of this first meeting includes a statement of how the rebuilding was to be done. In its wording it follows the instruction given by Parliament in the Act but is both more specific and more detailed:

> Dr Christopher Wren, Surveyor General of his Majesty's Works, Mr Robert Hooke and Mr Edward Woodroffe are hereby required to repair forthwith the aforesaid churches [the fifteen named in the Order] and take an account of the extent of the parishes, the sites of the churches, the state and conditions of the ruins and accordingly prepare fit models and draughts to be presented for his Majesty's approbation and also estimates proper to inform us what share and proportion of the money out of the imposition upon coals may be requisite to allow for the fabric of each church, and where any contracts have been already made by the churchwardens, the said Dr Christopher Wren and his assistants, are hereby authorised and required to call for the said contracts, and to examine what hath been already expended upon any of the said churches that thereupon we may the better judge what is further expedient to allow for the finishing of any such churches.

This was the authority for Wren and his assistants to begin their work on the parish churches, work which was to continue for almost half a century. In that period those churches which were reparable were repaired, some were reconstructed more or less to the pre-Fire design, and others were rebuilt to new and very different designs. Models (i.e. designs) were prepared, craftsmen contracted and the expenditure on building allowed and accounted for.

This statement of 1670 referred specifically to three men: Christopher Wren, Robert Hooke and Edward Woodroffe. The responsibility for rebuilding the fifty-one churches was to be uniquely theirs. None of the surviving records of the Commissioners give any indication of what their remuneration was to be, but the accounts show that in the period from June 1670 to the end of 1675 (to the death of Edward Woodroffe) the largest sum, approaching £1600, was paid to Wren.[2] This was followed by the quite considerable sum of £800 paid to Hooke, a similar amount to Woodroffe and only minor sums to others, confirming what can be inferred from the statement, namely that the burden of rebuilding the churches of the City of London was, as intended, shared by these three men and these three alone. It was to Wren, Hooke, Woodroffe and their successors that the City owed its new churches with their towers and steeples.

It is apparent that each of the three men was given the task and responsibilities of an architect in producing designs for the parish churches. The statement and subsequent orders of the Commissioners contain no reference to how these duties were to be performed, but the surviving parish records indicate that the three were also given the authority to make agreements with craftsmen and suppliers for the construction of these buildings, i.e. the power to act as contracting officers. Wren alone seems to have been given the responsibility for handling the money involved in payment for the work done. All sums required for this were obtained from the coal tax fund accumulating in the Chamber of London and paid to him personally before being disbursed by him or in his name to the craftsmen and others. His task of paymaster was not shared with Hooke or Woodroffe, and neither was that of accounting officer, in which Wren discharged his responsibilities to Parliament by accounting for both money spent and work done in a manner that Parliament would approve. The extent to which the three men (and with regard to Hooke and Woodroffe, also their successors) discharged their duties as architects is discussed below. Ability, aptitude and initiative were clearly important in deciding who did what, with each man doing what he was best at.

Wren personally does not seem to have undertaken much of the work as a contracting officer, nor could he have been expected to. The detailed discussions leading to the signing of contracts with the craftsmen were undertaken principally by Hooke, Woodroffe and the men who succeeded them. Discussion with parish authorities, on the other hand, was a matter for all three men. Parish records of the time contain many references to meetings with Wren and his two colleagues. There was, however, a difference in their relationships with the parishes – the churchwardens and other officers invariably meeting Hooke and Woodroffe on site. Wren was waited on at Whitehall, or entertained at some place of refreshment. Wren's status and office largely accounts for this, but the discussions Wren himself undertook were often very different: Hooke and

Woodroffe invariably dealt with practical matters related to the rebuilding, whereas Wren, the politician, was the man with whom the parish needed to negotiate for final acceptance of the design and as a preliminary to the approval of the Commissioners for work to begin.

There is no evidence that Wren was involved in physically measuring any of the work undertaken in the rebuilding of the parish churches for the purpose of payment. This, too, was a task that Hooke and, perhaps to a greater extent, Woodroffe would have attended to. Once this had been done payment according to the various contracts would follow, much in arrears. The more important craftsmen received their rewards as lump sum payments in the form of imprests.

As might be expected where Parliament had authorised the spending of money raised by taxation, detailed records were kept of all the expenditure incurred. From time to time arrangements were made for these accounts to be audited. No record now exists of any comments made by the auditor, Reginald Marriott, who also audited the St Paul's accounts; his remarks, if any, have not survived. Nevertheless, the existing evidence suggests that Wren attended to his duties as accounting officer as assiduously as he attended to all his public duties. The surviving Commissioners' Orders contain records of a number of occasions where decisions concerning expenditure were made only after seeking an opinion from outside the small group of individuals involved,[3] suggesting that Wren was conscious not only of the need to make good decisions but of the need to demonstrate that good decisions had been made. This also was one of the duties not shared with his colleagues.

At the start of the building campaign, Wren's skills as an architect were still largely undeveloped. The Sheldonian Theatre (1664–69) and the chapel at Pembroke College (1663–65) were his only major buildings at the time of his appointment to the post of Surveyor General of His Majesty's Works. His claim to the post was inferior to those of Roger Pratt and Hugh May, but in retrospect there is no reason to criticise the monarch's choice. Although a self-taught architect, as Kerry Downes has shown,[4] there never was a time when Wren could be considered an amateur. His approach was always conditioned by the view that he could tackle any kind of problem and, with his grounding in mathematics and astronomy, his solutions to problems were based on wide knowledge and practical calculation.

As an architect of the late seventeenth century Wren stands supreme – in inventiveness, in the quality of his work and in the individuality of his style. It is these qualities that are uppermost in our minds in seeking to unravel his personal contribution to the forty-seven years of church building under the Commission first appointed in 1670.

Wren, Hooke and Woodroffe were men of very different character. Academically Wren and Hooke had much in common, both were Oxford men of brilliance, both natural scientists and both Fellows of the Royal Society. They had both undertaken research in the rapidly developing physical and mechanical sciences of the time and both had made contributions to it. Hooke, indeed, was recognised as one of the most original experimenters of the time. He has been described as 'brilliant, cantankerous, secretive and always in ill-health',[5] but his quirks do not seem to have affected his relationship with Wren. He was employed as a surveyor by the City, although his skill as an architect was, until 1670, unpractised. They were friends and dined together regularly. Wren treated Hooke as his equal and Hooke's diary indicates the extent to which the two men discussed their common problems.[6] There can be no doubt that the designs for the churches would have featured in those discussions. Both were capable of invention and both capable of expanding that invention into plans and elevations for new and novel designs, even if they were not always precisely or meticulously drawn.

Like Wren, Hooke had no training as an architect. He was the son of John Hooke, Curate of Freshwater in the Isle of Wight and, again like Wren, attended Westminster School under Dr Busby. He made good progress and went up to Oxford as a chorister at Christchurch, matriculating in 1658 and taking his MA in 1663. In this period he became friendly with Wren, then at Wadham College. As Curator of the Royal Society, he was given the rooms in Gresham College, Bishopsgate, London, in which he lived for the rest of his life.

His career as a surveyor-architect did not begin until after the Great Fire, when he produced a plan for rebuilding the City for the Lord Mayor and City Aldermen. In October of 1666 he was appointed one of the three City Surveyors. The others were Peter Mills and Edward Jerman (or Jarman), with John Oliver replacing Jerman in 1668. Hooke was a highly competent surveyor, although the records of his work for the City have not survived. He is better known for the rebuilding of the City churches and for his design of a number of private and public buildings, most of which have now been destroyed. He produced a design for the Monument and was actively involved in its construction, although it is by no means certain if this is to his or to Wren's design.

Foreign influences noted in Hooke's architecture, particularly French and Dutch, may be attributed to his avid reading of the many books that are noted in his diary. Wren may also have seen these but, of the two men, Hooke seems to have been more greatly influenced by them. In his designs Hooke made frequent use of motifs generally associated with Holland, including Dutch gables and decorative elements. Dutch influences in the design and decoration of some of the City churches have generally been credited to Hooke with the suggestion, made by several authors, that his knowledge and love of these features was acquired from a visit to Holland. The existence, in a portfolio of drawings by Hooke in the British Library,[7] of a drawing of the Nieuwe Kerk of Haarlem, designed by Jacob van Campen (1645–49), with a roof support structure similar to that used at St Martin Ludgate, has been taken as evidence of a visit, but no confirmation of any such visit has been found.[8] Hooke is generally accepted as an architect of somewhat mediocre talent, but so few of his buildings have survived that this may be a harsh judgement. Competent but not outstanding may be a better assessment.

Knowledge of Hooke and his involvement in the rebuilding of the City churches is derived largely from his diary.[9] It is an incomplete document, with the most detailed part covering the years from 1672 to 1680. In it he lists numerous visits to the churches under construction. His brief notes indicate that he not only took 'views' of the building in progress, but signed contracts with the workmen and made decisions concerning the surviving fabric, as for example, to demolish the tower of St Bartholomew-by-the-Exchange and to clear the site ready for the rebuilding of St Martin Ludgate.[10]

Hooke visited a large number of the parish churches – over thirty of them are noted in his diary – some many times. Moreover, the churches that do not occur in it are largely those that were rebuilt before his diary begins in 1672, or were under construction in the period for which no diary now survives. It is not unreasonable to assume that he was a visitor to all or almost all of the parish churches between 1670 and 1693.

It has been suggested that Wren was much too busy with his work on St Paul's and elsewhere for him to have designed all the churches for which he, in *Parentalia* as elsewhere, has received credit. This view seems to have received general acceptance from architectural historians, and there are many who would accept that the churches not designed by Wren were by Hooke. There is, however, still the suggestion, repeated from time to time, that some of the churches may have been erected without design assistance from the two architects. Except for the few churches whose rebuilding began prior to 1670 (where any small amount of design work needed may have been provided by the contractors), no evidence has been found to support this suggestion. We may not know exactly how much designing was by Wren himself, but we may be reasonably sure that what he did not do was done by Hooke. The last payment to Hooke for his work on the churches was in 1693; his last recorded visits, also in 1693, were to St Dunstan-in-the-East and St Vedast Foster Lane, with demolition and reconstruction beginning on both sites shortly after. Hooke died at Gresham College on 3 March 1703, aged sixty-seven.

An indication that the design burden was not shared equally between Wren and Hooke emerges from a study of those churches whose construction was started by the Commissioners, before the death of Edward Woodroffe, in the period 1670–75: a total of eighteen parish churches. By far the greater number of these were in the north and eastern parts of the City. This unequal distribution is unlikely to have arisen by chance and must be due to a decision, made in 1670, on how the task of rebuilding was to be shared between the three men appointed to it. There is now no documentary evidence of this decision and few indications remain to suggest how it was implemented.

As noted above, in the rebuilding of houses and commercial premises after the Fire, the City of London employed three surveyors to stake out individual plots. These men, Robert Hooke, Peter Mills and John Oliver, each took a part of the City. Hooke had the eastern part, Peter Mills the western part and John Oliver the central area between the two.[11] A division of this kind was probably in the minds of the Commissioners in June 1670 when Wren, Hooke and Woodroffe were all appointed to design and rebuild the parish churches. Logically Hooke would have taken the same eastern part of the City, the area in which he lived (at Gresham College, Bishopsgate), with which he was by then very familiar and in which he would have already have met the parish authorities in setting out the boundaries of their various properties. Wren would perhaps have taken the western area which included St Paul's Cathedral and which was closest to his residence in Whitehall, leaving Woodroffe to take the area between.

With some such division of the City, Wren began on the designs for St Mary-le-Bow and St Bride Fleet Street in the western part of the City and Hooke on the churches in the eastern area. Woodroffe was by then fully engaged, not only as Surveyor of St Paul's and Westminster Abbey, but also in helping Wren with the Great Model and in surveying and measuring the work done on those churches which had already been started by the various vestries. Despite his many virtues, and his knowledge and experience of construction, Woodroffe was not a man of ideas and there is no reason to suppose that, despite his appointment to design and build the parish churches, he took more than a minor part, if that, in their design. The central area, for which he might logically have designed, must soon have been divided between Wren and Hooke, with Hooke taking the part to the north and east of a line stretching from Aldersgate to the east end of St Paul's, then along Cheapside, Poultry, Walbrook and Dowgate to the Thames.

In these years Wren was exceptionally busy and it must soon have become apparent that he simply did not have the time to produce the necessary designs for all the churches in the western part of the City. His attention, deliberately or otherwise, was given only to those few churches, such as St Mary-le-Bow, where for one reason or another it was appropriate. It was only in Hooke's area that much progress was made in producing new designs.

Of the three men named at the first meeting of the Commissioners, Edward Woodroffe is the least well known. His year of birth was recorded as 1622 on a memorial stone, formerly in the cloister of Westminster Abbey.[12] In his will he describes himself as of the parish of St Andrew Holborn.[13] However, many of the inhabitants of the City of London who were displaced by the Fire settled in the parishes on the northern boundary of the City and the Holborn parish records contain no entry relating to his birth or those of his four daughters.

He first emerged as Surveyor to the Dean and Chapter of Westminster Abbey in 1662. In 1668 he joined Wren as Assistant Surveyor at St Paul's Cathedral, becoming Surveyor to the Dean and Chapter in 1669, a post he held until his death in 1675. In 1670 he designed houses for three residentiary canons in Amen Corner but no other building to his design is known. In his early history, expertise and achievements he remains a shadowy figure. He was employed by Wren as a draughtsman – his use of ruled penwork and regular cross-hatching as seen in a number of surviving drawings is characteristic. They have some resemblance to drawings from the office of John Webb and it has been suggested that he worked in Webb's office and was perhaps trained there as a draughtsman.[14] He is known to have worked with Wren on the Greek Cross and the Great Model designs for St Paul's, as well as on the parish churches, but how much design work he undertook in any of these tasks remains unknown. He may have been trained to a particular trade or craft, but no record of any apprenticeship has so far been found – for this period neither the apprenticeship nor freedom records of the City of London were systematically kept (or if they were they have not survived). He may have been the 'Mr Woodrooffe Mason' named in a draft list of Office of Works personnel compiled in September 1658.[15] What is certain is that by the time he came to Wren he was a man of considerable maturity with a wealth of experience in the building industry. His position as Surveyor at both Westminster Abbey and St Paul's suggests that he was well able to take charge of the rebuilding of the parish churches. In the division of effort there was good reason for Woodroffe to be given responsibility for the practical side of the rebuilding.

There is no mystery concerning his appointment. Wren needed such a man; neither he nor Hooke had the requisite knowledge or experience of the building industry to enable them to translate ideas from their minds, and designs from their plans and elevations, into buildings of brick and stone. If Woodroffe had not been there, Wren would have needed to find someone of similar background, knowledge and experience. Although his style makes his drawings easily identifiable, only one by him is now known for any of the City churches, an elevation for the tower and steeple of St Mary-le-Bow of 1670 (Fig. 10).[16] The design may not have been his and he may have acted as no more than a draughtsman.

In March 1673, when he made his will, Woodroffe described himself as 'being sickly and weak in body but of good and perfect mind and memory'. He fell ill in August 1675, dying on 18 October. A replacement for Woodroffe was chosen by the Commissioners on 4 January 1676. Both Wren and Hooke must by this time have become very conscious of the extent to which progress was being made in the church-building programme in the north and east of the City and the corresponding lack of it in the west and south. Hooke's proposal – that Sir John Hoskins should replace Woodroffe – was designed to remedy this. Hoskins (or Hoskyns) was another friend of Wren and a man similar in many respects to both Wren and Hooke. His mind, we are told, was tuned to philosophical pursuits.[17] He had, like Wren, been educated at Westminster School under Dr Busby. He was called to the bar at the Middle Temple, although he seems not to have practised. He was elected President of the Royal Society in 1682 in succession to Wren – Evelyn retiring in his favour. There is no record of him receiving any training or experience in architecture, but in this he was no different to Wren and Hooke. Although we are not told, there can be little doubt that Hooke intended to continue his designing for the northern and eastern parts of the City, with Hoskins taking the rest, leaving Wren with a few, perhaps rather special, churches in the City.

We have only Hooke's side of the story, and not all of that. He affirmed that he and Wren were agreed on the choice of Sir John Hoskins, but it seems more likely that Wren (perhaps avoiding direct conflict with Hooke) preferred John Oliver. It was on Oliver that the Commissioners' choice fell. Hooke noted in his diary that in regard to Sir John, the Lord Mayor had 'by mistake excepted him'. In the practical business of getting the churches constructed, Wren must have appreciated Woodroffe's contribution and seen the need for a replacement by a man similarly experienced. He would also have realised that, in the period 1670–75, the sum of money available from the coal tax had scarcely been enough to maintain the existing rate of construction, and certainly not enough to support a larger design team including both Hooke and Hoskyns. What Wren needed was for Hooke to spread his effort over the whole of the City.

John Oliver was a craftsman, a glazier and glass painter by trade,[18] and a surveyor by profession.[19] He was born in about 1616 and died in 1701 at the age of eighty-five, at which time he was

FIGURE 10. St Mary-le-Bow. Project design for the tower and steeple, drawn by Edward Woodroffe. (*All Souls College, Oxford*)

living in the parish of St Michael Queenhithe. He succeeded Edward Woodroffe as Assistant Surveyor of St Paul's as well as in the rebuilding of the City churches. His name appears in the churchwardens' accounts of a number of churches indicating involvement in the building programme, but none of the extant drawings are known to be by him. Like Woodroffe, he was more concerned with the practical aspects of building than in the creation of new designs. Howard Colvin, in considering the rebuilding of St Mary Aldermary,[20] noted that work at the church was carried out under Oliver's direction. This church was rebuilt with the aid of a private benefaction, but the records do not suggest that Oliver did any more than he would have done if the church had been rebuilt with funding from the coal tax revenue. There is no indication as to who did the designing. Private funding did not absolve the Commissioners from their responsibilities under the Act of 1670. That Sir Christopher Wren was aware of this responsibility for the church was demonstrated in 1701–4, when the tower was rebuilt from the coal tax fund. It is reasonable to infer, if the cost of rebuilding the body of the church of St Mary Aldermary had exceeded the private donation, that Wren would have authorised payment of the excess from the coal tax revenue, as he did where other private benefactions were concerned, such as for St Dunstan-in-the-East.

The last recorded payment to John Oliver was in 1694, when he was about seventy-seven years of age, although, as the account ceased in that year, it is not possible to be sure when he stopped working. His place was taken by William Dickinson, whose name first appears in the records of the Commissioners in 1695. He was appointed at the age of about twenty-four, at a time when the work in rebuilding the parish churches of the City was all but complete. With the completion of the churches the amount of work outstanding decreased and there was no need for anyone other than Dickinson to control the remaining building projects, the towers and steeples. Eventually the Commissioners gave their approval to a small number of new projects: a substantial rebuilding of St Christopher-le-Stocks and the towers of St Sepulchre, St Mary Aldermary and St Michael Cornhill. The design work for these was supplied by Dickinson.

Robert Hooke's successor was Nicholas Hawksmoor (Fig. 11). His origins are somewhat obscure, but he is known to have been born near Tuxford in Nottinghamshire, probably in 1661. After local employment as a clerk, he entered Wren's service, probably in 1679, as his personal assistant or clerk. In no sense did he undertake a formal apprenticeship, but he rapidly acquired skills relevant to building, enabling him to serve as supervisor of the works at Winchester Palace and the Royal Hospital, Chelsea. He was appointed Surveyor to the Commissioners for

FIGURE 11. Nicholas Hawksmoor. Bust by Sir Henry Cheere. (*All Souls College, Oxford*)

Sewers for Westminster and Parts of the County of Middlesex in 1696 and Clerk of the Works at Greenwich in 1698. His early work in designing is largely unrecorded, although a small number of his drawings for the City churches survive in various collections. He produced drawings also for St Paul's Cathedral, but the extent to which he was responsible for producing the designs remains unknown.

Hawksmoor's career is well documented from the beginning of the eighteenth century, particularly his work for the Greenwich Hospital and for the 1711 Act Church Commissioners, producing the designs for six of the twelve churches built under the Act. He was associated with Vanbrugh at Greenwich Hospital, Castle Howard and Blenheim, a fruitful partnership in some of the grandest buildings of the age.

At the time of the departure of Hooke the only designing then apparently outstanding was in respect of the so-called late steeples. The renewal of the coal tax for a further period had created a need for steeple designs. Those built after 1693 would have been Hawksmoor's responsibility, although he may have been designing much earlier in his career. There is evidence from parish records, taken together with the building accounts, to suggest that the late steeple designs were produced several years before they were used. Certainly many were ready by 1700 or shortly after, completed while Hawksmoor was still employed by Wren and the Commissioners.

Hawksmoor's career as a fully-fledged independent architect flourished after 1700. He was then in full possession of his skills as a designer with a developed style of his own. As his training must have begun when he came to Wren in 1679, it might be expected that by about 1685 he was producing ideas of his own, if only in a derivative style. After 1685 his vision enlarged, his ideas developed and his abilities were seen conspicuously. It is exactly in this period that many of the late steeple designs were produced and it is among them that we must look for examples of his early work. It would be illogical to expect him to have become the master architect that he was by 1700 without a portfolio of work from the earlier years.

5

The Commission at Work

From the very first meeting of the Commissioners it was appreciated, at least by them, that the fifty-one churches of the City of London authorised by Parliament and named in the Act for rebuilding could not all be started at once. While some parishes would be fortunate in securing an early rebuilding, others would have to wait. They produced a list of fifteen which were to be the first to be rebuilt. These included some, but not all, of those where rebuilding had already started to the order of the parish vestries – St Christopher-le-Stocks, St Magnus the Martyr, St Michael Cornhill, St Sepulchre and St Vedast Foster Lane. None of these vestries had the resources to complete the rebuilding, and some at least may have been anticipating the work of the Commission:

> Christchurch Newgate
> St Anne and St Agnes
> St Augustine Old Change
> St Benet Gracechurch
> St Bride Fleet Street
> St Christopher-le-Stocks
> St Lawrence Jewry
> St Magnus the Martyr
> St Mary-at-Hill
> St Mary-le-Bow
> St Michael Cornhill
> St Michael Queenhithe
> St Olave Jewry
> St Sepulchre
> St Vedast Foster Lane

Nearly four years had elapsed since the Great Fire and in that time some of the parish vestries had already made a start in rebuilding their own parish churches. By mid 1670 major amounts of work had been done at St Sepulchre, St Michael Cornhill, St Christopher-le-Stocks and St Vedast Foster Lane. A start, but little more, had been made on the rebuilding of St Magnus the Martyr and St Mary-le-Bow, and some work had been done at St Mary-at-Hill, St Olave Jewry, St Peter Cornhill and probably also in other parishes. Some vestries had spent money in restoring or at least stabilising what was left of the fabric of their churches after the Great Fire. Wren and the Commissioners were therefore faced not with fifty-one churches waiting to be rebuilt, but with fifty-one in states ranging from largely rebuilt to others untouched since the Fire and still in ruins. The selection of fifteen included those that were nearing completion, but not St Dunstan-in-the-East nor St Mary Woolnoth. These were being rebuilt with the aid of private donations and were presumably omitted from the list because the Commissioners did not expect to pay for them.

This selection of fifteen did not stand for long. Clearly the churches on which a major amount of work had been done would need to be completed, but manoeuvring to place other churches on a priority rebuilding list began within days of the first meeting. At the second meeting it was reported that 'several parishioners of St Edmund the King in Lombard Street have earnestly requested the rebuilding of their said church and have offered to advance money'.[1] The Commissioners responded by agreeing to have a 'second class', a list of churches to be rebuilt after the fifteen already chosen. These were to be listed and the rebuilding started in the order in which the parish vestries deposited money by way of loans to the Commissioners.

Even at this early stage it was fully realised that finance would be a problem. It was the supply of money which would determine the rate of building, as the sums raised by the coal tax allocated by Parliament did not and would not flow into the Chamber of London at the rate at which churches could be rebuilt. Interest-free deposits – little short of enforced loans – in amounts of £500 were the first of a number of ways in which the Commissioners sought to match their building programme to the money available.

Within a month it had become apparent that the creation of a 'second class' in the rebuilding programme would cause difficulties for the Commissioners. They responded by retracting their earlier decision by which the fifteen named churches were to be rebuilt first. Good progress had been made with St Mary-le-Bow, St Sepulchre, St Michael Cornhill, St Christopher and St Vedast. These, it was reported, would be finished shortly and the Commissioners accordingly allocated further funding for work on them to continue. The list of ten churches remaining from the original fifteen was then scrapped and in its place the compilation of a new list agreed. This was to contain the names of those churches depositing money on loan to the Chamber of London, in the order in which the deposits were made. It was from this list that priority in rebuilding was to be determined. Establishing a position on it was to become the first step for each church in securing action by Wren and the Commissioners. The term 'second class' had become inappropriate and was replaced by the term 'ordinary', it being the ordinary way by which the churches were to be rebuilt. The deposits from the parish vestries were to be used directly to meet the rebuilding costs, each £500 being associated with a further £1500 allocated from the coal tax revenue.[2] The loans were repaid from the coal tax as the accumulated income from the fund reached levels determined by the Commissioners. In a number of instances, money repaid to a parish was immediately redeposited with the Chamber as a means of further promoting the rebuilding of its church. The Commissioners' papers give no indication of how these figures were derived. There may have been hopes that the aggregate of £2000 would have been sufficient for the repair or restoration of the smaller churches but, if so, it was to prove grossly inadequate.

Anxious not to lose its place in the building programme, St Mary-at-Hill was the first to make a deposit of £500,[3] followed quickly by St Edmund the King, whose proposal had been instrumental in the development of the scheme, and then St Mildred Poultry.

Although this scheme may have alleviated the immediate financial problems faced by the Commissioners, it must have been apparent that the sums available would still mean a protracted building period and that something more would be needed to persuade many of the vestries to be patient. The scheme devised was the provision of temporary churches or tabernacles. At their meeting on 7 October 1670 the Commissioners decided to spend some of the coal tax fund on providing ten of these temporary churches for parish worship until they were ready to proceed with more rebuilding. These tabernacles were to be made of cheap materials and 'of the least workmanship'. Most of them were of timber construction on brick bases and with tiled roofs. They were hastily thrown together and many were to need frequent repair over their lifetime. It was intended that they should be erected on the sites of the churches or their churchyards for no more than £150 each, although in the event some cost over £200.[4] The ten tabernacles were allocated to:

All Hallows-the-Great
Christchurch Newgate

> St Alban Wood Street
> St Anne and St Agnes
> St Bride Fleet Street
> St Margaret Lothbury
> St Mary Magdalene Old Fish Street
> St Michael Crooked Lane
> St Michael Queenhithe
> St Margaret New Fish Street
>   (united with St Magnus the Martyr)

Although the Commissioners agreed that one of these tabernacles should be provided for St Bride Fleet Street, there is no record in the accounts of any expenditure for it and the early rebuilding of the church made it unnecessary. The idea of having a temporary church was popular and in the succeeding months of 1670 and 1671 more tabernacles were agreed. In all twenty-seven were provided at a total cost of £4905, the most expensive being for St Mary Abchurch at £265 16s. 4d. Except for the one at St Mary-le-Bow, which was apparently only leased,[5] the tabernacles remained the property of the Commissioners. When the sites were required for rebuilding the tabernacles were pulled down and sold, mostly to craftsmen, for the materials they contained. Each of the tabernacles was provided with a communion table or altar and a pulpit, with other fittings and furniture provided by the parish vestries.

By early 1671 the Commissioners were aware that the coal tax fund at their disposal would need to pay for the rebuilding of St Mary Woolnoth and for part of the cost of St Dunstan-in-the-East. St Mary Woolnoth had been rebuilt by Sir Robert Vyner, a wealthy parishioner, later Lord Mayor, whose ancestors were buried in the church. He may at one time have intended to meet the cost of the rebuilding himself but, public funding being available, he recovered his expenditure from the Commissioners.[6] St Dunstan-in-the-East was rebuilt largely with a gift from Lady Dionys Williamson but, as the cost of rebuilding exceeded her donation, the balance was met by the Commissioners.[7] Both churches were rebuilt on the old foundations, largely if not fully to the designs of the pre-Fire churches. For St Mary Woolnoth some of the old walling was reused. At neither church was Sir Christopher Wren or Robert Hooke apparently involved in producing a new design.

The list of churches to be rebuilt on the ordinary continued to grow. By mid July 1671 it included the following:

St Benet Fink
St Bride Fleet Street
St Dionis Backchurch
St Edmund the King
St George Botolph Lane
St Lawrence Jewry
St Mary Aldermanbury
St Mary-at-Hill
St Michael Wood Street
St Mildred Poultry
St Nicholas Cole Abbey
St Olave Jewry

At this point the Commissioners closed the list. They decreed:

> We think it absolutely necessary, and do hereby Order that no more churches
> be begun, until a competent number of those that are in hand be finished and
> paid off. And to the end that no more depositions of new churches be received
> in the Chamber, a copy of this order shall be left and publicly affixed in the
> Chamber of London.[8]

Nevertheless, the parish vestries continued to raise money to make deposits
in the Chamber. In June 1672, despite their order, the Commissioners recorded
that deposits had been made by St Stephen Walbrook and St Bartholomew-by-
the-Exchange.[9] Unwilling to extend the list of churches to be built on the
ordinary, they created a new class of churches in which work could be started
and then carried on without any contribution from the coal tax fund. The
rebuilding was to be financed solely by the parish vestries until such time as the
Commissioners' financial position improved. In these the rebuilding was undertaken 'on the extraordinary'. The terms 'ordinary' and 'extraordinary' were taken
from the vocabulary of the Office of Works.[10]

Although the parishes were eventually to receive repayment of their loans,
they were in effect controlling the building by the rate at which they raised
money from their own resources, borrowing at interest if necessary. As would
be expected, such churches took longer to build. There is also evidence that
some were built rather more cheaply (for example, by using less ashlar), but
such pointers are not universal. St Stephen Walbrook, although built on the
extraordinary, shows no sign of any economy in the building.

For those churches to be built on the extraordinary, a clause was inserted into the contracts of the craftsmen to ensure that they fully understood that payment would be made only from the sums deposited by the parishes. The following example is from the carpenter's contract for St Bartholomew-by-the-Exchange:

> And the said Matthew Banckes doth hereby further agree to receive the value of his work when performed and measured out of such money as shall be deposited into the Chamber of London by ye Parishioners of the said Church. And in case the aforesaid Parishioners shall not deposite money sufficient for the completing the said Church, then the said Matthew Banckes doth notwithstanding agree and is content to stay for ye residue of his money while the said Church comes in course to be paid out of the money arising upon the Duty of Coales for the Parochiall Churches.[11]

The measures taken by the Commissioners still did not reduce the backlog of work to a reasonable level. It must have become apparent to the Commissioners that if fifty-one parish churches were to be rebuilt from the proceeds of the coal tax within the period 1670–87, as intended in the Act of 1670, some other measure of restraint would be necessary. This was introduced in October 1677 when they ordered:

> That the said tower [St Lawrence Jewry] be carried on, and no other but the steeple of Bow which is near finished and was formerly directed, and the steeple of St Nicholas Cole Abbey, which formerly wanted only the roof, and is small and stands conspicuous to the Thames. And that other towers for the present remain to the height of the churches . . .[12]

Until this time, in the authorisation of the Commissioners, there had been no distinction made between building the church and completing its tower, but from then on the towers were taken only to a convenient height, boarded over and left to be completed later.

In retrospect, it can be seen that the financial problems of the Commissioners were inevitable. The coal tax instituted in the Act of 1670 was collected only from 1 May 1670. By the time the first year's revenue was gathered, a great deal of construction work, some of it from as far back as 1667, had to be paid for. A delay in paying the major craftsmen (masons, bricklayers, carpenters, plumbers) of about four years soon built up and was to persist. The backlog of payments and pressure from individual vestries, anxious for early action to rebuild particular churches, made necessary some restriction and scheduling of the works. The measures adopted by the Commissioners were reasonable at the time and succeeded in spreading the building period over the half a century in which the revenue from the coal tax was eventually to become available.

Particularly in the early part of this period, there are references in the parish records of delays to individual churches due to shortages of money to pay the craftsmen, of craftsmen refusing to continue until payments were made, and of discussions concerning payments to craftsmen to induce them to continue. But given the system by which the churches were rebuilt by public funding from a tax revenue collected over a long period of time, Wren and the Commissioners were remarkably successful in managing the financial aspects of the enterprise without too much clamour or complaint from the parishes.

By about 1680 many of the churches had been completed and the distinction between those built on the ordinary and those on the extraordinary was no longer necessary and disappeared. The ban on completing towers also disappeared and vestries with incomplete towers to their churches soon began to petition for work to begin again.

The year 1680 provided a major landmark for the Commissioners and the City. In that year the tower and steeple of St Mary-le-Bow were completed and the scaffolding, which for ten years had stood in Cheapside, was removed to reveal the steeple in all its glory. Nothing like it was known in all England. It was the first classical steeple to be erected in the capital,[13] the subject of much admiration; human nature being what it is, the subject also of much envy. Other towers which had been rebuilt in the early days of the Commission rose, in general, to a height of about a hundred feet, although some were much less. Steeples, where they were provided, added further height, but other towers with steeples were far lower than that of St Mary-le-Bow, which now reached a magnificent 224 feet. The City skyline was to become dominated by steeples, but it was St Mary-le-Bow which both set the pattern and established its own claim to importance by holding its head higher than all the others.

Work on the churches continued for nearly two decades after 1666, with new ones added to the building programme as others were completed. Finally, the last five, All Hallows Lombard Street, St Andrew-by-the-Wardrobe, St Mary Somerset, St Michael Crooked Lane and St Michael Paternoster Royal, were started in 1686.[14] The aim must surely have been to complete the rebuilding of the fifty-one parish churches of the City from the revenue raised by the coal tax granted by Parliament for the period 1670–87.

The rebuilding of the churches was proceeding at the same time as the construction of St Paul's Cathedral, but by this time the tax on coal was running out, and the cathedral, unlike the parish churches, was nowhere near complete. In 1685 an approach was made to the House of Commons and leave given to bring in a Bill to extend the tax on coal to the year 1700, primarily to continue the work on St Paul's. The Commons referred the Bill to a committee (which included the new Member for Plympton, Sir Christopher Wren), who were empowered: 'to bring in a clause to be added to the said Bill, for Provision for Finishing of the Four Churches within the Walls of London'.[15] Royal Assent to the Bill was given on 2 July 1685, leaving the Commissioners and Wren in the entirely new position of having completed the rebuilding of most of the parish churches at the same time as having an assured and regular income to the year 1700. With this income Wren was able to complete the churches to which the Commons referred, to attend to the towers which had been boarded over, and to consider also what else remained to be done.

The building programme was not to proceed smoothly. The death of Charles II had little impact upon it, and at first neither did the accession of James II. It was not until the events of 1688, culminating in the flight of James from London and England, that there was major disruption in the capital. War with France no doubt contributed to it. There was general uncertainty over the outcome and building activity declined. Work on the remaining churches came to a halt by the end of 1688 with the last four churches still not finished. St Michael Crooked Lane was sufficiently advanced for it to be put into use, the others not. By the end of 1689 the crisis was over and life in the capital began to return to normal. Work resumed on All Hallows Lombard Street, St Andrew-by-the-Wardrobe, St Mary Somerset and St Michael Paternoster Royal in 1689–90, and the four churches were completed by 1694. The small amount of work necessary to complete St Michael Crooked Lane was not started until 1694 but was completed the following year.

St Andrew-by-the-Wardrobe and St Mary Somerset were particularly poor parishes. Wren agreed that the cost of providing them with pews, pulpit, reredos and other fittings should be met from the coal tax fund.[16] He had no authority of his own for this but the Commissioners presumably agreed to it, although no record of such agreement is known. The Commissioners would have been mindful that at this time the fund could afford to meet the cost and also that, as these were the last of the parish churches to be completed under the Act of 1670, the precedent would not rebound upon them.

Wren and the Commissioners were not the only ones to know that the coal tax fund, from being overstretched in the early days, was then in surplus.

Moreover, the building programme was no longer being driven forward by the demands of parish vestries anxious for their particular churches to be taken in hand. The churchwardens too must have been aware of the situation. They responded by persuading Wren to undertake work which, prior to the extension of the coal tax, would have been dismissed in the light of priority claims elsewhere. This included the construction of a vestry for St Benet Paul's Wharf;[17] a lantern for St Michael Wood Street;[18] a gallery and burial vault for St Stephen Coleman Street;[19] and repairs to other churches including St Mary-at-Hill.[20]

An even greater charge upon the coal tax was making good the deficiencies in the earlier work. The early repairs and restoration, undertaken by the parish vestries before Wren assumed control of the programme, had been done by local craftsmen, of varying skill and experience, possibly using poor materials and certainly unaware of the danger of latent fire damage to brick and stonework. This damage had later become apparent as cracks appeared in the fabric of the buildings, walls started to crumble and stone fell from the parapets.

St Vedast Foster Lane was one affected. It had been rebuilt in 1669–72 by the parish, although paid for by Wren from the coal tax revenue.[21] In its rebuilding it may have been the victim of poor workmanship and some or all of the other defects listed. This alone can hardly have justified what was almost a complete reconstruction to a new design requiring demolition of the tower and building a replacement in a new position. Nevertheless, the parish had seemingly been left with what was essentially a poor-quality church to a pre-Fire design which contrasted markedly with the later churches to be rebuilt. The vestrymen must have agreed to its replacement, and may even have proposed it, but the design and execution was the responsibility of Wren and the Commissioners who approved it. How much of the new building of St Dunstan-in-the-East, St Sepulchre and St Christopher-le-Stocks of that time was fully justified on structural grounds it is now no longer possible to judge.

In spite of these demands upon his resources, Wren's intention, following the renewal of the coal tax, must surely have been to adorn the already completed towers with steeples. This must also have appealed to many of the parishes whose towers had been left: some are known to have used the more relaxed financial position to press for a steeple. Unlike towers, it simply was not possible to erect steeples to anything like a standard pattern; and it was these designs that provided some of the more spectacular architectural achievements of the Commissioners. As for the cost, it cannot have been long before the total commitment, had all the churches been given new steeples, would have more than exhausted the money available from the coal tax.

At first the new steeples were mostly similar in style to those constructed earlier in the programme with turrets and cupolas, terminating with slender pinnacles or 'spikes'. Those erected later show a trend away from a strict classicism, towards the baroque of the early eighteenth century, raising questions of authorship which are considered later.

Shortly before the turn of the century it was time, once again, for the Commissioners to return to Parliament for a further renewal of the coal tax. The move was primarily intended to ensure the completion of the cathedral; the parish churches were mentioned only briefly in the petition. The churches themselves had all been completed and the comment in the parliamentary record that 'many parochial churches [were] not finished' must refer to their steeples.[22] In the event, Parliament voted to continue the tax on coals from 29 September 1700 to 29 September 1716.[23]

In its passage through Parliament the Bill attracted petitions from a number of parish vestries in the London area, each seeking access to the coal tax fund for the repair or rebuilding of its own church.[24] The House of Commons, it seems, had little sympathy with these and all were rejected except for that of St Thomas the Apostle, the parish church of St Thomas's Hospital, Southwark. St Thomas's claim, that it could not rebuild its church without diverting money set aside for the care of wounded soldiers and the sick, induced Parliament to include a clause in the Act making available £3000 from the coal tax revenue for the hospital.[25]

Whereas there is little doubt that the Commissioners met regularly as a formal body in the early days of the Commission, it seems that their meetings became fewer and fewer as time passed. There are, for example, none at all recorded in the order book for 1683–84. More and more of the instructions to Wren for work to be done seem to have been drafted for them to sign without a meeting. There is indeed a suggestion that Wren carried draft orders with him for signature at opportune meetings with individual Commissioners. Even this may eventually have been replaced by no more than a verbal agreement. Wren was increasingly in control of the programme. There is no reason to suppose that this met with other than approval from the Commissioners. They had other things to do than rubber-stamp proposals from Wren. Their acceptance was a measure of the trust they had in him. Regrettably, the orders produced in this way were not transcribed into a more permanent record. Those known to us from the later part of the programme have survived only by chance. The last order in the record book is dated 30 November 1685, although rebuilding of some of the churches and the provision of steeples was to continue until the money ran out in 1717.

The building campaign lasted for forty-seven years. In that time all the fifty-one churches named in the Act of 1670 had been rebuilt, almost all the work being charged to the tax on coal coming into the port of London. In spite of statements made to the contrary,[26] no evidence has emerged to suggest that the rate of church building was determined by the rate at which stone became available for building, or that it was affected by a shortage of craftsmen in the City. Only two controlling factors have been noted, both financial: the rate at which the coal tax accumulated to pay for the operations; and the extent to which the parish vestries were able to raise loans against a future repayment from the coal tax fund.

6

Parish Records, Patronage and Influence

It was Thomas Cromwell, Vicar General in the time of Henry VIII, who in 1536 required parish vestries to keep written registers. Few of these early documents now survive, some of the oldest being those of St James Garlickhithe, but many parishes have registers, churchwardens' accounts and vestry minutes from well before the Great Fire of 1666. The survival of so many suggests that their preservation from the Fire was considered important, for they must have been carried to places of safety at a time when the churchwardens had much else to think of. Following the Fire the written parish records, although at first somewhat sparse, continue almost without a break, with most of the parishes using the same books to record both the pre-Fire and post-Fire vestries, separated by no more than a page or two, if that. Most of these early records were surrendered to the Guildhall Library for safe-keeping; in the Second World War, although there was widespread destruction of the City churches, few of these old records were lost.

For the historian, there is no shortage of written records – just a shortage of information contained within them. Only where the vestries themselves made decisions do their minutes record the events of the time. It is for this reason that in some parishes these minutes make no reference whatever to the rebuilding of the church at public expense. Even where the rebuilding is mentioned, there is an almost total absence of information concerning the authorship of the designs. This absence is so marked as to suggest that such matters were general knowledge in the parish rather than only for discussion or debate within the vestry. Even in those cases where there is evidence to suggest that a particular vestry was much concerned with getting Sir Christopher Wren himself to design its new church, authorship is (with a single exception) not mentioned. Nor was Wren more explicit, leaving no claim to having produced the design of any of the City churches. Nor did his assistants, Hooke, Woodroffe, Oliver, Hawksmoor and Dickinson, make any personal claim for a part in the design process.[1]

The claim for Wren's authorship of all the fifty-one parish churches was made by his son, Christopher: 'Fifty-one parochial Churches of the City of London, erected according to the Designs, and under the Care and Conduct, of Sir Christopher Wren, in lieu of those which were burnt and demolish'd by the great Fire . . .'² It is now seen as a gross simplification, broadly true in only a very wide sense. Even the phrase 'under the Care and Conduct' is misleading for, as has been noted, a small number of the fifty-one churches were soon repaired, with Wren doing little more than meeting the bills with funding from the coal tax revenue. These, certainly, were repaired and reerected under the care and conduct of the parish officials.

The only parish church for which Wren is known to have claimed authorship is St James Piccadilly, in the City of Westminster. In a letter to his fellow 1711 Act Commissioners, in which he is commenting upon the design of parish churches, he wrote:

> I hardly think it practical to make a single Room so capacious, with Pews and Galleries, as to hold above 2000 Persons, and all to hear the Service, and both to hear distinctly, and see the Preacher. I endeavoured to effect this, in building the Parish Church of St James, Westminster . . . I think it may be found beautiful and convenient, and as such, the cheapest of any Form I could invent.³

The parish was not created until 1685 and its records contain no reference to how the church came to be designed or who was responsible for it. The evidence has been collected and reviewed by the *Survey of London*.⁴ It consists, apart from the claim made by Wren himself, of a study of his relationship with the Earl of St Albans, who was the prime mover in establishing the parish and the principal subscriber to the cost of the church. Wren had been given a letter of introduction to him when he visited France in 1665 and would seem to have been the Earl's natural choice of architect.

Documentary evidence of one sort or another is always attractive, especially if it provides what seem to be reliable and unequivocal statements. Nevertheless, if it is incomplete there is the possibility of giving a false impression. This is well illustrated in the parish records of St Stephen Walbrook. The churchwardens' accounts for this period have survived and the entries for 1673 and 1673–74 include the following:

> Paid to ye Survaer Gennarall by order of Vestry 20 Ginnes [guineas] for a gratuety to his Lady to incuring and hasting ye rebuilding ye church.

> Paid Mr Hook surveyor by order of vestry, 5 Guineas.

> Paid for a piece of plate by order of vestry for Mr Woodriffe, £5 5s. 0d.⁵

There is no mention of any design work or who may have been responsible for it, and the interpretation of these surviving accounts could be that the three men were jointly responsible for the rebuilding of the parish church, with Woodroffe, here as elsewhere, in control of the building operations, and with Wren, as we are told, active in 'incuring and hasting' the work. Hooke may have been responsible for the designing and for negotiating agreement on the design with the parish. If no other document existed (and the survival of any one particular document from this time is to some extent a lottery), this analysis could have formed the basis for arguing that Hooke was the designer of St Stephen Walbrook.

This conclusion, eminently reasonable in the light of this particular document-ary evidence, is however not in agreement with the vestry minutes, which, fortunately, have also survived:

> Ordered Dr Christopher Wren in consideration of his greate care & extraordinary pains taken in ye contriving ye designe of ye church & assisting in ye rebuilding ye same be presented him or his Ladey 20 ginneys, in a silke purse & Mr Woodrof ye Surveyor wth 5 ginneys . . .

> Ordered Mr Hooke ffive Gineys to be given him for his paynes in surveying & measuring ye ground yt belongeth to ye parish.[6]

A different story from that given in the accounts. There can now be no doubt that Wren 'contrived [made] the design'. Woodroffe presumably received his gratuity for his part in its construction. Hooke's five guineas were not, however, for any part in the rebuilding of the church but for surveying the parish land. This is, of course, not to say that Hooke played no part whatsoever in the design of St Stephen Walbrook, only that he was not rewarded for any. Hooke may indeed have helped Wren with the design. Collaboration was normal practice for the two men. But here at least we can accept that there is no evidence of any active involvement by Hooke in the designing. With regard to this particular church there can scarcely ever have been any doubt as to its author.

How the figure of twenty guineas for the gratuity to Sir Christopher Wren was derived is not apparent. Discusion within parish vestries concerning such matters is not recorded. It seems that the figure was considered an appropriate one, as a like amount was later given to Wren by the vestry of St Mary-le-Bow: 'Mr Hotchkins, Churchwarden, shall . . . present twenty guineas to Sir Chris-topher Wren for his courtesy to the Parish in forwarding the finishing of the Church.'[7] This falls far short of confirming any particular role in the rebuilding of St Mary-le-Bow to him. It could, for example, relate to his part in getting the Commissioners to buy additional land to the south and west of the old church in order to enlarge the building; for getting the City Corporation to pay for land on Cheapside used for the new church tower; or for his decision to pull down the old and crumbling tower and build a new one. The balance of view may well be that Wren received his gratuity in appreciation of all that he did for the parish, including providing the design. St Mary-le-Bow received a great deal of his attention, but this is not surprising. As the location of the Archbishop's Court of Arches and the headquarters of his interests in the City, it was the most important of the City churches after the cathedral. Whether or not the Archbishop, as one of the Commissioners, asked Wren to take a special interest in the church is immaterial. Wren, as their servant, would certainly have had regard to the Archbishop's interests and is likely to have viewed St Mary-le-Bow with more than normal concern, second only to St Paul's. The design is after that of the Templum Pacis, the Basilica of Maxentius in Rome, but on a much reduced scale.[8] It was the only one of the City churches to be given a new design with such a well-defined classical ancestry.

Apart from the general claim that his father designed the fifty-one City churches, Christopher Wren junior made a specific claim in respect of his authorship of the tower and steeple of St Mary-le-Bow: 'It was designed by the incomparable Sir Christopher Wren'.[9] It is the only part of any church erected in the Wren period for which such a further detailed claim was made. Nevertheless, as with St James Piccadilly, the existence of an original drawing for the church among the papers of Robert Hooke, and possibly by him, raises here also the question of whether Hooke contributed in some way to the design effort. Whilst it seems safe to conclude from all the available evidence that the design of church, tower and steeple was all by Wren, help from Hooke and from Woodroffe may well have been to hand. St Mary may indeed have been built by Wren with a little help from his friends.

Patronage and Influence

In its widest sense, patronage was a way of life in the seventeenth century, pervading all aspects of both private and official life. In the Court, the City and the Established Church it was not only widespread but completely accepted. Pluralism – the holding of multiple benefices, where the holder paid a junior to undertake the duties – was also common within the Church of England, and many of the richer livings were held by absentee clergy, including deans and bishops in other dioceses.

From time immemorial the benefices or livings held by the incumbents of the parish churches had been in the gift of a variety of patrons. When a living became vacant on the death or resignation of the incumbent, it was the patron of the living who presented his nominee to the Bishop for appointment to the post. In London these patrons ranged from the Archbishop of Canterbury (with his 'peculiars' in the City), the Bishop of London, the Dean and Chapter of St Paul's and the Dean and Chapter of Westminster to City Livery Companies, university colleges and even in a few cases private individuals. There was thus ample opportunity for the exercise of influence, although it must be said that in the written record of the rebuilding of the parish churches there is little evidence of it. The patrons of the living are seldom if ever named in vestry minutes; their low profile may have been from an apprehension that they would be called upon to contribute to the cost of reconstruction. The chancels of parish churches had long been regarded as their responsibility and, in the absence of clearly defined chancels in most of the new churches, they could reasonably have been asked to help with the new buildings, if only to contribute to furnishing and decoration. It is perhaps not surprising that they took back seats.

As one might expect, the patrons showing the greatest interest were those most concerned with the rebuilding: the Commissioners themselves, the Archbishop of Canterbury, the Bishop of London and the Lord Mayors of London in their years in office. In general terms, the Bishop had an interest in seeing that action, following the Act of Parliament providing for the rebuilding of all the fifty-one named churches in his diocese, was promoted as soon as possible. For only a few of these was the living in his own hands, but in a number of others the patronage was held by the Dean and Chapter of the cathedral. There is no indication from the surviving records that either Humphrey Henchman (Bishop 1663–75) or Henry Compton (Bishop 1675–1713) took any more than a general and formal interest in most of the parish churches. Compton's intervention, for example, on behalf of the parishioners of St Nicholas Cole Abbey, ('I desire Dr Wren to direct and order the building of the church of Cole Abbey') seems to have been entirely reasonable, given the unequal treatment of the parishes in the two parts of the City which until then had prevailed.[10] Moreover, the Bishop's intervention did not insist that the task should be personally performed by Wren. It could equally have been done by Hooke. Hooke was a frequent visitor to most of the City churches and his visits, seldom associated with any expenditure by the parish, would have passed unrecorded in both vestry minutes and churchwardens' accounts.

Henry Compton was active in promoting, and was possibly the biggest contributor to the cost of, a new church in Soho, which was then in the parish of St Martin-in-the-Fields. Like St James Piccadilly, it was created a new parish in 1685. The church was dedicated to St Anne in honour of the young Princess Anne, later Queen. The author of the design to which the church was eventually completed is uncertain. Several architects were involved, including Wren and Talman.[11] A design was certainly produced by the Wren Office at St Paul's (Fig. 12). Whether this was by Wren himself is far from clear, as is the extent to which these plans formed the basis of the construction. Due weight, but no more, can be given to the relationship between Wren and the Bishop, and this would certainly account for the existence of the surviving drawings from the Wren Office.

Action by the Lord Mayor in promoting or influencing the rebuilding of the churches is seldom recorded. One of the few examples is that of Sir Patience Ward, Lord Mayor and resident of the parish of St Mary Abchurch, who was apparently concerned that the rebuilding of his own parish church had long been delayed. In 1681 he inquired what the vestry required him to do towards its rebuilding.[12] The grateful vestry later awarded him two pews in the new

FIGURE 12.
St Anne Soho,
proposed east end:
design from the
Wren Office.
(*Conway Library*)

building. He was certainly regarded as instrumental in getting the church rebuilt, but there is no record of what it was that he did. The parish demonstrated its gratitude to Wren with a payment of twenty guineas and, stylistically, the church could be to his design. The arguments are, however, not entirely convincing and authorship remains unproven.

It is possible that successive Lord Mayors were more active in securing the rebuilding of the churches in which they worshipped, or had some other interest, than the surviving documents indicate. A letter from Sir Edward Clarke, Lord Mayor 1696–97, to Sir Christopher Wren concerning All Hallows Bread Street is a chance survival:

> I am informed by several of the parishioners of All Hallows, Bread Street that the steeple of that church is still unfinished. Now as I am particularly engaged in the service of that Ward and the same being situate in a public part of the City I do therefore earnestly recommend the finishing the same as speedily as may be.[13]

There may have been many more instances where pressure of this kind was applied, but there is now no evidence for them.

The living of St Stephen Walbrook was held by the Grocers Company. This, in common with other Livery Companies, had lost heavily in the Great Fire and was in no position to pay for the rebuilding of the church, or provide much by way of contribution. However it could, and probably did, use its position as one of the leading Livery Companies to provide moral support to the vestry and exert pressure on the Commissioners from the City. One influential Company member, later Master of the Company, was Sir Robert Hanson, Lord Mayor in 1672–73 and a Commissioner in his year of office. Whilst there is no record of any action on his part to secure the services of Wren in the designing and rebuilding of St Stephen Walbrook, he is recorded as one of those laying a new foundation stone for it – the only Commissioner or Lord Mayor so recorded. Here, as elsewhere, there is no explicit indication of how City patronage and influence worked, nor whether it led to the direct involvement of Wren.

Other Examples of Influence?

The examples given do not exhaust the list of churches where the personal involvement of Wren is or may be indicated. In particular there are a small number of others which are generally considered to have been designed by him and a few more where his involvement may be suspected. In each case the possibility exists that this involvement may have arisen through personal influence. These include St Andrew Holborn, St Bride Fleet Street and St Clement Danes.

There can be no doubt that Wren was personally involved in the reconstruction of the church of St Andrew Holborn, rebuilt through decrepitude rather than from Fire damage, in the period 1684–86. There are frequent references to him in the rebuilding accounts,[14] including such entries as 'according to the . . . direction of Sir Chr. Wrenn' (mason's contract), 'according to . . . [the] Estimate and Design given by Sir Chr. Wren' (carpenter's contract), 'as Schedule and design of Sir Chr. Wren' (joiner's contract). Wren also approved the accounts and allowed for 'overwork'. Certain minor matters were referred to him for a decision and he was named as one of those who would arbitrate in the event of disputes. The evidence, while perhaps not conclusive, is sufficient to justify attributing the design of the church to him, particularly as (unlike those churches destroyed in the Fire) Hooke had no reason to be involved. How Wren came to be involved is less clear, but the Rector was Edward Stillingfleet, Dean of St Paul's. Need we look further?

The tower from the medieval church was retained and later recased and heightened, probably in 1703–4; no evidence has been found to support any suggestion that the tower was by Wren. From the style, particularly the pinnacles and the bell-loft windows, it seems more likely to be by Nicholas Hawksmoor.

In 1670 the parish vestry of St Bride Fleet Street instructed one of its churchwardens to wait on Sir Christopher Wren.[15] There is no record of what took place at that meeting, but it may have been instrumental in securing for St Bride's a place among the first fifteen churches that were to be rebuilt. The church lost its place when the list was abandoned. The parish was then offered a tabernacle to be erected at the charge of the Commissioners, but this apparently did not meet the wishes of the parish. Instead, the parish raised £500 by way of deposit to the Chamber of London. This, on 28 January 1671, ensured a place for the new church in the revised or 'ordinary' building programme.

There was a further meeting with the parish on 15 August 1671 when both Wren and Hooke were entertained to dinner at the Globe Tavern,[16] but by then the design of the church had been settled and work on the site started. The building accounts give 16 January 1672 as the date of the first measurement of the masons' work to the value of £932 16s. 10½d.[17] This, allowing for the excavations that were needed for both church and tower, can hardly have been less than a whole year's work. Site clearance must therefore have started early in 1671. The mason's contract to take down the remains of the tower and all the surviving walls is dated 25 February 1671.[18] The designing of the church must therefore have been done in 1670 or very early in 1671. In this period, apart from the earlier meeting with the churchwarden, there is no record of any contact between the vestry and Wren or Hooke. This early date for the design of St Bride is confirmed by a Commissioners' minute of 1681, which is prefaced with the information that 'the church of St Bridgett alias Brides was begun to be rebuilt anno 1670'.[19]

Clearly there is much that we do not know about the early history of the designing of the church. Better recorded are the occasions, with the shell of the church completed, when the parish vestry sought Wren's advice and approval, particularly over the design and installation of the galleries in the church and the joiners' work in providing the pulpit, portals and 'other works at the east end'.[20] He had a clear personal commitment to the parish, although no special reason for this has so far been proposed. The personal contact may have been the Vicar, Paul Boston. He did not live to see the building completed, dying in 1672. He had been awarded the degree of MA from Oxford in 1642/43, but this link with Oxford is too early to have formed the basis for any personal relationship with Wren and none later is known. His subsequent career is poorly documented, with a gap from 1643 until 1666 when he was appointed to St Bride's.

The vestry minutes of St Clement Danes for the years 1677–86, in which the church was rebuilt (like St Andrew Holborn, from decrepitude), were destroyed in the war of 1939–45. The extent of the association of Sir Christopher Wren with the rebuilding can now be followed only from transcripts and other surviving documents. There is, however, a record of a tablet originally displayed on the north side of the chancel to the effect that the church,

> being greatly decay'd was taken down in the year 1680 and rebuilt and finished in 1682. Sir Christopher Wren, his Majesty's Surveyor, freely and generously bestowing his great Care and Skill towards the contriving and building of it.[21]

This tablet, no longer in place, indicates that the parish officials, who were responsible for it, had no doubt of Wren's work in designing the church, although he had no responsibility to the Commissioners or to Parliament for doing so. Details of Wren's personal involvement are tantalisingly few, although there are records of payments for his entertainment.[22] There is a note of his examining and abating a bill from Edward Pearce, mason and carver, for work in the body of the church, gallery, doorcases, stairs to pulpit, the pulpit itself, type and reredos, amounting in all to £412 5s. 9d.[23] Sir Christopher is also referred to in the articles of agreement signed by the masons, John Shorthose and Edward Pearce.[24] Would we be wrong in looking towards the Wren connection with Windsor, with the Rector of St Clement Danes, Gregory Hascard, Dean of Windsor? There are drawings for the church which, from their provenance in the Bute Collection,[25] must have come from the Wren Office at St Paul's, although they are not in Wren's hand. The steeple, projected but not built (Fig. 13), is close in design to that of St Peter Cornhill, which suggests there may have been collaboration with Hooke, although Hooke had no official involvement with either St Clement Danes or St Andrew Holborn.

Another church where influence may have been important is St Lawrence Jewry, whose Vicar, John Wilkins, was Warden of Wadham College, Oxford, at the time of Wren's residence there. Wilkins was a Fellow of the Royal Society and, like Wren and Hooke, a mathematician with an interest in natural science and astronomy. His vicariate at St Lawrence extended only until 1668, when he was appointed Bishop of Chester, but his influence with Wren may have continued until his death on 19 November 1672.

Other vestries which made gifts of the same or a similar amount to Wren included St James Garlickhithe and St Antholin. The gift of plate ('a ps of plat') to the value of £21 15s. 0d. is recorded from St Benet Fink and a hogshead of wine from each of the vestries of St Clement East Cheap, St Magnus the Martyr and St Martin Ludgate. The quality of wine and its price was, no doubt, as variable then as it is now. The cost to St Martin Ludgate amounted to £15 4s. 0d., recognition of some important unrecorded service.

All these gifts, although they demonstrate the appreciation of individual parishes for the services provided by Sir Christopher Wren, may not have been expressly for church designs. St Peter Cornhill gave him a total of £15 5s. 0d., but this is recorded as 'for his pains and furtherance about the tabernacle', with no record at all of who designed the church. St Mary Aldermanbury gave not only twenty guineas to Wren, but also ten guineas to Robert Hooke. This might be interpreted as Hooke having responsibility for the design and Wren being the intermediary with the Commission. But is this right?

Finally, the possibility remains that, where parish records now no longer exist, further examples of gratuities to Wren have been lost. We would dearly like to know what happened at Christchurch, where the parish records have been destroyed. The Vicar, Richard Henchman, was also Treasurer of St Paul's and would have known Wren well. Did he secure Wren's help in designing the new church in Newgate, or was he content with what Robert Hooke produced?

The small number of churches now personally attributed to Wren is unlikely to represent all that he was asked to design. He could and possibly did divert some of the requests that came his way to Hooke, leaving himself with those that he chose to execute as a favour or because it was expedient for him to attend to them personally. Wren's contribution to the rebuilding the parish

FIGURE 13.
St Clement Danes,
project design for
the west end.
(*Conway Library*)

churches in terms of design was numerically only modest, with Hooke having the greater part of the task and the greater number now to his credit.

Whereas there is a reasonable body of documentary evidence, reviewed here, for attributing some of the parish churches to Sir Christopher Wren, the equivalent documentary evidence for attributing any of the remaining churches to Hooke is non-existent. There are no instances where authorship of any was claimed by him, none where the parish attribute the design of their church to him and none where the vestry gave him a gratuity which can be specifically associated with design. No particular relationships have been observed to link his name with patrons, incumbents or Commissioners, although further research may be more revealing.

In summary, the evidence provided by the parish vestry minutes and church-wardens' accounts is of particular value in indicating indebtedness to Sir Christopher Wren and, occasionally, to Robert Hooke and John Oliver. Care is needed in interpreting such records and reaching an understanding of what it was that constituted that debt. An obvious conclusion, that twenty guineas given to Wren was associated with a design by him, is unlikely to be entirely true, although a useful indicator of his involvement. Taken in conjunction with other evidence, such payments nevertheless indicate the possibility that Wren himself may have been the designer of the parish church. The towers and steeples are a different story.

7

Architectural Drawings,
Illustrations and Models

The chance survival from medieval times of scratches on a prepared plaster surface, or tooled markings on a stone wall from antiquity, serve to remind that there has always been a need for the architect to make drawings and to communicate with the builder through them. The invention and widespread use of paper greatly simplified that process but, with the impermanence of paper, few such drawings survived once the building was complete and the need for that communication ceased.

Architectural Drawings

The production of architectural drawings in the England of the seventeenth century followed what was already being done in mainland Europe, where the technique of building according to a portfolio of drawings had been developed. They represented, in carefully scaled form, plans, elevations and sections of each new building, from which the craftsmen could work without requiring the constant attention of the designer. Such drawings became commonplace across Europe. This was nowhere more true than in London, where large numbers must have been produced for the new buildings for the burnt-out area of the City. The ones of greatest interest are those produced by Wren and his assistants for the new St Paul's Cathedral and for the City churches. This style of church-building was to set the pattern of design for such buildings well into the eighteenth century.

Although these drawings were the media through which London was to be redeveloped, as documents they remain elusive. Relatively few have survived, large numbers being lost: most were taken to building sites and repeatedly handled by the surveyors, craftsmen and lesser workmen, until they were dirty, torn and no longer of interest. They then disappeared into the general rubbish that accumulates on all building sites. Nor do we have any idea of how many were produced for St Paul's and the parish churches – hundreds certainly, thousands perhaps, if drawings for the detailing are included. We are grateful for those that are now left. They are the fortunate if chance survivors, owing their existence to events which rescued them from the building sites and preserved them in a drawer of an office somewhere, ignored and often forgotten.

Typical also is the survival of what has been called the office waste of discarded drawings, with ideas that were half formed or later superseded and then discarded, drawings never intended to be more than ephemeral. These brief sketches, the first thoughts, developing ideas and solutions to problems, were usually discarded almost as soon as they had served their purpose. Within the lifetime of the project at least, there can have been no intention of collecting or preserving them. A few were turned over and the reverse side of the paper used for new drawing, but most were simply set aside and then lost.

With the completion of St Paul's Cathedral, the Office was cleared and it was probably at this time that many such drawings for St Paul's and the surviving drawings for the City churches, all that remained of a much larger collection, were carried off by Wren. They represented much of his life's work, no longer wanted by anyone else.

Sir Christopher Wren's Drawings

In the collection of drawings in Wren's possession at his death, sketches for the early designs of St Paul's jostled with those of the City churches, the Monument, St Clement Danes and other buildings for which he had been responsible. We do not know what proportion of his total output of drawings was then represented by this personal collection. In number it amounted to rather less than a thousand, of which, as might be expected, those for St Paul's and the City churches predominated. At his death in 1723 these passed to his son, Christopher, and were eventually auctioned by Langford at his rooms in Covent Garden on 4 April 1749. Wren's books had already been dispersed, following a sale in October 1748, but his collection of architectural drawings and his son's numismatic collection, comprising 'Greek and Roman medals, medallions in silver and brass, antique marble statues, urns, inscriptions, bronzes, gems and other curiosities', then remained.

The interest which has since developed in these drawings and their later dispersal has tended to obscure the fact that there were many other Wren drawings outside his personal collection, which therefore did not feature in the sale. These included a great many more of the drawings for St Paul's, possibly left by Wren or the St Paul's Commissioners in the cathedral library, and drawings for the Royal Hospital at Greenwich, now in the possession of the National Maritime Museum. They reached their present locations by some route other than the 1749 sale. The RIBA drawings for Greenwich and a part of the collection in the Sir John Soane's Museum similarly cannot be identified in the sale catalogue.

Whilst there are in existence a number of important Wren drawings for the City churches, notably in the British Library, whose provenance cannot at the present time be traced, the greater number of these drawings came from Wren's personal collection. In the almost complete absence of any commentary from Wren and Hooke concerning the design process, it is these drawings which tell us much of what is known about the construction of the churches.

A total of five copies of the 1749 sales catalogue are known to exist. Of these, four – the two copies in the Sir John Soane's Museum, and those in the British Library and the British Museum – have similar annotations, leading to the suspicion that these markings were copied from one to the others and not all made at the time of the sale.[1] The fifth copy, now in the Bodleian,[2] has a larger number of annotations and gives the prices obtained and the names of buyers for most of the lots offered. It may well be the auctioneer's copy. The sale seems to have attracted little attention at the time, with most of the purchasers being interested in the coins and medals which constituted the bulk of the items on offer.

In the sale, the drawings comprised sixteen lots numbered 30 to 45:

30. 82 designs and 2 large prints of St Paul's in portfolio.
31. 114 large & finished drawings of St Paul's, Bow and other churches in London; also the Monument, Whitehall, Winchester Castle, Trinity College, Cambridge, etc. & 3 prints pasted into a large book.
32. 32 very large drawings of Whitehall, Windsor and Greenwich.
33. A Book of Astronomical Schemes.
34. 100 drawings and sketches of London churches in a Portfolio.
35. 66 drawings of Hampton Court.
36. 102 drawings & sketches of Kensington Palace, & miscellaneous architecture.
37. 101 ditto, in a cover.
38. 113 ditto, in a Portfolio.

39. 69 do of Hampton Court, Warwick church & other buildings in cover.
40. 7 large finished drawings of St Paul's, 1 of Monument, plan of London after the Fire.
41. Large Port Folio of finished drawings of Hôtel des Invalides.
42. 150 drawings and sketches of Winchester Palace, & Miscellaneous Architecture, with a parcel of papers relating to the subjects.
43. A large high-finished Drawing of St Paul's.
44. Ditto of the inside of St Paul's.
45. A long ditto of an intended New Palace at Westminster.

The individuals who purchased these drawings were identified in the Bodleian copy of the sales catalogue as 'Grover', 'Stack', 'Argyle' and 'Prowse'. No purchasers were identified for lots 35 (Hampton Court), 36 (Kensington Palace and miscellaneous architecture) and 41 (Hôtel des Invalides, Paris).[3] As the catalogue gives the sale prices for these items, it must be assumed that the purchaser's name (or names) was unknown to the annotator, rather than that the items remaining unsold.

John Grover, a Clerk at the House of Commons,[4] purchased lot 30 consisting largely of drawings for St Paul's Cathedral. These were later acquired by the printer Alexander Strahan and then by Robert Mylne for the use of St Paul's. They are now on deposit in the Guildhall Library, forming a major part of the St Paul's collection, catalogued by Kerry Downes.[5]

Dr Thomas Stack, Foreign Secretary of the Royal Society,[6] purchased 429 items in five volumes for which he paid six guineas. He disposed of them in 1751, when they were listed at £21 in a bookseller's catalogue.[7] They were purchased at that price for the newly completed Codrington Library of All Souls College, Oxford.[8] This constitutes the largest number of Wren drawings in a single collection. By far the greater number are for other buildings erected by Wren, but the collection also includes a few which relate to the church-building programme of the Commissioners appointed under the Act of 1711 for the Building of Fifty New Churches. In 1711–15 Wren was a Commissioner, appointed under this Act, and it must be presumed that these few drawings relate to the activity of those years. They include drawings by Dickinson, Hawksmoor and others.

'Argyle', the third Duke of Argyll, purchased 158 items in three lots, including drawings for many of the parish churches of London. He died in 1761 and his collection was acquired by the third Earl of Bute. It was believed to have been destroyed in a library fire at Luton Hoo in 1771.[9] The collection, then the property of the fifth Marquess of Bute, reappeared at Sotheby's saleroom in 1951 and was dispersed following the sale. Many of the most important church drawings were acquired by the National Art Collections Fund for British collections. A few have disappeared into private holdings.[10]

'Prowse' was almost certainly Thomas Prowse, a country gentleman, amateur architect and MP for Somerset. He seems to have had little or no interest in Christopher Wren's coins and medals and was the only purchaser at the sale interested solely in the architectural drawings. He acquired 102 drawings in three lots, including one hundred for London churches and two for St Paul's. He also bought a further lot, an unspecified number of drawings described only as 'Astronomical Schemes'. Despite an extensive search, none of these drawings has yet come to light. In the absence of further detail it might be concluded that it was the break up of this group which enabled drawings of the churches, notably their towers and steeples, to be acquired for the King's Topographical Collection,[11] but this is by no means certain, and in any case would account for no more than a dozen or so. It is more likely that all the drawings in this portfolio have been lost.

It is tempting to suggest, with so few buyers at the sale, that lots 35, 36 and 41 (to which no names are attached) may have been all bought by the same individual. Lot 35, the Hampton Court volume, is known as the album of drawings now in the Sir John Soane's Museum, having passed from George Dance the Younger to Sir John Soane in 1817. Arthur Bolton suggested that the purchaser was George Dance the Elder.[12] Although an eminently sensible suggestion, no evidence has so far emerged to support it. If these three lots were acquired by George Dance, what then happened to lots 36 and 41?

In 1926 the editors of the Wren Society, in their Volume 3, compared the lists of drawings known to them in various collections with those listed in the sale catalogue,[13] but found a numerical discrepancy, with only 584 that they could attribute to the sale, as against at least 924 in the catalogue. By 1954, following the Bute Sale, Fuerst felt that he could be more positive:

> it is gratifying to know that no important or considerable part of the material has been lost . . . no further major discoveries of hitherto unknown material are probable, and that it is highly unlikely that any documentary evidence, in the form of drawings, should yet come to light which would call for a revision and revaluation of the work of Sir Christopher Wren.[14]

There can be few architectural historians who would be so confident today. Although Fuerst's arithmetic suggests that the total number of drawings in known

Wren collections is not markedly different from the number disposed of in the 1749 sale, their contents do not match the descriptions of the sale catalogue. Nowhere, for example, can the Astronomical Schemes of lot 33 or the drawings for the Hôtel des Invalides of lot 41 be located.

The City Church Drawings

It is unlikely that we shall ever know, even approximately, how many drawings were originally made for the City churches. Between one hundred and two hundred are known to have survived, with another hundred from the missing lot 34. Of those in existence, only a handful have been identified as in Wren's hand. Rather more are likely to be by Hooke. Other names have been attached to a few, but by far the greater number are attributed to the 'Wren Office', that is to the draughtsmen and copyists working in the Office at St Paul's, whose function included converting the rough sketches provided by the surveyors into measured drawings and to duplicating these for the use of the craftsmen. Holes pricked through with a pin in some of the surviving drawings show how the copying was done. There is little evidence to suggest that 'office copies' of any of the drawings were made specifically for retention or future reference, a practice not adopted on any scale until the middle of the eighteenth century. Few, if any, of the drawings taken and used by the craftsmen and surveyors at the building sites can have been returned to the office. Hardly any of them have survived.

No drawings of any kind are known for those churches which were rebuilt by the parishes themselves, prior to Wren's involvement with rebuilding the City churches in 1670. These, excluding their later towers – St Christopher-le-Stocks, St Dunstan-in-the-East, St Michael Cornhill, St Sepulchre, St Vedast Foster Lane (and the church of St Mary Woolnoth) – may have been rebuilt entirely without drawings, but if any were made, there was no reason for them to have been sent to the Office at St Paul's.

The survival of drawings for the remaining churches is haphazard, with some churches (such as St Benet Paul's Wharf) represented by a number of related drawings, others by none at all. Where the parish vestries were content to leave Wren and his assistants and craftsmen to get on with the rebuilding, fewer drawings may have been produced, but there is no clear evidence for this. The drawings for some of the churches may simply not have survived.

The drawings for the churches are now widely scattered. By far the largest group, which with other Wren drawings amounts to not far short of 500,[15] is in the Codrington Library of All Souls College, Oxford. Others are in the collection of the Royal Institute of British Architects, with smaller numbers in the British Library; the Guildhall Library of the City of London; the Mrs Tweet Kimball Collection of Sedalia, USA; Sir John Soane's Museum; and a few more still in private hands.

Plans of the Destroyed Churches

The Commissioners' general accounts contain the names of two draughtsmen who 'took ground plotts of . . . churches yet unbuilt'.[16] William Walgrave was paid £2 10s. 0d. on 2 March 1674/75 for twelve plots and Henry Hunt £6 10s. 0d. for thirteen plots on 7 July 1677. Between them these two men drew the ground plans of about one half of those churches selected for rebuilding. No other individuals are noted as engaged in this activity, although others employed by Wren, including Andrew Philips, described as Wren's clerk, and John Scarborough, who was paid for surveying and measuring, may each have prepared more.

The ground plan of St Mary Somerset, one of the last of the City churches to be rebuilt, was probably drawn by William Kempster, mason. It is the only known instance where a craftsman can be identified as a likely author of a drawing. Sir John Summerson, commenting on the crudity of the plan, suggested that any connection with Wren's Office was unlikely and its purpose doubtful.[17] However, the plan must have passed through the Office to reach his collection. It seems that a crudely drawn plan was all that was required, providing a sufficient basis for the replanning that then took place.

Project Drawings

Project drawings are often of greatest interest to the architectural historian, since they are more likely to be in the hand of one of the architects, Wren, Hooke, Hawksmoor or Dickinson, and tell us something about the design process. They occasionally display features in freehand, making the identification of the author a little easier than the ruled drawings.

The drawings used for construction enabled the craftsmen and surveyors to interpret the approved design and the work to proceed without the presence of the architect. Very few project drawings have survived. Those for Christchurch Newgate are particularly important and are discussed in a later chapter. No draughtsman's name has so far been attached to them.

The general accounts record the name of Thomas Lane, who received a payment of £10 on 14 July 1677 for 'coppying the designs of several churches'. He was then paid further amounts varying from £5 to £10 in succeeding years to 1682 to a total of £82 10s. for his work in copying. His style has not been identified, but clearly he was responsible for a large number of the copies made, especially of the measured drawings needed for the craftsmen. Andrew Phillips and John Scarborough may have contributed others.

Presentation Drawings

It is apparent, from the first meeting of the Commissioners, that they intended to submit designs for the new churches to the King for his approbation. This practice soon lapsed and few presentational drawings can have been prepared for him. The only known survival is an elevation of the street façade, tower and steeple for St Edmund the King, which has the inscription 'With his Majties Approbation', indicating that the King had not only seen it but approved it. Other drawings which can be considered as 'presentational' include those of a few selected steeples which were prepared for engraving, but the original drawings for them are not now known. There is also a set of steeple drawings in a bound volume in the Guildhall Library, whose purpose is not entirely clear. Their neatness and general arrangement suggests that these too were prepared, about 1700, for presentation of some kind.[18] They consist largely of elevations of the towers and steeples with sections and cross-sections at various levels. This portfolio consists largely of designs by Hawksmoor and the possibility that they were intended for engraving cannot be dismissed.

Problems of Authorship

Elsewhere considerable emphasis has been placed upon the problems of identifying the various hands of the drawings, although this is particularly difficult with ruled drawings and office copies. It is the more so where two or more individuals have contributed. In making attributions reliance is often placed upon freehand features, including lettering and figuring, which are more characteristic, but they may not be by the individual who produced the rest of the drawing.

The drawings are important from several points of view: they sometimes give an idea of how the design evolved; they provide an indication of what the architect was thinking; they provide otherwise lost information related to the pre-Fire building and the way in which the site was to be reused; they give some information against which the reutilisation of any remaining walls can be considered; and in some cases they can indicate the architect.

Wren's authorship of the drawings for St Stephen Walbrook, an attribution by Summerson, is not surprising in view of the crediting of the church to him.[19] What is surprising is that no other drawings for the City churches have so far been realistically credited specifically to him.

Equally difficult to unravel is the extent of both drawing and designing by the young Hawksmoor. His work for the Wren Office encompassed everything from the copying of existing drawings to the production of new designs. The retirement of Hooke and the appointment of Hawksmoor in his stead must mark the completion of a process in which Hawksmoor became an architect in his own right, but when did it begin? Was there ever a time when the youthful, precocious Hawksmoor was not prepared to chance his arm with ideas of his own and drawings to illustrate them?

Later Plans and Illustrations

Although the surviving original drawings are of great interest for the information they provide about the design process, they do not necessarily give a precise or accurate picture of the buildings as they were constructed. Of the plans and elevations from Wren's personal collection, none can with certainty be said to represent what was built.

In the first two (or possibly three) decades of the eighteenth century, there was further interest in producing engravings of the Wren towers and steeples, possibly a joint venture by Hawksmoor and Wren's son, Christopher.[20] Whatever the project was, it remained incomplete. Only a small number of such engravings survive, and there are few copies of them, notably in the Pepys Collection,[21]

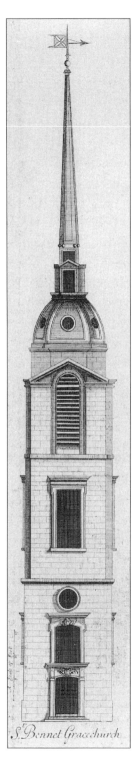

FIGURE 14.
St Benet Gracechurch,
tower and steeple.
(*Pepys Library*)

FIGURE 15.
St Augustine,
Old Change, tower
and steeple.
(*Pepys Library*)

which has engravings of the towers and steeples of St Benet Gracechurch (Fig. 14), St Augustine Old Change (Fig. 15) and St Martin Ludgate, all of which must date from no later than 1703.

A new edition of Stow's *History of London*, by John Strype in 1720, gave descriptions of the rebuilt parish churches, but the work was not illustrated. Later revisions and histories by other authors contain engravings of the elevations of many of the City churches. They are mostly small in scale and often not well drawn. Few ground plans were prepared and none engraved. Some of the earliest plans were those of St Christopher-le-Stocks, St Michael Crooked Lane and St Bartholomew-by-the-Exchange, probably all made or connected in some way with proposals to demolish these churches.

It may have been the loss of these three churches and the threatened demolition of others that prompted Frederick Crace to begin his collection of plans, sections and elevations of the Wren churches. Although incomplete and not always particularly accurate,[22] the Crace Collection represents the first systematic compilation of Wren church designs. As an interior decorator, the artistic side of the work appealed more to Crace than accuracy of detail. This work of his cannot be precisely dated but must have been produced over a number of decades, from some time after 1820 and continuing until his death in 1859.

Crace's project to record the Wren churches came at a time when very little other interest was being shown in them. Renewed concern for them, particularly among architects, seems to have originated with C. R. Cockerell, who drew a perspective of St Paul's and the City steeples in 1838 as a personal tribute to Wren. It was Cockerell who inspired another architect, John Clayton, to survey the Wren churches and produce measured and dimensioned drawings of them. Although without commentary, these drawings, published in 1848–49 and rearranged and republished by the Wren Society in 1932, remain the earliest guide to these churches in their the plans, sections, elevations and decorative detail. Occasional errors can be spotted in some of the drawings, but they are nevertheless of enormous value to present-day historians.

Complimentary to these drawings are the engravings, based upon drawings by competent artists and engraved by skilled engravers, to illustrate the churches of London in such nineteenth-century books as Clarke's *Architectura Ecclesiastica Londini*, of 1820; and Godwin and Britton's *The Churches of London* of 1838–39. Examples of both are included in the Gazetteer which constitutes the second part of this book. They succeed in conveying the atmosphere of the street scenes in a way that measured drawings never can, often with lowering clouds scudding across the skies and figures enlivening the foreground. They cannot be dismissed as mere artists' impressions, for they contain much architectural detail that has changed with time, particularly decorative detail and the positioning of doors and windows. They serve to remind us that the plans and elevations of John Clayton record the churches as they were in the mid nineteenth century, not necessarily how they were left by Wren.

Despite a revived interest in the Wren churches, their destruction continued to the end of the nineteenth century and into the twentieth, initially with inadequate recording of the demolished fabric and occasionally with no record at all, other than the casual observations of interested onlookers. Sudden destruction in the war of 1939–45 contributed further losses. More positively, post-war excavation by William Grimes, notably in the ruins of St Alban Wood Street, St Bride Fleet Street and St Swithin London Stone, added much, not only to the archeological record but also to the details of the constructional history in the rebuilding of the Wren period.

The Photographic Record

If there is cause to complain of the paucity and poor quality of surviving architectural drawings of the Wren churches, the same cannot be said of the photographic record. The photographs of Charles Latham, published in 1896,[23] are superb examples of the art and there is no shortage of snapshots recording these buildings ever since. There is also abundant other illustrative material, artists' impressions, sketches, and watercolours, testifying to the greater interest in the Wren churches in the past hundred years. However, the recent damage to St Mary-at-Hill and the loss of St Ethelburga have demonstrated all too clearly the inadequacy of the existing photographic and other types of record when faced with the task of rebuilding or reconstruction. There is a great contrast between the available photographs of carvings by Grinling Gibbons, for example, and those of architectural detail such as the mouldings of cornices, architraves and other features. Those constructional details which an architect would provide for a new building are seldom drawn or photographed.

Photographs taken in more than a century of photographic development have been assembled by the Royal Commission on Historical Monuments of England in the National Monument Record. These have now been supplemented by a more systematic photographic collection taken specially by their photographer,

Derek Kendall. Both his black and white and his colour photographs capture much of the splendour and sparkle of the buildings and their fittings. They provide an exciting extension to the Record, making many of the examples already in the collection look grim and second-rate. His work will undoubtedly be widely used.

Architectural Models

In contrast to architectural drawings, which were abundantly produced and used throughout the Wren building period, three-dimensional architectural models were little used in the entire campaign. They never assumed the importance that they had, for example, in the evolution of the designs for St Paul's Cathedral. Where the parish churches were reconstructed along the lines of the pre-Fire churches there would clearly have been no need of any model to assist in formulating designs. Where models might have been expected – for those churches which were erected to new and revolutionary designs – St Mary-le-Bow, St Stephen Walbrook, St Benet Fink and St Antholin – none has been recorded.

In accordance with the practice of the time, models of architectural features were sometimes made, presumably by the craftsmen involved, prior to undertaking their construction. At St Mary-le-Bow, William Grey (or Gray) was paid £1 4s. 0d. for a model of the steeple cornice; and Edward Pearce, mason and carver, made a wooden dragon for a model of the vane (he also made a cut out of the dragon in board 'to be preferred up to discerne the right bigness'). The masons Thomas Cartwright and John Thompson were paid £10 for models in connection with the building of the steeple, but no description of them survives. They were also paid for a model of pineapples.

Models were produced for a few of the more detailed and elaborate steeples, particularly those constructed following the 1697 renewal of the coal tax and the steeple-building that came with it. The earliest of these was the steeple of St Magnus the Martyr, for which John Thompson, mason, was paid £5 14s. 0d. for a model. Construction began in 1703 and was completed by 1706. Other models were produced by John Heisenbuttel for Christchurch Newgate,[24] by Samuel Fulkes for St Bride Fleet Street and Edward Strong junior for St Vedast Foster Lane. All these models seem to have been made well before the construction of the steeples was financially possible. None is known to have survived.

8

Design, Classification and Style

The prospect, faced by Wren and Hooke in the year 1670, of building fifty-one parish churches in the seventeen years for which Parliament had granted the tax on coal, was undoubtedly daunting. No campaign on such a scale had ever been mounted and, at the outset, the problems to be encountered were largely unknown. As far as the architecture of the churches was concerned, both architects were fully aware of the need to consider not only the nature of each site but also what remained of the fabric of the old churches left on each one. From these sites and these remains each new church was considered afresh, with no two designs alike. The change from medieval to classical architecture must have given many problems but, in designing these churches, one principle above all others emerged as uppermost in the minds of Wren and Hooke: the need to ensure that all the parishioners attending services could see and that all could hear. Wren's comment to this effect, made in a letter written in connection with the Fifty New Churches to be built by the 1711 Act Commission, was based upon his experience with the post-Fire City churches.[1] The maximum size was calculated and the dimensions then determined by the placing of the pulpit:

> A moderate Voice may be heard 50 Feet distance before the Preacher, 30 Feet on each Side and 20 Feet behind the Pulpit . . . By what I have said, it may be thought reasonable, that the . . . church should be at least 60 Feet broad, and 90 Feet long.[2]

Altars, described rather as communion tables, had by this time been removed from the naves, positions they had occupied during the Commonwealth, and placed against the east walls. They featured little in the ordinary Sunday and weekday services of the time, where the emphasis was on the spoken word, particularly the sermon, and Wren was not unique in insisting that everything should be heard. In contrasting the practice of the Church of England with that of the Roman Catholic Church, he commented: 'it is enough if they hear the Murmur of the Mass, and see the Elevation of the Host, but ours [churches] are to be fitted for Auditories'.[3] His churches and those of Robert Hooke were designed with this in mind. Whether they were large buildings, medium-sized or small, Wren's intention was the same – to create an 'auditory', a large uncluttered space in which seeing the preacher and hearing what he had to say were all important.

For the smaller churches the solution to the problem must have been fairly obvious. These churches were reconstructed much as they had been before the Fire, but with all obstructions to sound and vision swept away. Without the division into nave and aisles, with no piers, columns or arcades, the whole of the space inside each church could be converted into an open-plan, single-cell auditorium.

There was a limit to the size of church which could be converted in this way, a limit determined by the span of the roof. Wren knew as much about roof design as anyone; early in his career he had produced trusses for the Sheldonian Theatre spanning an exceptional seventy feet, with tie-beams each composed of seven pieces of oak in two layers, united with scarf joints,[4] demonstrating that he well understood the principles involved in spanning such distances. Such designs were, however, expensive to make and demanded a high standard of carpentry. At St Paul's he preferred to use trusses with king-posts, even for the nave spanning forty-five feet, with oak tie-beams consisting of single lengths of timber. However, he is known to have had difficulty in finding fifty oak trees long enough to provide the beams for this.[5] For many of his parish churches, as at St Paul's, he chose king-post trusses with tie-beams cut from single pieces of oak, but with spans of no more than about forty feet.[6] Greater spans would not only have required greater heights for the roofs, they would also have needed lengths of timber which were becoming increasingly difficult to find.

Churches wider than this were treated somewhat differently. In each of these, by combining the nave of the pre-Fire church with one of the aisles, he produced an auditorium of about forty feet in width which could be readily roofed. On one side of this and attached to it was the remaining aisle, much as it had been in the pre-Fire church, separated from the new auditorium by columns, arches and clerestories. This attached aisle was then provided with its own, separate, lean-to roof. Typical of these churches is St Vedast with a total span, north to south, of about sixty feet, forty of which were converted to the new auditorium, leaving a south aisle of about twenty feet.[7]

The creation of an auditorium, with or without an attached aisle, was not without its problems. In most of the pre-Fire churches the weight of the lead-covered roof was carried on the arcades and columns of the nave. With these swept away, the weight of the roof had to be transferred to the outer walls, which had formerly taken only the smaller thrust of the aisle roofs. These exterior walls were not usually strong enough to take the weight of the new, extended roofs: it became necessary to rebuild outer walls and in some cases also to provide new foundations for them.

The size and weight of the roofs of the largest churches made it impossible to convert the whole of their floor area into an open-plan auditorium; and the conversion of a part, as in the medium-sized churches, would hardly have made sense. With these it was necessary to provide greater support for the roofs, additional to the outside walls. The division of these churches into nave and aisles, much as they had been before the Great Fire, was inevitable. The choice of a basilican design, made first by Wren in respect of St Bride Fleet Street, set the pattern for these. Basilicas were historically large, classical, oblong buildings or halls with double colonnades and a semicircular apse often at the end, used for a court of justice or place of public assembly. From this it has more specifically come to mean a building of this type (more frequently now without apse), usually but not necessarily for Christian worship.

These three building types, galleried basilicas and single-cell buildings with and without attached aisles, were the basic designs to which most of the post-Fire churches were constructed. There were, in addition, two further groups of churches, those rebuilt with nave and aisles in the form of the pre-Fire building; and those where the architects, Wren and Hooke, introduced elements of central planning. These groups, which form the basic classification of the Wren parish churches, are considered together with the individual churches in each group in greater detail in the succeeding chapters.

Neither Sir Christopher Wren, Robert Hooke, the Commissioners nor anyone else in the seventeenth or eighteenth centuries would have considered making any kind of classification of these parishes churches. For them it would have been a pointless exercise; for us, without an understanding of how the designs arose, it can be a straitjacket. Nor does any classification based upon ground plans shed much light upon the personal contribution of the two architects, Wren and Hooke.

Discussion of who did what is hampered by the lack of any authoritative statement from either of the two men, or anyone else living at that time, concerning the division or allocation of the work. What is clear is the extent to which Sir Christopher Wren managed the whole operation. While his was the administrative responsibility, how much design responsibility did he also assume? The concept of an architectural practice, with the head of the enterprise accepting responsibility for all the work the team produced, had still to evolve. In the seventeenth century the work undertaken by each of the architects was by way of a personal rather than a corporate contribution. Even when the written evidence strongly suggests associating either Wren or Hooke with a particular church, it tells us nothing about the source of ideas for it. Nor is there an answer to the question of whether or not Wren officially approved the designs produced by Hooke and, if not, whether Hooke had complete freedom to proceed, even to the extent of not showing his designs to Wren.

A study of the style or styles in which the parish churches were built soon becomes a search for those features which can be used to characterise the individual work of Wren and Hooke. This study is undoubtedly confused by the fact that the two men helped each other with designs. Nevertheless, the end products of each man's designing seem to have retained an individuality which suggests each of them was solely or principally responsible for his own portfolio.

In Chapter 6 a number of churches have been suggested, from documentary and other sources, as the work of Wren himself. A consideration of the style of these buildings can be used to provide coherence to these attributions and hence a definition of the style used by Wren for his church-building. With Hooke, although there are other indications (the Dutch influence, for example), without documentary evidence this process cannot be used to define his style. It is necessary to consider those churches which have not been attributed to Wren, examining them for the existence of an alternative stylistic coherence. Inevitably, not all the parishes churches can be assigned to stylistic groups in this way and problems remain.

One feature of the churches so far attributed to Wren is that they are all regular in outline. Some may have been reconstructed by Wren on the foundations of late medieval churches which were themselves regular, but there is abundant evidence to indicate that others were made regular in the post–Fire rebuilding. These include St Bride Fleet Street, where the new east wall was laid square but at an angle to the old, irregular foundations of the east end to the church; and St Stephen Walbrook, where the old church was far from regular. Nowhere is this change to regularity more apparent than at St Clement Danes, where a brilliantly conceived and spatially satisfying building was created from an assembly of irregular nave and aisles.

Even a casual study soon reveals that there were parish churches rebuilt after the Fire where a realignment to give regular outlines would have been relatively simple to undertake. The east wall of St Mary Aldermary, for example, was and still is at an angle to the nave. No attempt has been made to make the east end square, although it seems that this could easily have been done. The east wall of St Vedast Foster Lane too could similarly have been brought to a right angle with the nave. There are other examples. In these cases conformity of the church to a geometrically regular outline clearly did not matter. It may have been the decision of the parishioners or the vestrymen, concerned primarily with getting their church rebuilt, but the distinction between the two groups of churches, the regular and the irregular, is so marked that it is tempting to suggest that it is between the new churches designed by Wren and those left with their medieval outlines by Hooke.

The group of churches with regular plans includes all those that have been particularly suggested by documentary sources as likely to be by Sir Christopher Wren: St Andrew Holborn, St Bride Fleet Street, St Clement Danes,[8] St James Piccadilly, St Mary-le-Bow and St Stephen Walbrook. These are linked not only by their regularity but by other features which suggest a common authorship. For example, they are all basilican in design, they all have plain exteriors, and most were faced with Portland stone. Other churches with rectangular plans include Christchurch Newgate, St Andrew-by-the-Wardrobe, St Mary Aldermanbury and St Nicholas Cole Abbey. They have features which suggest they could have been designed by Hooke, but the possibility that they are by Wren cannot completely be discounted.

Allied to considerations of regularity are those of proportion. Wren made no comment on this. He regarded his church of St James Piccadilly as the epitome of what a good church should be, commenting 'that it may be found both beautiful and convenient'. Despite the lack of any further comment, he was clearly satisfied with its proportions. Even a casual visitor, standing in the nave and pausing for a while, can appreciate this; one does not need to know the ratio of the short sides to the long, or the long sides to the height. It is a building where harmony is felt rather than measured. St Andrew Holborn, St Clement Danes and St Stephen Walbrook similarly all impress with their well-balanced dimensions. Regretfully it is no longer possible to stand in St Bride Fleet Street and appreciate the full the extent of the building. The screens separating the nave from the aisles hide the fact that this is a church where Wren was less successful in his proportioning and where he did not achieve the graceful relationships that he was later to provide at St James. Building on the foundations of the old St Bride's resulted in a church which could with advantage have been wider for its length or shorter for its width.

Such thoughts are perhaps not important in considering most of the churches rebuilt after the Fire, churches where the proportions of length to breadth were determined by the walls of the pre-Fire building still standing or by the foundations beneath. As with the regularity of outline, in these churches proportion was not a thing which mattered.

All, or most, of the medieval churches had chancels which at one time had housed their altar tables. Not all the chancels were separate structures with their own roofs, although some at least were. Wren's attitude to them can only be guessed but, in his 1711 letter, he commented that the new churches should have a chancel at one end. Small chancels can be found in his basilican churches, St Bride Fleet Street, St James Piccadilly and St Andrew Holborn, although not in the centralised churches of St Mary-le-Bow and St Stephen Walbrook.

Such features as chancels, regularity of outline and graceful proportions are not the only ones to distinguish those churches identified by documentary evidence as by Wren from those of uncertain authorship. We can also note the use of common motifs in the churches of this particular group. The unbuilt north door to St Stephen Walbrook, facing the Stocks Market, was to have been given an impressive entrance porch in the form of an archway characterised by a triangular pediment above a broken cornice. This was a motif commonly used by Wren but not by Hooke. It appears also in the east window of St James Piccadilly, the east window of St Bride Fleet Street, in doorways for St Mary-le-Bow and for the Dean's door on the south-west tower of St Paul's. Other motifs, although less frequently used, occur in the churches of this group, but not elsewhere: the large double-storied Venetian windows at St Andrew Holborn and St James Piccadilly; pairs of domed vestries at the east end of St Andrew Holborn,[9] and at the west end of St Clement Danes; and rusticated doorways at St Bride Fleet Street, St Clement Danes and especially St Mary-le-Bow.

A further characteristic of these churches attributed to Wren is the extent to which the decoration (apart from towers and steeples) is concentrated on the interiors. The exteriors, whether of ashlar, stone-rubble or brickwork, were all remarkably plain, with no urns or pineapples decorating the skylines and few festoons, swags, cherub heads and similar features to enliven flat walls. In Wren's churches there is the minimum of such decoration, with only cherub-head keystones at St James Piccadilly, festoons for the entrance of St Stephen Walbrook and carved work around the windows of the south and east fronts of St Clement Danes as exceptions.

The problems associated with style begin with Christchurch Newgate, which, although described as a galleried basilica, does not quite fit the pattern set by the others. This church, and that of St Andrew-by-the-Wardrobe which too is different, are discussed in greater detail in the following chapter. Here we can only wonder whether Wren would have produced such an economical church as St Andrew and whether both might not be by Hooke in Wren's basilican style.

Hooke's designs for the church-building programme are less easy to trace or define. The probability that he was responsible for St Martin Ludgate has already been recorded. The Netherlandish influences that can be associated with him have been noted elsewhere. A further indication of his work can be seen in the way that the churches erected at the beginning of the campaign, when Wren was particularly engaged elsewhere, were heavily clustered in that part of the City where he lived and worked. It seems plausible that Wren designed only those churches which he was particularly asked to. He also had a much freer hand in his designing – Rectors, Vicars, Lord Mayors, even the Archbishop of Canterbury, could hardly reject what he had produced for them as a favour. Unlike Wren, Hooke had no choice of which churches to design and which to leave. He had to contend with all kinds of parish authorities and reach agreement with them. A few may indeed have been enthusiastic about his new ideas, others not. He may have persuaded many to accept his schemes and designs, but with others there can only have been compromise. In these circumstances, is it surprising that he did not produce a portfolio of stunning designs? A resort to expediency seldom produces inspiration. Hooke's task was not to produce masterpieces, but to get the churches up and running. It is in the execution of that task that many of Hooke's designs were produced.

The greater number of churches completed for the Commissioners are those that do not bear the personal stamp of Wren, are significantly different from his in style, show foreign influences or, in one way or another, present evidence of a resort to expediency. Despite a lack of documentary backing, these may reasonably be attributed to Robert Hooke.

In most cases his churches were erected directly upon the foundations of the old and, as a consequence, reflect the plans of the pre-Fire buildings and retain the irregular shapes and odd angles in a way that Wren's do not. There is seldom addition to or subtraction from the area occupied by the church, except where post-Fire road widening has occurred. It is as a direct consequence of this that his churches are not so well proportioned as those by Wren. Nevertheless, the designs are so well-drawn and the buildings so skilfully constructed that we are scarcely aware of the irregularities and oddities. The blemishes, if that is the right word, hardly show and we become aware of them only by studying accurate plans or in taking measurements. Only then do we discover how geometrically irregular they are.

As a group, the City churches are not renowned for their exteriors. Most of them are or were on small crowded sites. Some had frontages to the streets, a very few were surrounded by their churchyards, but none stood isolated from their surroundings. Most had other structures built against their walls. There was no opportunity to create buildings that caught the eye and held the imagination – that function was reserved for the towers and the steeples intended to be seen above the houses, leaving the churches often with little fabric exposed, and that little having only the minimum of embellishment. The plainness of the church exteriors by Wren contrasts with Hooke's churches where, despite the limited opportunities, elaborate frontispieces were created and greater use made of decoration and variety. His vocabulary was, however, surprisingly small. For his long façades, like Wren, he used a series of simple, round-headed windows with moulded architraves but, unlike the Surveyor General, he invariably called for carved keystones and walls enlivened with festoons in carved stone. In some of the churches, All Hallows Bread Street (Fig. 16) and St Benet Gracechurch are examples, Hooke did not achieve a good balance between the size, shape and number of the windows, giving the impression that fewer but larger windows would have been more appropriate. For both these churches Hooke was probably repeating the bay size and number of the earlier church. One wonders how much freedom he had in this matter.

The same decorative elements, festoons and carved keystones, can be seen to even greater effect on his short façades, used where the parish churches had an east or west end as street frontage. St Dionis Backchurch (Fig. 17) was a particularly good example, with a massive keystone having an impressive carved face over and an array of festoons and drops. This front had elements, repeated elsewhere, which together bound the front into a more formal presentation, in this case the paired Ionic pilasters with a pulvinated frieze placed on either side of a large round-headed window below a triangular pediment. This centre section was balanced by outer bays which marked the aisles of the building,

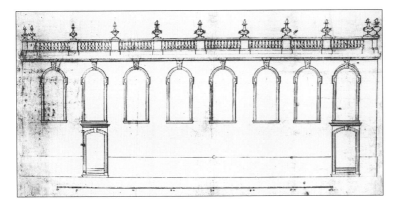

FIGURE 16.
All Hallows Bread
Street, design for the
north front.
(*All Souls College,
Oxford*)

FIGURE 17.
St Dionis Back-
church, east front.
(*Clayton*)

each with a round window, an entrance door below and a plain cornice and parapet over. The central east window was somewhat similar to a Serlian or Venetian window but enlarged with an outer semicircle.

The basic façade composition appeared elsewhere with but slight variation. The centre was invariably broken forward, the side bays often with round-headed windows. At St Mary Aldermanbury the central window, round-headed and without keystone, was supported by large carved volutes adding to the decoration, here without the festoons (Fig. 18). The centre bay was marked by a plain triangular pediment. At St Mary-at-Hill the central Venetian window and the round-headed windows of the side bays had festoons and possibly also drops provided by the mason to the architect's design, although these were never

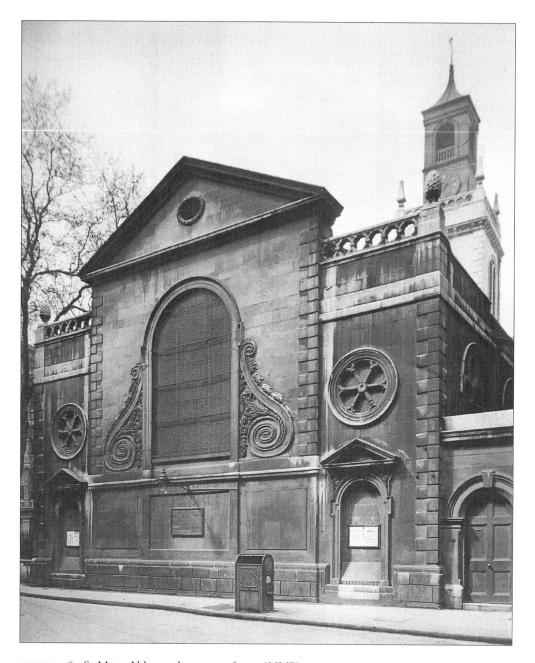

FIGURE 18. St Mary Aldermanbury, east front. (*NMR*)

recorded and were later removed. It had a plain, triangular pediment covering the central bay. This was broken and a semicircular window inserted by James Savage in the nineteenth century.

No two churches were alike in their frontispieces: St Stephen Coleman Street had a segmental pediment containing a carved cock; St Swithin London Stone a similar pediment but broken to contain a cartouche; and St Lawrence Jewry a triangular pediment over the central three bays of a five-bay façade. A similar five-bay front, with the centre three bays broken forward, occurs also at St Peter Cornhill, one of the most developed with an arcade of five round-headed windows, similar to that at St Matthew Friday Street, but as the lower of a double-story elevation. St Mildred Poultry had a highly decorated front to the street, in this case the south side of the church. Elements of a formal frontispiece appear also in the two churches probably by Hooke which have their towers incorporated into the street elevations – St Edmund the King and St Martin Ludgate (Fig. 19).

Another decorative feature widely used by Hooke was the use of urns and pineapples on the parapets of his churches. A number

FIGURE 19. St Martin Ludgate, project design for the street façade. (*All Souls College, Oxford*)

of these have since been lost, while at St Mary-at-Hill, although intended, they were never provided. Christchurch Newgate, St Edmund the King, St Martin Ludgate, St Peter Cornhill and St Stephen Coleman Street are amongst the churches that have or at one time had them.

As always in considering these churches, caution is needed in making attributions based upon simply decorative features. They are not unique to Hooke, appearing generally elsewhere as well as in the vocabulary of Wren, particularly in his early days, and notably for the Sheldonian Theatre.

What now remains is to bring together those features described in this and earlier chapters which can be used to support individual attributions, particularly for those churches where documentary evidence of any kind is missing.

9

Who Did What?
Problems of Attribution

Wren's definite contribution to parish church design, as indicated by documentary evidence (parish records, payments to him, patronage and so on) amounted to no more than about half a dozen churches. For most of the others no clear evidence of authorship has been found. It is these other churches which now need examining for indications as to which of the two architects was responsible. Evidence of some kind, indicative but far from convincing, exists to suggest that a few more may be by Wren. The rest may be by Hooke, but there also remains the possibility, or even probability, that some of these designs are the result of a collaboration between the two men.

Evidence for Hooke's involvement in the church-building programme beginning in 1670 is overwhelming. Quite apart from his appointment by the Commissioners for this purpose, his name appears in the records of a number of parishes. His own diary records many visits by him to church sites while the rebuilding was in progress and more particularly in the formative stage, prior to the rebuilding, when the details of the various designs were being produced and agreed. The wide extent of his contribution cannot be doubted; it is the nature of that contribution which is difficult to discern, and more particularly how it can, if at all, be separated from that of Wren.

This separation is not easy to make, especially as Hooke was involved in Wren's own designing. The evidence for this comes from two sources: that of surviving drawings in Hooke's hand; and his diary. Of the parish churches, St Mary-le-Bow has long been accepted as Wren's work and there is no reason to doubt this. Yet among Hooke's papers is a plan for the site between the body of the church and Cheapside (Fig. 20),[1] a site which was eventually used for a vestibule to the church and for the tower. Hooke's plan represents what may have been the first thoughts for using this area. It is not the work of a draughtsman illustrating the ideas of someone else but of a man participating in the design process. Whether the suggestion for using this site came from Wren or from

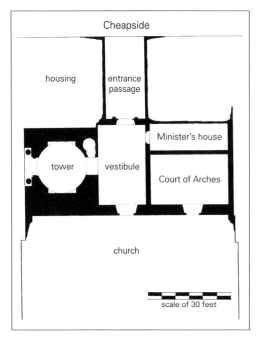

FIGURE 20. St Mary-le-Bow, plan for the site on Cheapside. (*PJ*)

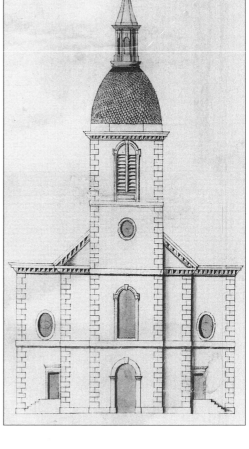

FIGURE 21. St James Piccadilly, project design for the street façade. (*All Souls College, Oxford*)

Hooke is now impossible to determine, but it was Hooke who in this drawing was suggesting how it should be used; Hooke serving as Wren's right-hand man. Similarly, at St James Piccadilly a surviving original drawing for the tower and steeple is also probably in Hooke's hand (Fig. 21).[2] Wren's claim to have designed the church is not in question, but he seems to have left the design of the tower and steeple to Hooke. Although the steeple was not built to Hooke's design, the drawing was a major contribution to the initial design of the building. In the absence of any comment, both the nature and the extent of cooperation between the two men elsewhere in the programme remain unknown. It presumably ranged all the way from a general discussion of ideas over dinner to making design contributions sufficiently large to make attribution difficult.

Apart from such collaboration, Hooke, in accordance with the instruction of the Commissioners, undoubtedly produced designs of his own. It was his duty and he was paid to provide models and drawings for the King's approbation. His discharge of that duty can be seen in the surviving design for St Edmund the King (Fig. 22) in the form of an elevation for the street façade in his hand, which bears not only Wren's initials but an inscription stating that it had received the King's approval.[3] The system by which such designs were submitted to Charles II for his approval did not last long, but this one example indicates that Hooke had started on the task imposed by the Commissioners, and was producing designs in a style which was recognisably his own.

The greatest number of visits paid by Hooke to any one site was to St Martin Ludgate, which he visited on thirty-one occasions, mostly in the years 1674 and 1675. It was precisely in this period that the design for the church was generated, discussed, perhaps changed, revised, amended and finally agreed with the vestry; leading to the approval for rebuilding given by the Commissioners on 20 September 1676 and to a start with the rebuilding probably in 1677. It is particularly noticeable that Hooke's diary records no visits at all to the church in 1677 or 1679 and few in 1678 and 1680. His involvement was therefore greatest in the period during which the design was created, evolved and agreed. Thereafter, during the period of construction, his attendance was minimal. In any other circumstances, thirty-one site visits by an architect would be regarded as overwhelming evidence for design responsibility and, on this basis, St Martin Ludgate must

FIGURE 22. St Edmund the King, street façade. (*All Souls College, Oxford*)

be credited to Hooke, although the construction of it does not seem to have been supervised by him.

Other churches which received several visits from Hooke included Christchurch Newgate, St Anne and St Agnes, St Bartholomew-by-the-Exchange, St Lawrence Jewry, St Magnus the Martyr, St Michael Bassishaw and St Peter Cornhill. There may have been others not recorded in his diary in the incomplete state in which it is known to us. The authorship of Christchurch Newgate and St Lawrence Jewry is discussed below and that of St Magnus the Martyr explored in Chapter 10. For the rest, these visits support the view that they too were likely to have been designed by Hooke.

The suggestion made in Chapter 4 that, in order to share the design burden, the intention had been to divide the City into areas of responsibility – with each of the three named individuals, Wren, Hooke and Woodroffe, taking a sector – cannot now be proved. Nevertheless, it is apparent that the churches designed in the first five years of the campaign can be separated into two geographical groups: the churches in the southern and western parts of the City (St Bride Fleet Street and St Mary-le-Bow, both by Wren, and St Nicholas Cole Abbey); and those in the eastern and northern parts of the City, those parts with which Hooke was best acquainted (St Bartholomew-by-the-Exchange, St Benet Fink, St Clement East Cheap, St Dionis Backchurch, St Edmund the King, St George Botolph Lane, St Lawrence Jewry, St Magnus the Martyr, St Mary Aldermanbury, St Mary-at-Hill, St Michael Wood Street, St Mildred Poultry, St Olave Jewry, St Peter Cornhill and St Stephen Walbrook). On stylistic grounds, the design of most of the churches in this latter group can be attributed to Hooke.

The continued involvement of Wren, not only with St Paul's Cathedral but also with the many other duties of his official post, suggests that, for the parish churches, he would have made the most of Hooke's services. His own involvement would have been limited to designing those churches which were particularly important, for whatever reason, and those where pressure of some kind was brought to bear upon him. Churches where the parish vestries were far from active in seeking an early rebuilding, and those which were content with a rather run-of-the-mill rebuilding rather than a grandiose redesign, were likely to have received the attention of Hooke rather than Wren.

With these factors in mind, we can now turn to the various groups of churches and consider their authorship. In this chapter they include the churches rebuilt with nave and aisles to the pre-Fire design, the basilicas and those with open auditoria. The churches with elements of central planning are considered in the next chapter.

Churches to Pre-Fire Designs

Those churches whose rebuilding was started by the parish authorities before the Act of 1670 gave authority for public funding do not here concern us. Their architects, if any, remain unknown. Our concern begins with those where, for whatever reason, the pre-Fire designs were recreated by Wren or Hooke for the Commissioners. However, both groups reflect the traditional plan and have some of the gothic style and character of their predecessors. Some, possibly all, had classical features in addition. Those rebuilt by the parishes were probably closest to the pre-Fire originals. For these, no attempt was made to clear the sites of any remaining walls and, after removal of any obviously fire-damaged material, what was left formed the basis for reconstruction. No new foundations were required, and rapid progress was possible so that all six churches, St Christopher-le-Stocks, St Dunstan-in-the-East, St Mary Woolnoth, St Michael Cornhill, St Sepulchre and St Vedast Foster Lane, were in use within a very short space of time.

The churches, rebuilt with nave and aisles under the direction of Wren to the plan of the pre-Fire church, might under other direction have included the majority of the City churches. It would have been surprising if the new, classical style of architecture had appealed immediately to all churchwardens. Left to their own devices and resources most of the parish vestries would probably have rebuilt their churches in the old style. The City has seldom been a trend-setter and, even with Wren holding the purse-strings, there must have been many inhabitants who looked askance at the churches then rising. The extent to which the post-Fire churches departed from their late medieval form is a measure of the influence exerted by Wren, by Hooke and by the Commissioners. Even so some parishes resisted what they regarded as an alien style, while some settled for compromise. These included St Alban Wood Street, St Augustine Old Change, St Bartholomew-by-the-Exchange, St Dionis Backchurch, St George Botolph Lane, St Mary Aldermanbury, St Mary Aldermary, St Michael Bassishaw and St Peter Cornhill. There was little uniformity among them, other than the clear resemblance of each to its own pre-Fire building. They had pillars or columns which, with arcades or straight entablatures, formed a well-defined

nave, mostly with clerestory windows. In some the addition of classical features –
pilasters, columns, capitals, corbels, plaster work and windows, could all be seen
as an updating rather than a change in design. The churches remained as they
always had been, traditional in plan and with a forward emphasis from west to
east, corresponding to the liturgical axis.

Here the question is about who may have designed these churches. With the
exception of St Augustine Old Change, all are or were in Hooke's area, the
eastern and northern parts of the City. Payments to Wren were made by some
of them, but they do not necessarily indicate that he designed the church. The
vestry of St Peter Cornhill made two payments to Wren, one of five guineas,
the other of ten pounds,[4] but both were specifically associated with his part in
providing the parish with a tabernacle. Such generosity in connection with the
tabernacle could lead one to suppose that the absence of any gift for his part
in the rebuilding of the church indicates that the church was not by him. There
was no payment to Hooke but, as City Surveyor, he would have known the
church well, having been involved in the widening of Gracechurch Street which
took parish land from the east end of the church. A surviving drawing for the
east end of the church is probably by him.[5] The design for the building, based
very largely upon the pre-Fire structure with a shortened east end, may well
be his.

The parish of St Mary Aldermanbury, one of the first to have its church
rebuilt by the Commissioners, was also generous. The vestry presented Wren
with a gift of twenty guineas and Hooke with ten, both for 'expediting the
Building of the Church'.[6] Hooke's contribution may have been in producing
the design, a conclusion which might also have been reached on stylistic grounds.
Apart from his usual duty of forwarding the case for the rebuilding, what then
did Wren do?

Doubt remains concerning three of these churches, St Augustine Old Change,
St Alban Wood Street and St Mary Aldermary. At St Augustine Old Change,
the only church of this group in Wren's area and close to the south-east corner
of St Paul's, the church was rebuilt much as in the pre-Fire design, except that
the columns were repositioned and the tower rebuilt to a smaller dimension
north-to-south. There may have been an intention of providing a large auditorium by combining the nave with the north aisle, leaving the south aisle with
the tower on its south-west corner. This is suggested by the report of a meeting,
attended by the Bishop of London, Wren, Thomas Strong (the mason who was
to build the church) and a Mr Lisle, who owned the property to the north of

the church which had a party wall to it, but not apparently by Hooke.[7] At this meeting it was decided to rebuild the north wall of the church to a certain thickness on its old foundation, a decision that could well have been taken by Wren alone, if not by Thomas Strong himself. The need for the Bishop's presence is nowhere explained and the decision certainly did not require his attendance. The agenda must have included something else, possibly the building a single-cell auditorium, a project then abandoned. Hooke's absence suggests that the church is more likely to have been by Wren.

In a note to the Commissioners referring to St Alban Wood Street, Wren commented: 'I find an irregular peece of ground & not fit for a chargeable Fabrick. Yet it may be brought to a decent & useful Church . . .'[8] The ground plan of the pre-Fire church (Fig. 23a) was irregular, and much could be done by incorporating the land on the south-west corner into the church, enabling a large auditorium to be created, as in Fig. 23b. Wren's intention, if that's what it was, cannot be proved, but he may have had something of this kind in mind. Instead, the church was rebuilt with the tower on the north-west corner, but with nave and aisles and much of the detail it had before the Fire (Fig. 23c). No

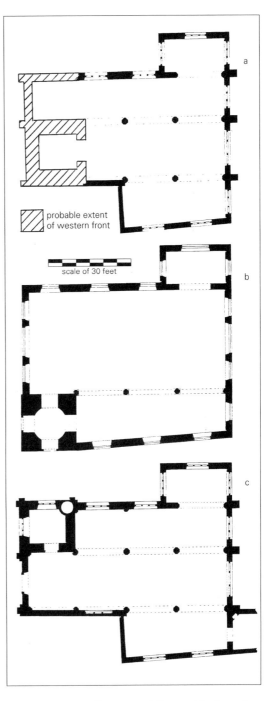

probable extent of western front

scale of 30 feet

FIGURE 23. St Alban Wood Street: (a) plan of pre-Fire church; (b) plan for 'a decent and useful church'; (c) plan of the church as rebuilt. (*PJ*)

evidence has been found to connect Hooke with the rebuilding of the church and the vestry minutes do not record any meetings with him.[9] The minutes record a substantial number of meetings with Wren and there was a payment of £10 15s. od., assumed to have been to him, 'to hasten the building of the church'.[10]

There seems to be no direct evidence to connect the designing of St Mary Aldermary with either Wren or Hooke and a stylistic analysis of the fabric has not proved helpful.[11] Wren may have had St Alban and St Mary Aldermary in mind when, in a letter to the Dean of Westminster, he wrote:

> I have among the parochial Churches of London given some few Examples (where I was oblig'd to deviate from a better Style) which appears not ungraceful, but ornamental to the East part of the City.[12]

but it is not clear if he was referring to himself as architect, or to the churches erected under his care.

The Galleried Basilicas

As noted earlier, from the documentary evidence there can be no doubt that Wren designed St Bride Fleet Street, St James Piccadilly, St Clement Danes and St Andrew Holborn. They were all big churches of large, important and affluent parishes with large congregations. The liturgical axis was in all cases in the east-west direction and there is no suggestion of any cross-axial planning except possibly at St James Piccadilly. The authorship of the designs for St Anne Soho has not been confirmed; they seem likely to be by Wren, although the drawings are not in his hand.

All the basilican churches were severely damaged in the war of 1939–45. Christchurch Newgate has not been rebuilt, the interior of the ruined church remaining as an open space laid out as a garden (but with the east end taken for road widening). St Anne's church has since been rebuilt to a very different design after severe war damage. The remaining five have been rebuilt largely as they were in the post-Fire Wren rebuilding. In external form they look much as they have done for 300 years, but in that period extensive changes were made to the interiors and none is now recognisably as it was in seventeenth century. In their reconstruction St James Piccadilly and St Andrew Holborn are little changed internally, while at St Clement Danes the general arrangement remains

unaltered, although adapted to serve as the central church of the Royal Air
Force. The greatest changes have been made to St Bride and St Andrew-by-
the-Wardrobe which have been the subject of much reordering. Although these
seven churches have sufficient in common for them to be considered and studied
as a group, Christchurch Newgate and St Andrew-by-the-Wardrobe show
differences suggesting that they were more likely to have been designed by
Hooke than Wren.

The pre-Fire church of Christchurch Newgate occupied the east end of the
former conventual church of the Friars Minor, or Greyfriars, the Franciscan
priory in Newgate. In its original form it is hardly likely to have rivalled St
Paul's in its splendour, but in any case much of its glory, including its fine
tombs, had disappeared in the sixteenth century. The priory was surrendered
to Henry VIII in 1538, and in 1546 the east end of the church was released to
the Corporation of London to serve as the church of a new parish comprising
the former old parishes of St Nicholas-in-the-Shambles and St Ewen in Newgate
Market,[13] with that part of the parish of St Sepulchre which lay within the City
walls added. Although only the east end of the priory church was used, it was
even then still the largest parish church in the City. It also served the children
of Christ's Hospital School, which had no chapel of its own.[14] The hospital
occupied the buildings to the north of the church, the former domestic quarters
of the priory.

There are a number of surprising features about the church. In the light of
experience at St Bride, it might have been expected that Christchurch would
have been designed with elevations of two stories and galleries supported on
piers, but instead there was a repetition of the design used at St Bride, with tall
columns on high bases at floor level and elevations with a single story. Immediately
before the Fire the church had galleries, but the new church was initially erected
without them. They were used by the children of Christ's Hospital and there
must have been an understanding, at least on the part of the school governors,
that new galleries would be erected for them.[15] The galleries came later when,
in 1685, officers of Christ's Hospital made an approach to Wren: 'concerning a
Gallary to be built in Christ Church for the Children of this Hospital to sit in.
He promised a Gallary should be built at the Publick Charge, as soon as convenient
may be'.[16] The galleries then erected were somewhat smaller than those known
to us from pre-war photographs and drawings and originally did not occupy the
full length of the church. As constructed they were not of equal breadth with
the aisles, but were increased by subsequent additions.[17]

Christchurch was the only church of the period to be erected with exterior buttresses, provided only for the east and west walls. In the construction of the new church some of the old foundations had been reused and, in all probability, some of the old walling with the existing buttresses to it on the north and south fronts swept away. The six-bay elevation, using six bays of the pre-Fire church, was also unusual, underlining the fact that the architect was working not, as at St James Piccadilly, on a virgin site but with the remains of an existing building. After the Fire much of the medieval fabric was apparently still largely intact and there was some expectation that the pre-Fire church would be restored.[18]

Work on the new church began in the following year with the clearance of what was left of the old tower and the piers which had supported the roof. It has generally been assumed that the church erected in 1677–87 occupied the same area as the pre-Fire church. However, there is a plan for the post-Fire rebuilding which suggests that this assumption may not be correct. This drawing (Fig. 24) is an early design, made following the Fire,[19] but is unlikely to date much before December 1676 when the parish made its deposit of £500 to the Chamber.[20] It is notable for its length, its rectangular tower, a large chancel, galleries, and the hidden corners where the schoolchildren could remain unseen and would certainly be unable to see or hear any part of the service. Such a church is unlikely to have been designed by Wren and it may safely be concluded that it is Hooke's design for a reconstruction of the pre-Fire church with nave and aisles, making much use of the surviving fabric.

Perhaps the most curious feature of this plan is that it was not used. The existence of duplicate copies, ready for the craftsmen to begin work, suggests that building was intended. It seems that there was then a change of mind, but by whom? It is unlikely that the vestry would have objected to a rebuilding of its pre-Fire church, and there is no evidence to suggest that the Commissioners ever personally concerned themselves with the design of their new buildings. Did Wren, perhaps with Hooke at his side, pacing the ruins with the plans for reconstruction in his hands, shake his head and ask 'what are we doing, setting out to build a church for a congregation which will not fill it, with an enormous chancel which is not required and a vestibule with no significant use?' The plan was shelved, to come to light only when the drawings from the Bute Collection were sold in 1951. If this suggestion is correct, we can expect that the two men would then have discussed the alternatives. The broad features of a new design would have been formulated in line with current thinking – more open, more

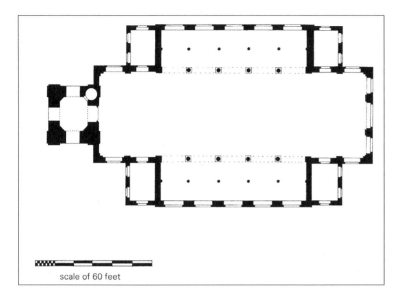

FIGURE 24.
Christchurch
Newgate, plan for
proposed rebuilding.
(*PJ*)

scale of 60 feet

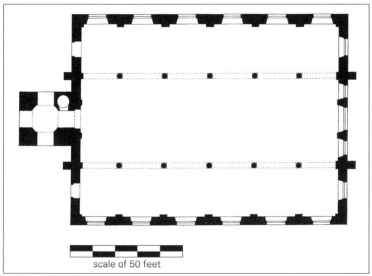

scale of 50 feet

FIGURE 25.
Christchurch
Newgate, plan of the
rebuilt church. (*PJ*)

compact and reduced in size.[21] There was to be no separate chancel or vestibule and the galleries were omitted, reducing the capacity.

The plan to which the church was built is shown in Fig. 25. As far as the detailed designing was concerned, Wren is unlikely to have taken it out of Hooke's hands. There must therefore be some presumption that Hooke, having produced the first design, continued to produce later ones. Building on the extraordinary started in 1677; the parish is recorded as making only one deposit with the Chamber. This suggests that there cannot have been any great parish enthusiasm for the rebuilding. It seems unlikely that the vestry would have pressed Wren to be personally involved in the detailed designing. None of the motifs noted earlier as associated with his rebuilding elsewhere has been seen at Christchurch. There is a lack of keystones and the 'ears' of the window architraves seen on all the remaining basilicas. The east and west fronts had pediments decorated with pineapples (those at the west are still in place), a motif associated with Hooke. Thus, although the spirit of this church is decidedly that of Wren, the design may be that of Hooke.

There have been many changes to St Andrew-by-the-Wardrobe, with much of the detail added to or changed, particularly in the nineteenth century, although externally it is, and always was, a very plain church, constructed of red brick with little stonework. This church of St Andrew is the most difficult of the basilicas to attribute. With no documentary evidence, no record of any payment to Wren and no hint of the exercise of any patronage, the case for Wren as its author is slim. The parish was poor and unlikely to have exerted pressure for him to take a personal interest in designing the church, nor can any reason be seen for the joint involvement of the two men. These facts suggest Hooke as the more likely architect, but stylistically the design is closer to St James Piccadilly, St Clement Danes and St Andrew Holborn by Wren than it is to Christchurch. However, there are a number of features – the absence of a chancel, the lack of western vestibules, the positioning of the tower on the south-west corner and the replacement of columns by piers – which, taken together, suggest that the church is not a development of Wren's basilican design; rather it is an adaptation of it which Hooke might well have produced for a church destined to be built with the utmost economy, not knowing if funding would be available to complete it.

Open-Plan Churches

In the post-Fire rebuilding there are more churches with an open plan than to any other design. Those in the single-cell group, All Hallows Bread Street, All Hallows Lombard Street, St Benet Gracechurch, St Edmund the King, St Mary Magdalen Old Fish Street, St Mary Somerset, St Matthew Friday Street, St Michael Crooked Lane, St Michael Paternoster Royal, St Michael Queenhithe, St Michael Wood Street, St Mildred Poultry, St Nicholas Cole Abbey, St Olave

Jewry and St Stephen Coleman Street, all owe much to the pre-Fire churches on their sites. It would seem that the biggest problem facing the architect in designing the churches was the lack of scope afforded for any change, a limitation not only in the shape and size of the plot, but probably also in such matters as door positions, window patterns and the locations of the towers.

No other group of the Wren period churches has been so sadly decimated. These, the smaller churches serving minor parishes, inevitably had small congregations. making them vulnerable at a time when the size of the congregation was what mattered. Even so, this group does seem to have been particularly unfortunate, with only three now surviving: St Edmund the King, St Michael Paternoster Royal and St Nicholas Cole Abbey, none now as designed or built. St Edmund the King was the only church of this group to survive the war intact, although it had earlier suffered some damage in the war of 1914–18.

None of these churches are or were of exceptional architectural merit or had unusual features, except perhaps St Edmund, one of the few churches of the period with a well-defined chancel lit partly from surrounding windows and partly from a large semicircular lantern. It was the only one of the post-Fire churches orientated with its liturgical axis north-south. Presumably some thought was given to the possibility of changing this but, with the long narrow site of the church, it is difficult to see what else could have been done.

In considering and analysing the architecture of the post-Fire churches, most authors have given greatest attention to the galleried basilicas and those churches with elements of central planning. In contrast, the single-cell churches have been little studied and received little attention. This (and the early destruction of some of them) has resulted in poor and uneven recording with, for example, no measured drawings at all of St Christopher-le-Stocks or St Michael Crooked Lane. By comparison with the drawings which Clayton drew for the basilicas, those for All Hallows Bread Street, St Mary Somerset, St Olave Jewry and St Stephen Coleman Street are selective, poor and lacking in detail.

There is no documentary or other evidence to link Wren with designs for any of these churches. There are no surviving drawings attributed to him for any of them and there is no record of any payment in appreciation of his services. There is thus good reason to suggest that he is unlikely to have been the architect responsible for them.

A possible exception is St Nicholas Cole Abbey, which is the only church on this list from 1670–75 in the southern part of the City. It is possible, although unrecorded, that Wren was involved in discussions concerning the use of the fire-ravaged St Nicholas as the site for a new church to be erected and used by a Lutheran community for services in the German language, a proposal opposed by the parish and eventually abandoned.[22] A plan for a rebuilding of the church, now in the RIBA,[23] suggests that pre-Fire church was considerably narrower than the post-Fire building. The change to a wider church may have been made to accommodate the parishioners of St Nicholas Olave, whose parish was united with St Nicholas Cole Abbey, but the enlargement gave a better-proportioned building and points, perhaps, to Wren. However, the exterior of the building does not have the plainness associated with his rebuilding of, for example, St Bride Fleet Street, and there are none of his motifs. The external decoration of the windows with lintels and the design of steeple, which belongs to the same group as St Edmund the King and St Martin Ludgate, suggest it is by Hooke.

The first visit of Hooke to the site recorded in his diary was on 19 September 1676, by which time the church must have been essentially complete. Any involvement by him in the design of the church must have entailed several earlier visits, but these would have taken place prior to 1672, when construction began and Hooke's diary commences. However, the vestry meetings contain several references to meetings with Wren, Woodroffe and Oliver, but to none with Hooke. An attribution to Wren is not convincing, but neither is there sufficient evidence to suggest that the church is by Hooke, even though the style of the architecture points towards him. This may well be a church whose design was initiated by Wren but completed by Hooke.

The group of single-cell churches with attached aisles has fared rather better than the groups without them, with all but All Hallows-the-Great surviving. St Lawrence Jewry and St Vedast Foster Lane were rebuilt following extensive damage by fire-bombing in December 1940. The group includes All Hallows-the-Great, St Benet Paul's Wharf, St Clement Eastcheap, St Lawrence Jewry, St Margaret Lothbury, St Margaret Pattens and St Vedast Foster Lane.

All Hallows-the-Great and St Benet Paul's Wharf seem to be special cases, where the form of the churches was dictated by the design of the pre-Fire churches they replaced, that of All Hallows in particular determined by the early restoration of its tower in the middle of the aisle on the north side of the church. Except for St Benet, all the churches of this group were in Hooke's area, the eastern or northern parts of the City. No documentary evidence of authorship has been found, nor any indication of patronage which might suggest a particular architect. The clearest evidence for Hooke as architect is stylistic, but visits paid by him to All Hallows-the-Great, St Lawrence Jewry and St Vedast prior to the commencement of rebuilding lend support to this.

Hooke's diary is incomplete, and the building of St Clement Eastcheap, St Margaret Lothbury and St Margaret Pattens took place in a period where there is a gap in this record. St Benet is one of the few churches erected in a period for which Hooke's diary exists but for which no visits are recorded. It seems hardly likely that he would have designed a church without making a visit, yet the design of St Benet shows strong Netherlandish influence, generally taken as evidence of his involvement. A series of original drawings of this church, now in the United States of America, warrant further study.[24] A more detailed comparison with other drawings known or suspected to be by Hooke may be revealing.

There is some doubt concerning the authorship of St Lawrence Jewry. The east front recalls Wren's work at St Paul's Cathedral but the ground plan, with its irregular outline, acute and obtuse angles, the rebuilding of the late medieval tower with its old irregularities and the overall design of the church, in which a single aisle was retained, all suggest the hand of Hooke.

There was a dispute between the parish and the City Corporation concerning the ground to the south west of Guildhall Yard which, before the Fire, was the north-east corner of the church.[25] The Corporation were anxious to acquire it in order to extend Guildhall Yard. Although the Aldermen would have been within their rights, as given to them in the Act of 1670, in taking this area, they declined to act without the agreement of the parish vestry and referred the matter to Wren and Hooke for arbitration:

> The parishioners of the said parish have pressed this Court that the same [north-east corner of the church land] may not be taken in [by the Corporation] but continue to be built as formerly upon the old foundations. This Court doth not think fit to grant the said petition, but doth refer it to Sir Christopher Wren and Mr Hooke to contrive the building . . . as may best answer the desires of the said parishioners, and without disappointment or hinderence, to the conveniency and ornament intended to the said Court.[26]

The Aldermen got their way and Guildhall Yard was enlarged by taking in the church land (compare the plans of the pre- and post-Fire churches (Figs 26 and 27). The parish received its cash compensation, leaving us to wonder what it was that persuaded the vestry to change its mind. There is no written record of it. Was it a promise from Sir Christopher to attend personally to some of

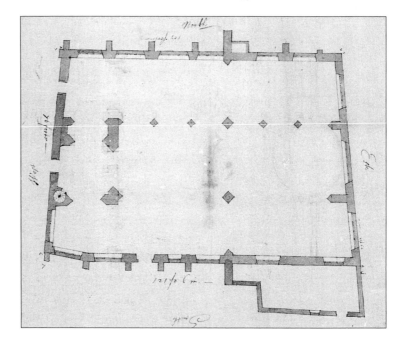

FIGURE 26.
St Lawrence Jewry,
plan of pre-Fire
church.
(*Conway Library*)

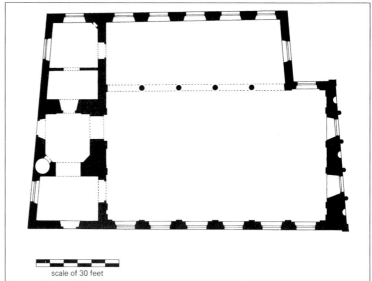

FIGURE 27.
St Lawrence Jewry,
plan of rebuilt
church. (*PJ*)

the designing for them? Is this the origin of its splendid east end? Was this a
church by Hooke with help from Wren? The parish was indeed grateful for his
services, whatever they were, for in the vestry minutes of 1679 the churchwarden
was ordered: 'to give Sir Christopher such gratuity as he thinks fit, not exceeding
30 guineas'.[27] Confirmation of the payment is lacking, no corresponding entry

in the churchwarden's accounts being found. Even if payment was not to the full amount authorised, the possibility remains that it was in recognition of a substantial contribution to the rebuilding of the church. With the east end before us, need we look for more?

A gratuity was presented to Wren by the vestry of St Clement East Cheap. This amounted to seven guineas, hardly a vast sum.[28] Was this in appreciation of his work in designing a new church or, perhaps equally possible, for his efforts in resolving a dispute over land to the east of the church which was used for extending the church?[29]

In summary, many of the post-Fire churches considered in this chapter, the four basilicas in particular excepted, are likely to have been designed by Hooke, although confirmatory evidence for this is thin. A few – St Alban Wood Street, St Augustine Old Change and St Mary Aldermary – may well have been designed by Wren. He must surely have been involved in some way with designing for others, notably St Lawrence Jewry and St Nicholas Cole Abbey. The authorship of St Benet Paul's Wharf remains unresolved.

10

Elements of Central Planning

In the sixteenth and seventeenth centuries thoughts of building churches with elements of central planning were not new. The Pantheon, which had been converted for use as a Christian church, provided an example and inspiration, but many others were devised and constructed. Both Wren and Hooke must have been conscious of the extent to which Italian and other foreign architects were producing such designs. Wren, on his visit to Paris in 1665, was witness to the extent to which designs with prominent domes crowning the central space were featuring in French church-building of the mid century. These included those of the Sorbonne, the Val de Grâce and what is now the Palais des Quatre Nations. In England, the building of churches with domes did not begin until the seventeenth century, with the construction of Wren's St Paul's Cathedral as the supreme but not the only example, although there had been an earlier, unbuilt design by Webb.

In the early years of the post-Fire church building campaign between 1670 and 1675, Wren was much occupied with designing for St Paul's Cathedral, in particular with producing the Greek Cross and the Great Model designs. His thoughts, even when not focused on the cathedral, can never have been far from ideas of central planning. It is not surprising that examples of it are to be found in the rebuilt City churches. These include churches with domes, churches built to a cross-in-a-square design and churches having nave and aisles but also a well-defined cross-axis. These ideas too must have featured in the many discussions over dinner between Wren and Hooke. There is no reason to suppose that all the City churches having or based upon these elements were the individual work of either man.

Except for St Stephen Walbrook, which can hardly be described as experimental, there is a certain tentativeness about the central planning in London at this time, almost as if Wren and Hooke were aware of the concept but unsure of how best to make the most of it. It creeps in almost unnoticed, as it were, when the need for it arises, into the otherwise longitudinal, east-west orientated designs. As the campaign proceeded it was used with greater confidence, but the limitations of the sites and the hesitancy of the parish vestries can have done little to inspire great designs among the City churches.

Whatever thoughts Wren and Hooke may have had on central planning, they are not recorded. It was a concept which seems to have appealed not only to them but to all sections of organised Christianity. For the Catholic Church it provided ample opportunity for ritual and for the enhancement of ceremonial connected with it. For Dissenters such churches provided a greater involvement of the congregation who, because they could see better, were much more aware of what was taking place. This is, perhaps, what appealed most to Wren, who was anxious that all should both see and hear.

Cross-in-a-Square Designs

Cross-in-a-square designs, with axes orientated north-south, were used in a number of the newly reconstructed churches. Those where these axes feature as prominently as those in the more familiar east-west direction include:

> St Anne and St Agnes
> St Mary-at-Hill
> St Martin Ludgate
> The French Protestant Church in the Savoy

Experimenting with central planning seems to have begun at the start of the building campaign, with the reconstruction of St Mary-at-Hill beginning in 1670, although it is doubtful if the ideas had by then been formalised in the minds of either Wren or Hooke. The pre-Fire church of St Mary had a strong east-west emphasis with a well-defined nave supported on two rows of columns, the side aisles being covered with lean-to roofs. Much of this old church remained after the Fire and certain features of it were adapted for the rebuilding in a form which amounted to some kind of central planning. These features included the transepts (present in the church since medieval times, although their exact location in the church and their extent is nowhere described) and entrances in the centre on both north and south fronts, which together must have given what was in effect a north-south aisle or cross-axis.

The church spanned about sixty feet and the first proposal for roofing was to dispense with most of the columns, the arcades and clerestories, using a grid of timber supported upon four giant columns,[1] thus converting the church into

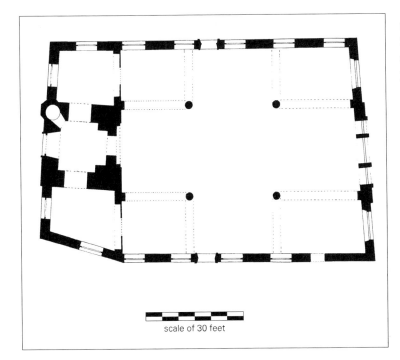

FIGURE 28.
St Mary-at-Hill, as
rebuilt, 1670–74
plan. (*PJ*)

scale of 30 feet

FIGURE 29.
St Mary-at-Hill,
north front as
rebuilt, 1670–74.
(*Reconstruction by
Richard Lea, 1996*)

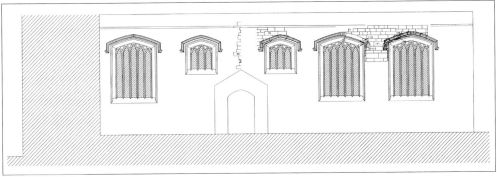

an open auditorium, with only minimal obstruction from the four columns. It
was a concept in keeping with what Wren and Hooke were to do elsewhere.
At some time between 1670, when this timber grid roof structure was proposed,
and 1671, when the carpentry for the roof was completed, the design was
changed. Instead, the four giant columns were used to support eight beams,
each extending from one of the four columns to the exterior walls (Fig. 28).
On the north and south these beams rested on wall plates, but on the east and
west pilasters were provided. The north and south walls, with their existing late
medieval windows repaired, were merely heightened and a roof of low pitch
provided to cover the entire building (Fig. 29). Pilasters could not be provided

on the north and south walls, as the beams from the four columns were positioned directly above existing windows – a most unsatisfactory arrangement. The centre of the ceiling area was given a shallow, saucer-shaped dome supporting a large lantern, an experiment which was not to be repeated elsewhere. The church is now known for its round-headed windows, pilasters supporting the beams on all four walls, an intersecting barrel-vaulted ceiling and a semi-circular dome. These are all features introduced by James Savage in the repairs of 1827. The present design of roof is his, as also the tall, narrow lantern, although the structures are replacements following the fire of 1988. Savage also moved the doors from the centres of the north and south fronts to vestibules which had been created in the campaign of 1670–74 on either side of the tower against the west wall.[2]

Other cross-in-a-square designs were St Anne and St Agnes; and St Martin Ludgate. In these, as well as in St Mary-at-Hill, there was an inherent structural problem arising from the vertical forces from the roof giving an outward thrust to the walls, a thrust not adequately contained by the tie-beams of the roof trusses. The increasing pitch of the roofs, from St Mary to St Martin, suggests that the architect was aware of this problem, even if he did not find a solution.

As far as central planning is concerned, St Mary-at-Hill can be seen as somewhat of a hybrid design, evolved to meet the local circumstances, but then forming the basis for subsequent designing at St Anne & St Agnes and St Martin Ludgate. The name of Robert Hooke is coupled with all three of these designs, although not for the same reason. It would be surprising if he had not discussed them with Wren. How much the basic roof design depended upon Jacob van Campen's Niewe Kerk at Haarlem is now impossible to say. The existence of a drawing of the Haarlem church among Hooke's papers indicates that he was certainly aware of this building with its innovative roof. It is one of the examples, frequently quoted, of Netherlandish influence in England at that the time, particularly upon Hooke, and there seems to be no reason to dissent from that view.

A ground plan of the pre-Fire church of St Anne and St Agnes, probably drawn from what remained of the church after the Fire (Fig. 30),[3] shows the building with nave and aisles separated by rows of columns. The east end was irregular, with access to the rectory on the south-east corner. In 9 March 1677 the Commissioners asked Sir Thomas Bludworth, the former Lord Mayor, and Sir Thomas Exton to agree a sum as reasonable compensation to the Rector for relinquishing his claim to the rectory site in order that the church could 'be

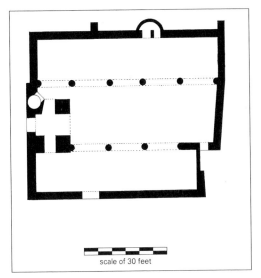

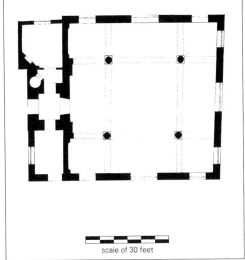

FIGURE 30. St Anne and St Agnes, plan of pre-Fire church. (*PJ*)

FIGURE 31. St Anne and St Agnes, plan of rebuilt church. (*PJ*)

made square, uniforme and lightsome'.[4] A sum was agreed and the new church constructed to a regular plan (Fig. 31). Hooke visited the site on a number of occasions before the building started and it can be assumed that the design is his. The Netherlandish influence is seen in the high Dutch gables; the extensive use of brickwork (mostly rebuilt) lends support to this.

As noted in Chapter 9, the many visits paid by Hooke to the St Martin Ludgate site in the years when the design was settled provide a strong indication that the church was by him. The façade resembles the street elevation of St Edmund the King attributed to him and the steeple recalls others which may also be by him.

Although the two churches are basically similar, they have many small differences, notably that St Anne and St Agnes has its intersecting barrel-vaulted ceiling supported on four Corinthian columns, where at St Martin they are Composite. St Martin's church is taller, giving an impression of greater grandeur, an impression which is enhanced by the high quality of the woodwork closing the three arches to the south of the church and by the galleries over the vestibule. The four columns are here raised on exceptionally tall bases, which must have dwarfed the box pews. It was a church flooded with light from round-headed windows on three sides, although those on the west side are now blocked.

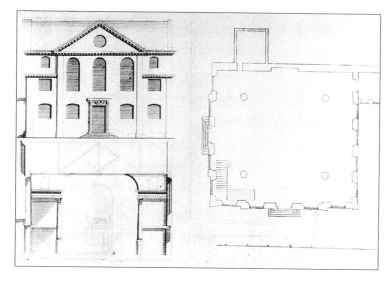

FIGURE 32.
French Protestant
Church in the
Savoy. (*PRO*)

The Protestant Church in the Savoy (Fig. 32) (the equivalent of a parish church for the immigrant French community) was relatively simple in its construction, with four columns supporting the roof, which was pitched in two directions at right angles, leaving flat roofs at the corners.[5] The church proposed for Lincoln's Inn Fields was designed but never built. It is here referred to as 'St Mary-in-the-Fields' and was to have had a similar basic construction, but surmounted by a large central dome supported on eight double columns with smaller domes over the four corners.[6] Externally both churches had giant orders, that of the church in the Savoy having pilaster strips to the corners of the façade of the building and also marking the central three bays, which were broken forward. The Savoy church was simple and unpretentious in the crowded precinct of the Savoy Hospital, whereas 'St Mary-in-the-Fields' would have been much more resplendent. It is discussed in greater detail below.

Cross-Axial Designs with Nave and Aisles

With many of the Wren City churches the changes made in the past 300 years have tended to obscure details of the original design. Nowhere is this more true than at St Magnus the Martyr. The more obvious changes include the loss of the two bays at the west end of the church in 1762, taken to widen the approaches to Old London Bridge, with the pathway passing through the base of the tower. These were not, however, the first changes to be made, as others, largely of an unknown character, were made in 1760 following a fire which began in a neighbouring oil store and destroyed the roof. There is now no record of how the church was originally vaulted. Other changes include the blocking of the north door on the inside of the church, changes to the fenestration and, as late as 1924, the insertion of an additional pair of columns into the arcade, in a position opposite the no longer visible north door.

Even when these changes are unpicked, it is still a difficult church to understand. The closest and best attempt is by Summerson,[7] which is based extensively upon a study of a plan and section for the church formerly in the Bute Collection (Figs 33 and 34).[8] These show the church as an aisled building with the tower intruding into the west end of the nave. The north front has nine bays, the centre three broken forward, emphasising the importance of the central door. As Summerson recognised, there is no acknowledgement of this symmetry in the interior of the church shown in these drawings. He suggested the possibility of an open market or piazza to the north to account for this appearance of the north front, but this seems unlikely, as Thames Street to the north was always an important thoroughfare and was in fact widened at this point by the taking in of parish land. Thames Street and the transport along it effectively isolated the church from any activity to the north.

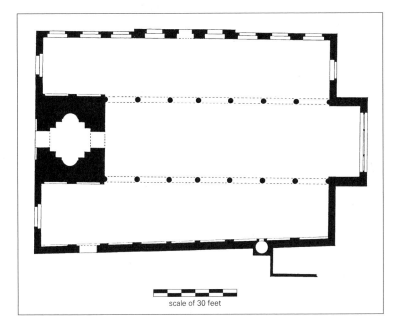

scale of 30 feet

FIGURE 33.
St Magnus the
Martyr, plan of
proposed church.
(*PJ*)

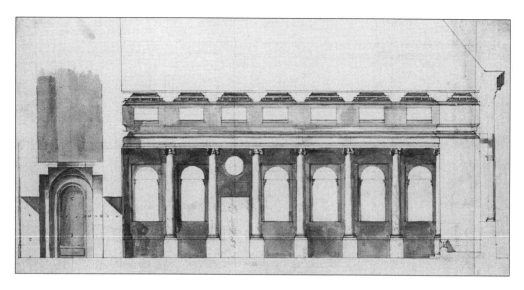

FIGURE 34. St Magnus the Martyr, section of proposed church. (*Conway Library*)

Summerson's difficulties were increased by the knowledge that the intercolumn-iation of the arcade was irregular, varying from nine feet seven inches to eight feet two inches, reflecting the unexplained variation in the bay width of the north front, with the narrowest interval in the centre bay containing the doorway.

It is still not possible to explain this irregularity, but it can be seen in a different light when it is realised that this north front is not to Wren's (or Hooke's) design. A vestry minute of 1671 ordered the churchwardens to 'get in money disbursed in raising the north wall'.[9] There would have been no need for the parish to disburse money in raising the wall if it had been built by Wren using money from the coal dues. The wall was in fact built no later than 1669, as the building accounts indicate: 'Rubble wall and foundations in the north wall wherein is comprised the North dore to the top of the Frontispiece and the walls on either side . . . bill dated 16 May 1669.'[10] The Commissioners ordered the cost to be repaid in 1672.[11] No architect's name has so far been associated with this work.

It is now impossible to judge to what extent this rebuilt north wall may have resembled the north wall of the pre-Fire church, especially as the taking of land to widen Thames Street is likely to have swept away what was left of the old wall. All we can be certain of is that the bay width of the north wall shown on the drawing from the Bute Collection is derived from the rebuilding of 1668–69 and that the irregular intercolumniation followed from it. This drawing may have been produced in the Wren Office, but it seems more likely that it was produced in connection with the earlier start to the rebuilding and was then inherited by Wren; and that the alterations, tentatively indicated on the plan, were his first thoughts for changing and completing the design. These show a moving away from the simple basilican design to one incorporating a square central area, marked in pencil with diagonal lines, in a position opposite the north door. Wren, if the church was indeed by him, was therefore thinking in terms of a design with some kind of central planning, similar in certain ways to what was later to be done by Hooke at St Martin Ludgate.

In the absence of a ceiling plan it is not possible to decide what may have been intended for the roof of the church, although there are indications in a further drawing from the Bute Collection of what seems to be a later elevation of the interior of the east end. This shows that the church would have been barrel-vaulted with lunettes to the north and south, probably at the crossing. We do not know how far this design was pursued, as the destruction of the roof in 1760 has removed the evidence, but the intercolumniation existing prior to the insertion of the additional columns in 1924 suggests that something of this kind was not only intended but built.

The elevation of the east end is said by Summerson to be in Wren's hand and there is no reason for doubting this. His authorship of the design of the church would presumably follow and the gift to him of a hogshead of wine, valued at £15 14s. 0d., would seem to confirm it. The vestry minutes contain no reference to Hooke, although his diary records that he visited the church several times in 1672 and again in 1675–79. The latter visits may well have been in connection with his designing of the tower and steeple, but the former probably relates to designing for the church, constructed in 1674–78. The available evidence thus suggests that the design was the work of both Wren and Hooke, in collaboration.

There is now little evidence remaining of any cross-axial planning in the church, with only the door visible on the north front serving to remind that it did at one time exist, even if it soon vanished. As with other similar parish churches, the churchwardens accepted a design which they did not understand, did not know how to use and which, over the centuries, they progressively changed into a traditional nave-and-aisles church, with the centralising elements almost totally obliterated.

St James Garlickhithe is another church where Hooke's diary shows that he made several visits. These were in 1677–78, by which time the design for the rebuilding had already been settled. The churchwardens' accounts record several occasions when Wren visited the site and more when the parish officials called upon him. He was, apparently, more involved with the rebuilding of this church than with many others. The evidence is far from conclusive but, in the absence of any other, does lead to the suggestion that Wren may have been the architect of the design.

Although the roof of St James Garlickhithe is not original, much having happened to this church, particularly in the present century, the ceiling is presumably to the original design. It does not reflect the arrangement of the furnishings within the church which, like St Magnus the Martyr, has long since abandoned all pretence of cross-axial planning. The large windows in the centres of both north and south fronts (now changed from round-headed to circular) and the remains of a doorway on the north front, visible only from the outside, confirm what can be deduced from the arrangement of the columns and entablatures: that this church, like St Anne & St Agnes and St Martin, had intersecting axes. This is the more curious in that it is one of the few of the City parish churches to have retained a separate chancel, a feature promoting a strong east-west liturgical axis. This may reflect a conflict between the architect and the vestry, or perhaps a desire to retain elements of the pre-Fire church, but even so is difficult to understand.

Just as St Magnus the Martyr and St James Garlickhithe retain redundant doors, visible only on the exterior of the buildings, so does St Mary-le-Bow as evidence of its original cross-axis. Here too it is a doorway visible only on the exterior of the south front, but much above the level of the lane at the side of the church. While it must always have been at this high level, the exact purpose of the door remains unclear. The church may have been designed to permit a processional use of this north-south axis, possibly in connection with the Court of Arches. Such use, if intended, has long since vanished.

The Basilica of Maxentius or Constantine, known in Wren's time as the Templum Pacis (Temple of Peace), stood towards the west end of the Via Sacra in Rome. Its ruins are there now and still impressive. It was a very large building and casual visitors to the church of St Mary-le-Bow are unlikely to associate the two. But for the information provided by Christopher Wren junior in *Parentalia*, the source of Wren's design for St Mary might have remained unknown. Not only is the scale very different, the proportions too have been changed. The original was never seen by Wren but the building would have been known to him from published plans and descriptions, such as those by Serlio and Palladio.

No doubts have been raised concerning the authorship of the design for St Mary-le-Bow, although, as indicated in Chapter 9, a contribution of Robert Hooke to the design of the tower is likely.

Churches with Domes

The list of Wren churches contains eight that had, or were intended to have, domes. These include the unbuilt church to be built by private subscription on a site in the centre of Lincoln's Inn Fields and referred to here as 'St Mary-in-the-Fields'. St Mary-at-Hill, in the form designed by Hooke and built in the years 1670–72 with its shallow saucer-shaped dome, is best considered as a church to a cross-within-a-square design. Of the seven built, only St Mary Abchurch and St Stephen Walbrook have survived in anything like the form in which they were constructed, with the dome of St Stephen rebuilt after its destruction in the war of 1939–45, and that of St Mary Abchurch extensively restored. The list is:

> St Antholin, Budge Row
> St Benet Fink
> St Mary Abchurch
> St Mary-at-Hill
> 'St Mary-in-the-Fields'
> St Mildred Bread Street
> St Stephen Walbrook
> St Swithin London Stone

The initial design for St Mary Abchurch included a hemispherical dome without a lantern. The dome was to stand on columns and pilasters in a church considerably larger than that which was eventually built. The design is known only from a surviving plan and elevation (Figs 35 and 36). When the church was built a more lightweight dome was provided, a construction that did not need the support of columns. The reason for the change to a smaller building is not known – perhaps by then it had become accepted that a larger building was not required.

One of the most interesting of the designs in this group is that for St Benet Fink, which had a decagonal plan. The pre-Fire church was rectangular in shape

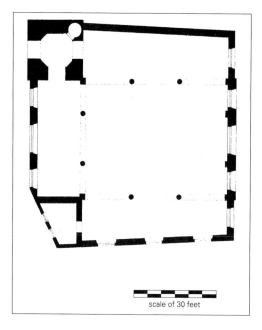

scale of 30 feet

FIGURE 35. St Mary Abchurch, plan of proposed church. (*PJ*)

and had its principal axis aligned approximately north east to south west along Threadneedle Street. The church could not, however, be reconstructed to this plan as the north-west corner of the site was taken by the Corporation for the widening of Threadneedle Street, thereby creating an irregular site and limiting what could be done with it. The polygonal church can be seen as the response to this limitation. Despite the problems which this imposed upon the building, it enabled an east-west orientation to be given to the church. The exterior of the building had a form which strongly reflected that of the interior, but later construction against it obscured much of the delicacy that this building originally possessed.

The problem of building on an irregular site was also encountered at St Antholin Budge Row. Here the south front was on Watling Street which, at that point, curved to join Budge Row, leaving the church site with a truncated south-west corner. For this irregular site, another domed, polygonal building was designed, this time contained within a shell whose exterior did not reflect its interior form. The church, when viewed from the east along Budge Row, showed no trace of its internal symmetry. From this direction it appeared much like churches with rectangular plans; its polygonal shape was apparent only when viewed from Watling Street. Although its dome could be seen, it was only from the inside that this also had decagonal symmetry.

The pre-Fire church of St Swithin London Stone was rectangular in shape, with the tower on the north-west corner. In the rebuilding it was converted to square by moving the tower to a position further north. This enabled the church to have a regular octagonal dome of wood and plaster. It dominated the interior of the building, creating a strong sense of central direction, ruined (certainly in Victorian times and possibly in the seventeenth century) by the parallel rows of pews facing the altar. The all-pervading sense of theatre-in-the-round seems to have been largely lacking also at St Mildred Bread Street, where

FIGURE 36.
St Mary Abchurch,
design proposed for
the east front.
(*All Souls College,
Oxford*)

a semi-circular dome was provided for a small single-cell rectangular building.
A dome was, perhaps, not the obvious solution for such an auditorium and one
wonders why it was adopted. Here, as with other domed churches, the response
of the churchwardens to any element of central planning seems to have been
to ignore it.

The most developed and intricate of all the domed churches was and still
is St Stephen Walbrook. A description of it as a domed church with nave
and four aisles does not adequately sum up the ambiguities and complexities
of the design, in which Wren succeeded in fusing these basic elements together
into a remarkably homogeneous building. It is undoubtedly a masterpiece and
a good example of a centrally-planned building which manages to retain also
an unequivocal and dominant east-west axis. The north-south axis led from
a north door where Wren intended a grand entrance portico facing the Stocks
Market. This was never built, although there was apparently a north door of
some kind whose position is still marked in the masonry of the north front.
The reason for abandoning the project is not entirely clear, but may have
been connected with the nature of the stalls in the market. The Shambles,

the area devoted to the slaughter of animals, and to the preparation and selling of meat, was notorious for the odours it generated. It seems that a door on the south side of the church was never intended. The property on this side and to the east of the church was owned by a Mr Pollixifen and there can never have been any intention of developing a full cross-axis.[12] Pollixifen's right to light was infringed by the building of the church so, in compensation, he was given a burial-vault on the south side of the church.[13] The central area of the church is clearly defined, functioning as a focus for the whole building beneath its plaster dome, which has often been said, without reason, to be a model for the dome of St Paul's.

This emphasis on the central space is particularly marked now that the pews have gone and Henry Moore's large, circular travertine altar occupies the space beneath the dome. Opinions about it vary greatly, from those who feel that it is a travesty that should never have been allowed, to those who feel that the central area is a suitable place for it and that it responds admirably to the building and the building to it. It is far from what Wren intended, nor would it have been in any way appropriate to the church of his time. Then the box pews obstructed the view of the central area from all but those close to it and those advancing towards it from the cardinal points. It was a meeting-place, a place to which people came and from which they went. When all were in their places the church became, like so many others, a building with nave and aisles filled with a congregation facing the altar which, with the pulpit, then formed the foci of the building. For all its suggested appropriateness, the block of travertine is now the one and only focus, occupying and blocking the meeting-place and causing the congregation – or more often visitors – to flow around it. The ambiguities of the building, and its careful arrangement of vistas that changed as one entered and advanced towards the altar at the east end, are no longer apparent. The fenestration around the dome now seems quaint, the auditorium barren and the seventeenth-century altar and pulpit irrelevent.

At 'St Mary-in-the-Fields' Wren was required to create a design that was not only functional but externally impressive. His church for Lincoln's Inn Fields, an area then being developed with large houses for affluent inhabitants, had to be appropriate for the site in the centre of the great square, requiring emphasis to all four fronts. None of the City churches had to meet this criterion, none was exposed to four-square public gaze. It is true that it was said to have been intended only as a 'singing chapel', rather than a parish church, but this can have deceived few. The first step in creating a new parish was to provide a church for it. This was only the first of a number of attempts to provide a church on this site.[14]

The church, projected only, is known from a drawing in the Westminster City Archives,[15] and engravings in the Pepys Library.[16] There are some differences between the designs from these sources: the most elaborate, with the west front featuring attached giant columns, is that from the Westminster Archive. It shows

FIGURE 37. 'St Mary-in-the-Fields'. Lincolns Inn Fields, elevation design proposed for church. (*Westminster City Archives*)

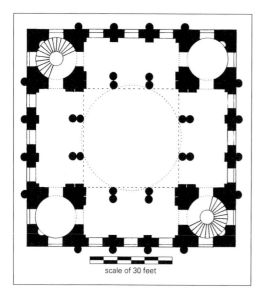

FIGURE 38. 'St Mary-in-the-Fields', Lincolns Inn Fields, plan of the proposed church. (*PJ*)

a church raised over an open basement resembling the church in Lincoln's Inn, to a cross-in-a-square design having a prominent dome carried on eight paired columns and capped with a lantern and small spire. It is a true quincunx design, with domes over the corners. It is shown in elevation in Fig. 37 and in reconstructed plan in Fig. 38. It would certainly have been one of the most significant and magnificent of parish churches by Wren, showing what he could do on an unencumbered site and with a free hand.

In comparison with Wren's St Stephen Walbrook and 'St Mary-in-the-Fields', the remaining domed churches are all relatively simple in their design. They do not show, for example, any ambiguity in how they should be read: none of them has any great axial emphasis and in all of them the focus is, or was, immediately below the dome. While St Stephen Walbrook and 'St Mary-in-the-Fields' are unquestionably by Wren, the same cannot be said for the remaining domed churches, where the authorship is as yet uncertain. Wren received payments or gifts from the vestries of St Antholin Budge Row, St Benet Fink and St Mary Abchurch, and it is tempting to suggest that he may have designed all three. However, the Netherlandish style and motifs of St Benet Fink might well be taken as pointing to Robert Hooke as the author. St Mildred Bread Street was built with a façade having pineapples on plinths above the cornice and a large urn above the segmental pediment, which also suggest Hooke as the architect. No payment to Wren has been traced for this or St Swithin London Stone. Hooke's diary lists visits made by him to St Antholin, St Benet Fink and St Swithin but not to St Mary Abchurch or St Mildred Bread Street. None of this can be regarded as conclusive evidence for authorship, but neither can the possibility of collaboration between Wren and Hooke be completely disregarded. Until further evidence is uncovered, little more can be said.

11

Towers and Steeples

As with many cities, the skyline of medieval London was dominated by the huge bulk of its cathedral. Its preeminence was even greater when the crossing-tower had its spire, rising to to a height of about 540 feet. In 1561 it was struck by lightning, caught fire and crashed through the roof of the building, setting the roof timbers alight as it fell. The stone tower on which the spire had rested was repaired, but the spire was not rebuilt. The tower provided the building with a new silhouette, still massive and impressive, particularly when viewed from south of the river. Away from Ludgate Hill and the dominance of St Paul's, the cityscape was determined more by the towers and steeples of the parish churches, most of which rose above the surrounding houses, with their characteristic spires, pinnacles and parapets in the views recorded by Wyngaerde and others. All this was destroyed in the Great Fire. The London skyline was never again to be so thickly populated.

Even before the Fire there was no uniformity in the design or size of the steeples. Just as the churches ranged from very small to excessively grand, so they had anything from a short, plain stump to a highly-decorated tower or a tall spire. Differences in towers and steeples reflected differences between the parishes. They had never been equal: all too often what distinguished one from another was the wealth of its inhabitants contributing to its upkeep. No two parishes resembled each other before the Fire and no two were alike afterwards. It was often the richer parishes with the loudest voices which were most able to demand the best for their new churches, to pay for the finest furnishings and to seek steeples that reflected their view of themselves as most deserving of recognition. What better way was there than having a steeple that was higher or more magnificent than your neighbours'. St Bride Fleet Street, St Magnus the Martyr and St Michael Cornhill all showed their parish pride with magnificent towers and steeples, obtained as a result of concerted efforts to influence the Commissioners and their architects.

Many of the London churches were renowned for their bells: they kept the curfew and they tolled the passing of the dead. Occasions civil and military, official and private, were marked by their sound. Few churches had full peals of eight, ten or twelve, but all had two or three that regularly called their parishioners to worship. They were part of life in the capital; churches without bells would have been unthinkable and bells needed towers. Although the rebuilding Acts of 1667 and 1670 made mention of neither, it was taken for granted that the rebuilding of fifty-one parish churches would include a rest-oration of their towers and the provision of new steeples. The replacement of the bells was left to the parish vestries to organise and pay for.

Although towers can be decorative, their principle function is utilitarian, providing space for bells and facilities for bell-ringing, accommodation for clocks and for the display of their dials. In addition, they provide viewing-points for ceremonial and other occasions and, at a lower level, rooms for vestry meetings and other parish functions. The purpose of steeples is purely decorative, to draw attention to themselves as locating and identifying the site of the parish church. The distinction between towers and steeples, each as a separate part of the combined structure, works well for the churches of the Wren period. In the cases of most of them, the two were constructed at different times with an interval between; but, even when designed and built together, the join between tower and steeple needs no defining – it is there to see.

Church Towers

Engravings of the City made immediately after the Fire show that in the conflagration the steeples vanished. A skyline still dominated by towers remained. Made of brick and stone, the towers survived the Fire. With their interiors gone, they stood empty, bereft of windows and open to the sky. Their wooden floors, staircases, ladders, roofs and bell-frames had all been consumed. The towers acted as chimneys, providing a draught for the fire, causing bells to melt and molten metal to drip to the ground. The chimney action took the heat upward away from the walls of the tower and saved much of their lower parts from severe damage, but the parapets inevitably crumbled and the tops of the towers suffered badly from calcination and spalling of the stone. The lead coverings of the towers and steeples disappeared with the bells, as drops into the dust and ashes of the fire.

Nevertheless, because a substantial part of many towers survived, it was usually the part of the church to receive first attention from the parish vestries.

Roofs, first temporary then more permanent, were thrown across and flooring installed to create parish rooms. Until the tabernacles were built, these served as vestry meeting-places and probably also for some services. The towers were the one part of many churches which could quickly be brought into use, providing a focus to reestablish local government at the parish level. For some of the towers the cost of repair was met by the sale of lead and bell-metal recovered from the debris of the Fire, although not all parishes parted so readily with their bell-metal. For some, the restoration of the tower was followed almost immediately by a recasting of one or more bells, or a purchase of new ones, to call the parish to worship once again or to mourn its dead.

The first group of churches to be brought into service – those repaired by the parish vestries (St Christopher-le-Stocks, St Dunstan-in-the-East, St Mary Woolnoth, St Michael Cornhill, St Sepulchre and St Vedast Foster Lane) all had towers which were repaired. This pattern was to continue with Robert Hooke producing new designs for other churches where the pre-Fire tower remained and could be repaired. The churches of St Anne & St Agnes, St Mary Aldermanbury, St Mary-at-Hill and St Michael Bassishaw were reconstructed with the pre-Fire towers restored, with no thought given to any other course. Pulling the towers down in order to rebuild them would have been seen as extravagant and unnecessary. Even at St Mary-le-Bow Wren had no intention of demolishing what was left of the pre-Fire tower on the north-west corner of the church. Because it still stood, there was a presumption that it could be repaired. Money and effort were therefore spent in attempting to preserve and restore it. When signs of instability became apparent, iron bands were employed to hold the fabric in place.[1] It was after the failure of these bands to hold the tower that Wren decided to pull it down. Only then did he consider the advantage of rebuilding it on an adjacent site in Cheapside.

In deciding to have the tower on a new site, the prime consideration seems to have been one of visibility. This may also may been in Wren's mind at St Stephen Walbrook, where he proposed to place the tower on the north side, facing the Stocks Market, a position of some prominence.[2] The tower of any particular church was not necessarily designed by the architect of the church. For example, the tower of St James Piccadilly does not appear to have been by Wren. The tower of St Clement Danes was constructed earlier than the church, probably to a design by Joshua Marshall and Stephen Switzer, while that of St Andrew Holborn was a recladding of the medieval tower, probably by

Hawksmoor. The tower of St Stephen Walbrook, as rebuilt, was not part of the original design by Wren and not by him.

Church Steeples

The simple steeples placed on the first towers to be restored, consisting of bell-cages or turrets, mostly wooden and lead-covered, were probably very similar to those destroyed in the Fire. It cannot be said that much thought or ingenuity was expended on these designs. All were produced early in the life of the Commission and some at least had disappeared before the end of it. They were illustrated by Gerald Cobb in an arrangement which drew attention both to the similarity of the visual shapes and the differences between them.[3] Even where a basic similarity exists, as with St James Garlickhithe, St Michael Paternoster Royal and St Stephen Walbrook, the variations provide quite different silhouettes and illustrate the complexity of the designs.

Nowhere in the papers of the Commission are the architects of individual steeples named and other contemporary sources are silent. The long-held view that they were all by Wren is not now sustainable; recent literature has acknowledged that some of them (St Edmund the King is the one most frequently named) are probably by Robert Hooke. It is not difficult to see him as the author of this and more; confirmation of his work on most of the individual churches is lacking but, on stylistic grounds, most of the early steeples must be by him.

The year 1670 marked not only the beginning of the Wren church-building programme with designs based upon classical ideas, but also the introduction to England of classical towers and steeples. There were no precedents to which Wren and Hooke could turn and few examples abroad providing suitable models. Even in Holland, where towers were conspicuous features not only of churches but of town halls, town gates, weigh-bridges and other buildings public and private, there were few examples that were other than gothic in spirit and execution. In Flanders, Holland's Catholic neighbour, the lead in church and tower design was taken by the Jesuits, with baroque architecture emanating from Rome. The design of their churches has much in common with the Gesù in Rome, their spiritual home, but their towers and steeples are more original, fusing the northern, Netherlandish tradition of tall, gothic steeples with classical and baroque elements from further south.

Early Flemish essays in the baroque include the heptagonal church of Scherpen-heuvel, begun in 1609 by Wenceslaus Coeberger, the Jesuit church in Brussels by Jacob Franckaert of about 1616 and the Begijnage at Mechelen, also by Franckaert, whose tower of about 1620 has a steeple that rises in octagonal stages and is completed with a cupola and lantern. But the most successful and influential of the baroque towers and steeples was undoubtedly that of St Charles Borromeo in Antwerp.[4] There is no doubt that its design was known to Wren and Hooke, but probably not from direct acquaintance. They may have known, or even possessed, a particular drawing of the tower, now in the Sir John Soane's Museum (Fig. 39).[5] It is in an unknown hand and shows the east façade with the tower and steeple largely as built. Although the original design for the tower is attributed to Huyssens, it is now generally accepted that, as built, it owes much to Rubens.[6]

The borrowings from St Charles Borromeo for the City churches are too blatant to be ignored, with individual features from it appearing in a number of the towers and steeples, with that of St Magnus the Martyr a near-direct translation of much of the design. St Mary-le-Bow has the same pilasters, paired at the corners at the bell-loft stage, as does St Bride Fleet Street. The combination of a conical cap or pyramid with an octagonal lantern over a small dome is repeated at St Benet Fink, St Benet Paul's Wharf and St Martin Ludgate; and in unexecuted designs for St Antholin, St Clement Danes and St James Piccadilly. The lantern with conical cap was used at St Mary Magdalen and St Michael Bassishaw. Even the cross from St Charles Borromeo, with four tulip heads springing at right angles from a rosette, appears on a design by Wren for St Paul's Cathedral.

Although a less direct borrowing, the influence of St Charles Borromeo can also be seen in a drawing of an unbuilt steeple for St Benet Gracechurch (Fig. 40).[7] St Benet was one of the fifteen churches that the Commisioners decided, on 13 June 1670, should be the first to be rebuilt. It was located in the eastern sector of the City and Hooke probably began work on the design immediately following the decision. On 13 July, with the abandonment of the list, the interest in St Benet Gracechurch evaporated, the drawing was put aside and no further work undertaken either on the design or on the church itself for the next ten years. Executed in Hooke's hand, the drawing showed what was probably the first classical steeple to be designed in England. The details – rustication, portal, round window decorated with swags, a pedimented window supported with scroll work, louvered window with shell niche – all testify to a radically new approach to tower design, as also do the panelled dome and slender spire. Although its

FIGURE 39.
St Charles Borromeo,
Antwerp, tower and
steeple.
(*Sir John Soane's Museum*)

FIGURE 40.
St Benet Gracechurch,
an early design for the
tower and steeple.
(*Sir John Soane's
Museum*)

features are from St Charles Borromeo, in outline it looks back to the pre-Fire tower of St Benet Gracechurch, which had a lofty spire. The rebuilding of St Benet was not started until 1681. In that time not only had Hooke's ideas evolved but funding had become tighter and the tower and steeple, although still with a lofty spire, were a great deal simpler in design with much of the decorative detail removed. In particular the columns of the bell-loft stage had gone, although the corners remained indented.

The next design to be produced by Hooke was probably for St Edmund the King. Although this church did not feature on the list of the first fifteen, the parish obtained an early place on the rebuilding programme. A new design was therefore required and, since it lay in his sector of the City, Hooke produced it. The only drawing for the church known to have survived is one which carries Wren's initials in the tympanum of the doorcase and the inscription 'With his Majties Approbation'. The requirement to submit designs for the King's approval was soon to lapse, confirming that this is an early drawing, probably of 1670.

The entrance to St Edmund the King was on Lombard Street and Hooke combined it with a tower as a formal street façade. The model is Dutch in inspiration, with large wings supporting the tower decorated along their outer edges with festoons of fruit and leaves. The steeple, rising above the tower, was quite simple, consisting of an octagonal lantern surmounted by a small dome or cupola. This, together with the festoons from the wings, was removed later in the building campaign. The octagonal lantern and dome were nevertheless features that Hooke was to deploy elsewhere with increasing deftness and greater finesse.

On 14 October 1670 the parish of St Benet Fink made its first deposit of £500 with the Chamber of London. This was another parish in Hooke's sector and his design for the church must date from about that time. It was a small church with a squat tower having large oval windows, decorated underneath with stone festoons. It was surmounted with a convex, tetragonal lead-covered dome topped with a small lantern (Fig. 41). The church had large round-headed windows with carved drapery over, giving the whole building a Netherlandish air.

Another early design was that for St Mary-le-Bow, for which there is no reason to dispute Wren's authorship, although he may have received help from Hooke. The earliest drawing for the tower and steeple is by Woodroffe. It shows the portal based upon Mansart's Hôtel de Conti (Figs 10 and 42), which Woodroffe is unlikely to have known and which he was presumably instructed

FIGURE 41. St Benet Fink, tower and steeple. (*Niven after Clayton*)

to incorporate – his role being that of draughtsman. The drawing of the tower and steeple cannot be earlier than April 1671, but must have been produced soon afterwards.

The rebuilding of St Nicholas Cole Abbey was ordered by the Commissioners in August 1671, with its design presumably dating from then or early in 1672. The steeple consists of an octagonal, concave cap of lead-covered timber, with a small gallery towards its apex. This cap was mounted on an octagonal base at the top of an unremarkable tower, having a low parapet in place of a balustrade but with urns on corner plinths. It is reminiscent of St Edmund the King and the vocabulary is typically that of Hooke.

The design of St Martin Ludgate was developed in the period 1673 to 1676. Hooke sited the tower on the street frontage of the church on Ludgate Hill and incorporated a formal façade, as he had done at St Edmund the King, to which it has some resemblance. Here, too, the tower is supported by wings but in the form of scrolls. This is another lead-covered timber steeple. It has an octagonal cap rising to a galleried platform with a lantern surmounted by what was intended to be a short spire. As a consequence of the Commissioners' decision, the construction of the tower and steeple were delayed. When building was resumed the steeple was given a taller spire.

In this part of the building campaign, steeple-building can thus be seen to have consisted of a design by Wren for St Mary-le-Bow, tall, elegant and completely different from anything by Hooke, together with a group of designs by Hooke, all for towers and steeples of medium height. The decoration of his towers and steeples, like that of his churches, tended to be Netherlandish but with the steeples themselves all much simpler than continental models. They have a common vocabulary of domes, lanterns, spikes, balustrades, urns and

FIGURE 42.
St Mary-le-Bow,
entrance portal,
based on Mansart's
Hôtel de Conti.
See also Fig. 10. (*PJ*)

pineapples, all motifs that he was to use again when tower- and steeple-building resumed in the 1680s.

This later phase of tower- and steeple-building was similar to the earlier – no design was repeated although all used the same vocabulary. None is particularly remarkable. Stylistically there is no break between the steeples of this and the earlier period: designing may have continued without a break, even though construction had ceased. There are no more steeple designs that can clearly be identified as by Wren, although the steeple of St Peter Cornhill, which closely resembles an unbuilt design for St Clement Danes, may conceivably be by him. The alternative, that both are by Hooke, is equally plausible.

Throughout the eighties Hooke continued to produce steeple designs, including in all probability those for St Mary Abchurch, St Mary Magdalen, St Michael Queenhithe, St Mildred Bread Street and St Swithin London Stone. A surviving drawing, showing a steeple for St Antholin Budge Row, is also in his hand. It might have been expected that he would have produced a design for the steeple of St Mary Somerset, but neither St Mary nor St Antholin were built to his design; they simply do not have the vocabulary associated with him. The urns are somehow less renaissance and more baroque, the spires and spirelets have become noticeably more like obelisks and the feeling is altogether much more eloquent. At St Antholin, of 1687–88, the profusion of windows in the spire, decorated with flaming urns or flambeaux, was similar to the assembly used later at both St Margaret Pattens and St Edmund the King. At St Mary Somerset, 1685–94 (with the tower towards the end of this period), the design of pinnacles and urns is more baroque than anything produced by Hooke and recalls those provided later for St Augustine Old Change. These, together with the carved masks and faces, foreshadow the use of old and young faces on St Michael Cornhill. Here, for the first time, one can sense an input from the fledgeling but precocious Nicholas Hawksmoor. How much he was allowed or encouraged to do at this stage is uncertain, but there can be no mistaking the fact that he was doing something, if only providing detailing for his elders.

By the time he retired Hooke's designs had become somewhat stereotyped and there is no difficulty in recognising his hand in the designs for St Margaret Lothbury and St Michael Bassishaw. Both were timber-framed and lead-covered, St Margaret with a tetragonal dome surmounted by a panelled spire and St Michael Bassishaw with an octagonal lantern on a high base topped with a concave pyramidal cap. The steeple of St Michael had been repaired early in the life of the Commission, but this was not, it would seem, well done. By the end of the century the church was shored up and in need of repair. In 1692–93 the vestry employed a surveyor to inspect the church and also lobbied Wren, although no work was done. In 1700–1 the vestry waited on the Commissioners and Dickinson later viewed the church. Work in 1711–13 included repairs to the roof, upper parts of the wall and the tower. The steeple was added at this time. The work was supervised by Dickinson but the steeple is unlikely to be by him. The design may have been produced by Hooke about 1693, when the parish appealed to Wren.

The steeple of St Magnus the Martyr is another completed by Dickinson, probably to a design by Hooke. Work on the tower was originally in step with that of the church but, in response to the Commissioners' order, work on it ceased in 1678. It resumed in 1680 and the tower was completed in 1684 with the addition of the parapet but without the spire. John Thompson, mason, was paid £5 14s. 0d. for making a model of a spire and in 1685 the Commissioners ordered its construction. The existence of both a design and an order was one thing, but getting the work done was another – by the end of the century it had still not been started. Following the 1697 renewal of the coal tax, the parish vestry lobbied Wren and the Commissioners, spending forty guineas: 'properly disposed of for Secrett Services for the benefitt of the Parish, & in procuring the Steeple to be finished'.[8] Work on the steeple began in 1703 and was completed by 1706. In its outline it resembles St Charles Borromeo but is very different in its detail (Fig. 43). The octagonal lantern rises from a tall plinth and is surmounted by a convex dome, a further octagonal lantern and a concave spirelet.

The retirement of Robert Hooke in 1693 marked the completion of the church-building programme. By then the fifty-one parish churches of the City of London which Parliament had decided should be retained had all been repaired, restored or rebuilt, although the further rebuilding of St Vedast Foster Lane had still to be put in hand. A few towers, notably those of St Alban Wood Street and St Michael Crooked Lane, remained to be completed and many of the church towers were lacking their steeples.

At that time the construction was being financed by the Act of 1685. The amount of money that this would make available to Wren in the period 1693–1700 would certainly have been known to him; it is reasonable to assume that he also knew how he intended to spend it. The programme of work was not, however, entirely of his choosing. The Commissioners were still in charge and they were under pressure from individual parishes still hopeful of getting

FIGURE 43.
St Magnus the
Martyr, north front,
tower and steeple.
(*NMR*)

more work done at public expense. Wren, too, repeatedly received repre-
sentations from the vestries, pressing their cases to his attention. The forward
programme cannot have remained unchanged for long.

Wren, fully aware of how Parliament operated, is likely to have assumed that
the revenue from the coal tax would not continue beyond the year 1700. In
the event, Parliament approved further revenue from 1700 to 1716, enabling
work on the steeples to continue until 1717. In this period the parish records
repeatedly record the name of William Dickinson. He was the Commissioners'

surveyor most concerned with the construction of their steeples. He was the man entertained by the churchwardens and the one who received small gifts in appreciation of his work. On stylistic grounds, however, some of the most characteristic of the late steeples are unlikely to be to his design. His task, initially at least, was in overseeing construction, like John Oliver and, before him, Edward Woodroffe. The authorship of the steeples which he constructed now remains to be considered, in particular the following:

St Dunstan-in-the-East	1695–1701
St Augustine Old Change	1695–1696
All Hallows Bread Street	1696–1698
St Margaret Pattens	1698–1702
St Bride Fleet Street	1701–1703
Christchurch Newgate	1703–1704
St Edmund the King	1706–1707
St Vedast Foster Lane	1709–1712
St Michael Crooked Lane	1709–1714
St Michael Paternoster Royal	1713–1717
St Stephen Walbrook	1713–1717
St James Garlickhithe	1714–1717

Of these churches, five have since been demolished: Christchurch Newgate, St Augustine Old Change and St Dunstan-in-the-East, all following destructive damage in the war of 1939–45, together with All Hallows Bread Street and St Michael Crooked Lane taken down in the nineteenth century. The towers and steeples of St Dunstan, St Augustine and Christchurch remain.[9]

The twelve late steeples of this list are noteworthy for a significant change in design that took place principally after Hooke's departure. It had already been foreshadowed by such designs as the tower of St Mary Somerset, pointing towards the involvement in designing by Sir Christopher Wren's clerk, Nicholas Hawksmoor. In these late steeples there is a greater variety of outline with interesting shapes such as the 'elongated flask' or 'onion' of St Augustine Old Change and St Michael Crooked Lane, together with wider use of new decorative motifs and a lightness of touch in the treatment of the architectural forms, particularly at St Dunstan-in-the-East and St Bride Fleet Street.

The last three to be erected, on the towers of St James Garlickhithe, St Michael Paternoster Royal and St Stephen Walbrook, all have arrangements of grouped columns beneath an entablature broken forward, possibly inspired by Roman models such as the towers of St Agnes in Agone in the Piazza Navona or Bernini's bell-towers for St Peter's. This general design appears also on the west towers of St Paul's Cathedral, although on a grander and far less intimate scale, built between 1705 and 1708. As with the rest of St Paul's Cathedral, they are generally credited to Wren and are used to support the suggestion that, as he grew older, his architecture became increasingly baroque and more responsive to the influences spreading from France and Rome. An alternative explanation is that, as he grew older, Wren was content to leave an increasing amount of the work to his junior, Nicholas Hawksmoor. It is possible that the designs for both the west towers and the late steeples may represent the interaction of the two men, Wren and Hawksmoor, perhaps their joint work. Yet, having produced no more than a handful of designs for churches, all early in the programme, it seems unlikely that Wren would, at the age of nearly seventy, once again have become involved in designing. Just as in the earlier stages of the programme he had left most of the church designing to Robert Hooke, and the building to Woodroffe and Oliver, so he could have left the late steeple designs to Hawksmoor and their building to Dickinson.

St Dunstan-in-the-East had been repaired by the parish soon after the Fire. The earliest report that all was not well from this early restoration is in the vestry minutes of 1693 which record that 'the church and steeple are defective and may be rebuilt at public charge', suggesting that agreement had by then been reached for rebuilding.[10] The design may date from this period. The old tower was pulled down in 1695, the church extensively repaired and the new steeple constructed under the supervision of William Dickinson in 1698–1701. A gift of wine was sent to Wren, a small payment made to Dickinson in 1697 and a larger payment to Hawksmoor in 1696.[11] Hawksmoor was probably also the recipient of eight guineas in 1695 as 'Sir Christopher Wren's clerk'. The steeple is gothic in spirit, the only one of this group that was, presumably at the insistance of the vestry (Fig. 44). It does have a few classical touches, with carved masks or faces both as decorative features and corbels.

Among the surviving original drawings for the parish churches are a number for St Augustine Old Change. One of these includes an elevation of the tower and steeple by Robert Hooke, but this remained unbuilt.[12] The ideas from which the final design of the steeple were developed can be seen in a drawing long recognised as by Hawksmoor (Fig. 45).[13] The outline of the pine cone and its superstructure can be seen in the structure of the lead-covered bulbous spire, although the detailing of the cone has vanished. The motif derives from a pre-Fire design by Wren for a dome to St Paul's,[14] which in turn looks back to old St Peter's. Not shown in his drawings are Hawksmoor's final design for the corner obelisks of the steeple which each had four masks or faces looking to the cardinal points, a motif used by him at Castle Howard for the 'Four Faces' garden ornament.

The vestry of All Hallows Bread Street attended the Commissioners in 1696 'to promote an order for finishing the steeple'. It must be assumed that they were successful in this, as work on it began in 1697 and was completed in 1698. Wren was presented with a chest of wine and another of 'florence' (wine despatched from Florence, probably Chianti) to the value of £12, Hawksmoor with £11 and Dickinson £5 10s. 0d., reflecting their presumed roles with

FIGURE 44. St Dunstan-in-the-East, design for tower and steeple. (NMR)

FIGURE 45. St Augustine Old Change, steeple design by Hawksmoor. (Conway Library)

FIGURE 46. St Margaret Pattens, tower and spire, drawn by J. Clayton.

FIGURE 47. St Bride Fleet Street, project design for a steeple. (*All Souls College, Oxford*)

Dickinson as constructor and Hawksmoor as designer.[15] The steeple had a balustrade with corner plinths and obelisks with decorated panels rising from acanthus leaves, a design that Hawksmoor was to use elsewhere. The upper part of the tower was completed at the same time. Each face had three round-headed arches with large keystones in the form of human faces or masks.

The churchwardens' accounts for St Margaret Pattens record several occasions when 'Sir Christopher Wren's clerk', not named but presumably Hawksmoor, was entertained and when small payments were made to him. The steeple, built in 1698–1702, is in the form of a lead-covered panelled spire with supporting corner pyramids or obelisks, panelled and rising from acanthus leaves (Fig. 46).

The tower of St Bride Fleet Street was constructed in 1671–78. One of the surviving drawings for the steeple shows a polygonal, bell-shaped cap, inscribed 'St Brides offer' (Fig. 47).[16] It probably dates from about 1676–77, with the intention that its construction should follow that of the tower. Work on the project stopped when the Commissioners ordered a temporary halt to towers and steeples. When work resumed, St Bride's vestry was no longer content with a tower having no more than a bell-shaped cap; it lobbied the Commissioners and, in 1681, obtained an order for a 'tower or spire'. Nothing, however, was done. The already completed tower of St Bride had been left open in 1678 and was not covered until 1697, probably in response to further lobbying from the vestry, anxious for a new spire and complaining that the tower was deteriorating. Two drawings for a new steeple survive,[17] neither as built but both showing the way in which the architect's ideas for a 'wedding-cake' design were evolving. One of them still has the bell-shaped cap, now very much smaller. The drawings presumably date from 1697–1700, soon after the lobbying by the vestry. The first stone was laid on 6 October 1701 and the steeple completed in 1703. The origin of the design for the steeple can be seen in the Warrant Design for St Paul's Cathedral, although in its final form the proportions were much changed. The four pairs of urns at the base of the steeple have the 'Four Faces' design used for St Augustine and at Castle Howard (Fig. 48). They provide the strongest evidence for suggesting that the design was by Hawksmoor.

The tower of Christchurch Newgate was built with the church in 1677–87. It rose to a main cornice over the colonnaded bell-loft with segmental-headed

FIGURE 48.
St Bride Fleet Street,
'Four Faces' design
of urns.
(*Warburg Institute*)

FIGURE 49.
Christchurch New-
gate, west front,
tower and steeple as
originally constructed.
(*All Souls College,
Oxford*)

plinths supporting urns on each face (Fig. 49). The steeple was added in 1703–4 when the first task facing Edward Strong junior, mason, was the construction of 'four great arches . . . to bear the spire', indicating that the added steeple was not a part of the original design. Alternative designs for completing the steeple date from about 1700 show a terminal pyramid or obelisk rising from acathus leaves, again suggesting Hawksmoor (Fig. 50).[18]

The steeple of St Edmund the King, constructed with the church in 1670–74, was undoubtedly designed by Robert Hooke, but it did not survive in that form. In 1705 the vestry reported the imminent 'repairing the steeple and building a spire . . . at the publick charge'.[19] The dome of Hooke's steeple was removed, together with the festoons decorating the wings of the tower, and a new spire added in 1706–7. This was concave, lead-covered and octagonal, with an assemblage of urns at two levels and additionally urns and pineapples on the parapet.[20]

There is no written confirmation of the authorship of the steeple of St Vedast Foster Lane but the architectural style, convincingly baroque, points directly to

FIGURE 50. Christchurch Newgate, proposed design for completing the steeple. (*Guildhall Library*)

Hawksmoor (Fig. 51). It was erected in 1709–12 after fabrication by Edward Strong junior at Greenwich. Constructed of Portland stone, in design it fore-shadows the later work of Hawksmoor for the 1711 Act Commissioners in the interplay of contrasting forms, convex against concave, and in the changing pattern of light revealed in lines, planes and volumes.

The tower of St Michael Crooked Lane was completed in 1697–98 with an open-work parapet and stone pyramids to each corner. The steeple was added in 1709–14. It was timber-framed and lead-covered, consisting of three circular concentric drums rising one above the other to a platform with three steps and a flask-shaped finial reminiscent of St Augustine Old Change. There are further reminders of St Augustine in the cut-away wings to the drums and of both St Antholin Budge Row and St Edmund the King in the tiers of urns with flames.

FIGURE 51.
St Vedast Foster
Lane, tower and
steeple from the
south west. (*NMR*)

In summary, the evidence for Hawksmoor's authorship of these late steeples is patchy, amounting to a few drawings by him, some payments to him, a vocabulary of motifs that we have come to accept as typical of him and stylistic evidence that varies from uncertain to, in the case of St Vedast Foster Lane, convincing. Taken together, however, they provide sufficient support to remove most if not all of the doubt concerning his work for the Commissioners in the period 1695–1701. In a period in which Hawksmoor's style was developing, one must not expect to see the full extent of rugged grandeur that he was later to deploy in his designs for the 1711 Act Commissioners, with its massive simplicity and eloquent, powerful, even overpowering steeples. But one would expect to see him developing his ideas, his forms and above all his motifs, those little details that announce him and which occur again and again in his mature work. One can point particularly to his use of carved human faces, to the use of obelisks and pyramids, to baroque urns, to drapery in eloquent stone and to curious steeple forms. Gone are the opulent cherubs, richly-decorated swags and gilded pineapples. The architecture of a solidly assured Restoration, classical but static, bland and not overtly religious, has given way to a lighter touch with an appeal to the imagination and the emotions. The stage has been set for the dramatic architecture of the 1711 Act Commissioners. We should not entirely shut our eyes to the possibility that Wren, too, in his last years as a designing architect, may have been subject to the influences of the time and have been moving slowly but significantly towards the new, emotive architecture of the baroque. It is perhaps in the later work at St Paul's that one should look for evidence of this. Distinguishing between such late work by Wren and that by Hawksmoor, at St Paul's and elsewhere, may always be difficult.

With the realisation that designs were prepared long before they were used, it is possible that the brief period between Hawksmoor's emergence as an architect and his disappearance from the parochial church rebuilding programme about the year 1701 was devoted to the production of one design after another, enabling him to leave behind in the office a cache of drawings for the remaining work. He may have felt secure in the knowledge that the design requirements to the end of the coal tax imposition were provided for.

The building of the late steeples to designs by Nicholas Hawksmoor brought almost to an end the church-building era that followed the Great Fire of 1666 – almost, but not quite. What Hawksmoor did not forsee was that new demands were to be made on the Commissioners, demands particularly from those parishes whose churches and towers had been rebuilt soon after the Fire and which by the end of the century were again crumbling: St Christopher-le-Stocks, St Mary Aldermary, St Mary Woolnoth, St Michael Cornhill and St Sepulchre,. What is noteworthy about these is that, together with St Dunstan-in-the-East (which had already been extensively repaired and the tower rebuilt) and St Vedast Foster Lane (which had been entirely rebuilt), they were all churches or towers repaired by the parishes themselves.

There is no doubt that the towers of these churches were in poor condition, with vestry minutes recording a number of incidents where damage had been inflicted by falling masonry on adjacent property. It would seem that in the earlier rebuilding there was a lack of appreciation of the extent to which the stonework of the walls and particularly the tops of the towers had been damaged by the Fire, with latent defects revealed only long after their restoration. Nevertheless, the fact that all these seven needed rebuilding again after so short a time suggests some other reason. One cannot but help wondering if the rebuilding would have been so extensive, or perhaps even have taken place at all, if public funding had not been available. Was there perhaps an element of envy – if St Dunstan and St Vedast could acquire new and exciting steeples at public expense on the second time round, why not the others?

After St Dunstan and St Vedast, the first of these towers to be rebuilt was St Mary Aldermary. Its tower had, seemingly, suffered little damage in the Great Fire and was patched up by the parish at a cost of £74 9s. 6d., paid by the Commissioners in 1675. The church itself was later rebuilt from the shell of the old building with the aid of a private benefaction. In 1701–3 the vestry secured a total demolition and rebuilding of the tower at a cost to the Commissioners of £6352 13s. 8d. William Dickinson was the man entertained by the church-wardens and small gifts were made to him.[21] He was undoubtedly responsible for supervising the reconstruction and, on the basis of a resemblance of the elongated bottle-shaped pinnacles of the tower to those that he was later to design for Westminster, Colvin also attributed the designing to him.[22]

The vestry of St Christopher-le-Stocks appealed to the Commissioners to have its church and steeple repaired in 1703. The work was undertaken in 1711, with a large part of the church and much of the tower taken down and rebuilt. Similarly, the Commissioners accepted the case for major repairs to the tower of St Sepulchre, whose vestry appealed to them in 1706. This work also began in 1711. The pinnacles and upper parts of the tower were rebuilt and extensive repairs made to the windows of the bell-loft, the middle- or clock-loft and the ringing-chamber.

The church of St Michael Cornhill was apparently sound but, by the end of the century, the tower was shedding stone and needed repairing if not rebuilding. In 1703 the vestry petitioned the Commissioners and in 1704 obtained an order for the work to be done. However, the parishioners soon complained that they could not get the order complied with.[23] In 1711, with the work still not started, the parish petitioned the House of Commons but without success. In 1715 they approached William Cowper, the Lord Chancellor, 'whose Ancistors ly interr'd in the Cloyster of our Church', and with his help obtained another order from the Commissioners.[24] Work on the tower then began. This was once again supervised by Dickinson and it seems likely to be to his design – a drawing for it, signed and dated May 1716, survives in the British Library.[25] By December 1717, however, the churchwardens reported that 'the workmen had left off going on with the steeple'. The money from the coal tax levied for rebuilding the City churches after the Fire was finally exhausted.

As a result of a further petition to the House of Commons, the construction of the tower was completed by the Commissioners appointed under the Act of 1711 to a design that can only be by Hawksmoor. It gives a distinct impression of gothic splendour, although an examination reveals classical and baroque features. The carved faces of the panelling at the belfry stage, alternating young and old, are reminiscent of Hawksmoor's work elsewhere.

The churches of St Christopher-le-Stocks and St Michael Cornhill, although nave-and-aisles in plan, had some classical features – the aisles, for example, having round-headed windows. It is therefore not surprising that, in the repair and rebuilding, the lower stories of the towers should have been given classical windows with moulded architraves. The tower of St Sepulchre rose from the body of the church with the lowest level open to the nave on all sides and therefore without windows, but the upper floors of the towers were given pointed windows, gothic in style. The steeples of all three towers were somewhat similar, with tall corner pinnacles rising from octagonal bases and with decorated parapets to all fronts. It is not difficult to see them all as the work of William Dickinson, who had a great deal more sympathy for the gothic style than either Wren or Hawksmoor.

St Mary Woolnoth was another of the small group of churches rebuilt or patched up by the parish (in this case for the parish by a parishioner, Sir Robert Vyner). In 1705 or 1706 the vestry again approached the Commissioners but the outcome is not recorded. There is no record of any further work undertaken by Wren or the Commissioners, nor of any design produced for the church at this time. In 1707 the parishioners appealed to Parliament and succeeded in getting a clause added to a St Paul's Bill (a Bill to get the dome of St Paul's covered with British copper), in which the Commissioners were empowered to rebuild 'such parts of the church . . . as should be necessary'. This Bill failed when the House was prorogued. In 1712, in a further attempt, the parish succeeded in getting a clause added to another Bill, a clause which would have enabled the Commissioners to rebuild the church from surplus money from the duty on coals levied for the purpose of finishing St Paul's, once the cathedral had been finished and adorned. By 1715 it was apparent that the Commissioners were not going to have any surplus money, at least for the time being, and the parish turned once again to Parliament, obtaining yet another clause to a Bill, enabling the 1711 Act Commissioners to rebuild the church, recovering the cost from the St Paul's money at a later date. The church was then rebuilt by the 1711 Act Commissioners to a design by Hawksmoor.

The repair and rebuilding of the last four churches and their towers was undertaken at a cost of over £15,000, a sum which would have enabled the Commissioners to provide steeples for several of the churches still without them. It is known, from the parish records, that Wren and the Commissioners were planning steeples for All Hallows-the-Great, All Hallows Lombard Street and St Mildred Poultry, steeples which, for want of funding, were then abandoned. Other churches for which steeples may have been planned (although no records of any proposals now survive) include St Andrew-by-the-Wardrobe, St Clement East Cheap and St Matthew Friday Street, all of which had been left with very plain towers.

A catalogue of drawings dispersed in the Hawksmoor sale of April 1740 records that he left about 2000 drawings. Of these, about 300, possibly more, were church designs. Is there a cache of Hawksmoor drawings waiting to be discovered? If so, will it include drawings for these unbuilt steeples?

12

Christian Worship:
The Liturgy, Fittings and Furnishings

The purpose of a parish church is to provide a place for a particular congregation to gather for an act of communal worship. In those churches rebuilt after the Fire, this worship was in accordance with the practice of the Church of England, a practice which had then by no means settled after the upheavals earlier in the century. The form of the building, and the arrangement of the interior, style and disposition of the furniture and fittings, all reflect the ideas of worship as they then existed, although in the late seventeenth century this pattern was changing rapidly. The simple rituals of the Commonwealth were giving way to a more elaborate, formalised and presentational form of worship. It was not until the early eighteenth century that this change can be seen in the architecture of new church-building, although it is reflected in some of the fittings of the late Wren period.

Few churches had been built in or around London in the early part of the seventeenth century and in England there were scarcely any examples of classical buildings that could be studied. City churches rebuilt earlier in the century included St Alban Wood Street (1633–34), in late gothic style, and St Katharine Cree (1628–30), with mixed decorative elements. The Queen's Chapel, by Inigo Jones (1623–27), was not a suitable model for a parish church. St Paul's Covent Garden, also by Inigo Jones (1633), was the outstanding classical building, with its huge portico facing the piazza and its unencumbered interior providing a preaching-box large enough to accommodate all the parishioners who wished to attend. These virtues made it an unsuitable model for the City, with its narrow streets, restricted sites and mostly small parishes, whose churches were unsuited for temple fronts. Most did not need a vast interior. There were no examples of centrally-planned churches whose advantages and disadvantages could be considered by the parish vestries. John Webb's drawings for a small centralised church, now in Worcester College, remained largely unknown.[1]

Mid seventeenth-century London had seen the building of a large number of Dissenting chapels, but details of most of them have not survived. Notable Anglican chapels of the period included the New or Broadway Chapel in Westminster and another in Poplar, later St Matthias.[2] These were cruciform in plan, with a principal east-west axis, but by virtue of a roof with cross-vaulting had at the same time a strong north-south emphasis, reflected in the seating. They were chapels for Protestant worship but it is doubtful if they were seen as suitable models for the increasingly formalised services of the Church of England.

As completed by Wren and his assistants, the parish churches of the City were bare boxes, without furniture, without fittings. Even before the Commissioners' craftsmen moved out, the parish craftsmen moved in to begin the work of installing the oak panelling known as wainscot to a height of between eight and eleven feet. Where recent examination has revealed the earliest coats of paint, the walls can be seen to have been painted a pale stone colour. The east walls, or at least the centres of them, may have been treated somewhat differently, if only to draw attention to the altars which, in the first churches to be completed, were not provided with the elaborate altar-pieces which developed as the century progressed. At St Mary-at-Hill the centre bay of the east wall was painted a chocolate brown colour, against which the 'Tablets' (the Decalogue, Creed and Paternoster) were fixed. Although subsequent alterations at the east end now prevent any real assessment of what it was like, the parish vestry minutes record the painting of portraits of the Virgin Mary and St Andrew (for St Andrew Hubbard) on the wall; also a painted curtain, drawn aside. Such painted curtains were a feature of many City churches, some surviving long enough to be recorded in illustrations, although none in photographs.[3]

Wren and the Commissioners provided doors but not screens, paving but not pews. Nothing in the Act of 1670 enjoined them to equip the churches with pews, pulpits, fonts or altar tables. These, and the remainder of the items then considered necessary, were obtained and paid for by the parishes – the usual procedure being for this task to be overseen by a parish committee or, when parishes had been united, by a joint committee of the two parishes. These committees were often empowered by the parent vestries to choose designs, contract with craftsmen and apportion the sums involved between the two parishes, leaving each vestry to recommend a parish rate to pay for them. In two cases, St Andrew-by-the-Wardrobe and St Mary Somerset, the parishes were too poor to raise the necessary sums and the fittings were provided from the revenue of the coal tax. These were exceptions: in all other cases it was the responsibility of the parish to choose its fittings and to pay for them. In the exercise of parish choice there was frequently more than religious fervour. Parish pride, keeping up with neighbours, or even going one better, all played a part. Having been given new churches at public expense, money could usually be found by most parishes to fit them out in a lavish manner. A few parishes were fortunate in having private benefactors. Their gain is our loss, in that the records of such gifts tell us nothing of the men who made these pieces, nor how much they cost.

The fittings and furnishings of the churches are now so closely associated with the architecture of the churches that it is often assumed that the buildings were designed with their interior fittings in mind. Only to a very limited extent is this true. The tall plinths provided for the columns supporting the roofs were clearly conceived with the idea that the column bases would be visible above the box pews that were to fill the auditories. These box pews have since been cut down or removed entirely. While this may have resulted in improved and more comfortable seating, and certainly improved the view of the worshippers (and made them conspicuous if they slept through long, tedious sermons), it has meant that the church interiors are seen with a disproportionate height, and with what now seems to be exaggerated plinths fully visible. This effect is particularly noticeable in St Martin Ludgate.

What neither Wren nor Hooke could have foreseen was that, even in their own time, changes were to be made to the design of the fittings and furniture which made a nonsense of certain aspects of their architecture. The altar-pieces,[4] for example, were soon to reach a size where they completely obscured the east windows, many of which were then or later blocked. This led, eventually, to the search for new ways of lighting the space before the altar. Even before this, the equipping of the buildings with pews, rigorously pursued to maximise the income from renting, made a nonsense of all elements of central planning in the churches. As far as we can now tell, pews were even then laid out, as they always had been, row upon row facing the altar, with only those around the walls as exceptions. Such churches as the polygonal St Benet Fink and St Antholin, where some other arrangement might have been more sympathetic to the architecture, still conformed to this pattern, presumably because the churchwardens knew of no other or the clergy wanted it that way. Demand for the traditional arrangement effectively prevented anything by way of experimentation at those churches with north–south axes and these, long redundant, eventually disappeared.

The use of galleries in churches was not new: a number of London churches destroyed in the Great Fire are known to have had them, some constructed solely for private pews. They were not provided in the first churches to be designed in the post-Fire rebuilding. In general most of the parishes, even where amalgamated, were still quite small and did not need the extra accommodation that galleries could provide. St Bride Fleet Street was an exception. It was a large parish and even the building of a large church may not have provided enough space for all who wanted to rent the pews.

It is commonly believed that on the Restoration of Charles II there was a command that the churches should display the royal arms (Fig. 52). If such a command was ever issued, no record of it has so far come to light, despite much searching. The royal instruction is increasingly seen as unfounded and the large numbers of royal arms in the City may owe more to custom than command. The gallery fronts were a convenient place for some of these displays, others include siting on the altar-piece, above doorcases and even fixed directly to church walls. The royal arms, together with their supporters, a lion and a unicorn, were sometimes painted and sometimes moulded in plaster but more frequently carved in wood. The examples that appear in the City churches are mostly what are known as 'undifferentiated Stuart' ('undifferenced Stuart', or just 'Stuart'), in use from the time of James I to 1707 in the reign of Queen Anne, and having the three lions of England quartered with three lilies of France in the first and third, and quartered with the lion of Scotland and Celtic harp of Ireland in the second and fourth.[5]

FIGURE 52. St Andrew-by-the-Wardrobe, Stuart royal arms. (*NMR*)

The change subsequently made to the seating, with the loss of the box pews in the parish churches, is but one example of the changes to the fittings and furnishings that have taken place in the course of 300 years. This evolution, sometimes arising as a result of changes in the liturgy, sometimes not, is a continuing process whose recent results can be seen, for example, in bench seating arranged east and west in so-called collegiate style, and the installation of Henry Moore's travertine altar at St Stephen Walbrook. In looking at the furniture of the Wren churches it is important to see the various items in relation to the purposes for which they were acquired, and how they served in the worship of God according to the rites of the Church of England at the time. We can then look at the many changes that have since occurred and ponder what is to come next, as the buildings are used less frequently for worship and more for secular purposes.

Parish Services

As one would expect, the principal assemblies in the church were for the Sunday services held in the morning and afternoon, taking advantage of natural light. When it became necessary to provide lighting, it was from arrays of candles in metal candelabra standing on the floor. A City church would have had a few of these, perhaps as many as four or six, known from their shape as branches. Candles and candlesticks were not used for decorative purposes; they were placed on the altar only when required for reading. There was no heating in the churches in the seventeenth or early eighteenth century; open coal-burning fires had yet to come, although fire-places were being installed in the parish vestries. Very few of the new churches had porches, ensuring that the buildings were not only cold but draughty, especially as leaded windows did not long remain wind-proof. The windows did however have plain clear glass, providing abundant natural light in the hours of daylight. Stained and painted glass was not unknown in the churches of the time, mostly for memorial and commemorative windows, but its use on the scale of medieval times did not return until the eighteenth century. Few examples are recorded in the churches of the late seventeenth: it is not known how much was installed and virtually none of it has survived. An early example was a panel containing the arms of Queen Anne, after the Union with Scotland (1707), in St Edmund the King (now destroyed), illustrated by Gerald Cobb.[6]

Accommodation in the churches was in the form of high box pews, each enclosed and usually with a lockable door. In some cases keys were provided, in others parish officials were appointed as pew-openers to make sure that only the rightful renters entered. Pew rents were an important source of parish income, with position in society and authority in the parish reflected in the way pews were allocated. The parish poor would stand or sit on benches. Charity children were frequently placed in galleries, away from the more affluent citizens. In the eighteenth century additional galleries, placed above the west gallery, were often used to accommodate these children. Not all the City churches provided such upper galleries and none now remains.

In addition to the normal Sunday services there were regular weekday services and lectures, often endowed. In all these, including the Sunday services, the focus of attention in the church was not the altar but the pulpit and the reading-desk. These were invariably sited together in a position where all could hear and most could see, usually against a wall in the smaller churches, against

FIGURE 53.
St Stephen
Walbrook, pulpit.
(*NMR*)

a column in the larger. In the eighteenth century there was a vogue for moving the assembly, including the pulpit, into a central position in front of the altar. The three-decker pulpits with reading-desk and clerk's desk have now all disappeared, leaving the pulpit still in a prominent position but not now obscuring the altar. The place of the reading-desk has been taken by the lectern, some examples of which have been constructed from woodwork which had previously served some other purpose. The surviving churches now have a wealth of carved woodwork, mostly of oak and much of it rearranged and reused, culled from the churches that have gone. A few churchwardens' pews remain with their carved fronts and staves or wands, symbols of their particular authority in the parish.

The pulpits of the period were fine examples of seventeenth-century joinery, constructed like almost all the furniture of oak – mahogany had still to be widely adopted and there was no shortage of good quality oak (Fig. 53). They were usually hexagonal, panelled and with extensive carved decoration. Most had sounding-boards, sometimes referred to as testers, also of oak and also much decorated. There are some superb examples remaining in the City churches, including those of St Magnus the Martyr, St Stephen Walbrook and All Hallows-the-Great, the latter now in St Margaret Lothbury.

It was customary for the Lord Mayor, at some time in his year of office, to attend one of the parish churches in state, accompanied by his officers and preceded by the City Swordbearer. The church chosen was frequently in the ward of which the Lord Mayor was Alderman. For the service, the City sword was placed in a sword-rest (also 'sword iron' or 'sword case') attached to the pew front (Fig. 54). Such sword-rests are now characteristic features of the City churches: most have one, some have several. The earliest recorded is

FIGURE 54. St Magnus the Martyr, sword-rest. (*NMR*)

from 1574–75.[7] A notable example, constructed in wood, survives at St Mary
Aldermary. The remainder, of which there are many examples, are of wrought
iron and have plaques painted with coats of arms,[8] up to four in number
(occasionally five or more if they record the visits of more than one Lord Mayor):
the royal arms, the arms of the City, the arms of the Livery Company to which
the Lord Mayor belonged and the personal arms of the Lord Mayor. Although
such formal attendances by the Lord Mayor are now discontinued, occasional
visits by him (or her) can still be marked by the introduction of new armorial
plaques for existing sword-rests.

In a few of the churches the sword-rests are accompanied by lion and unicorn
supporters. These are post-Wren introductions, marking the division between
nave and the area set aside to serve as a chancel. They are sometimes referred
to in the parish records as 'the beasts'. The reason for the choice remains
obscure – one might have expected that, rather than the royal supporters, the
dragons of the City of London would have been chosen.

Services of holy communion (not then referred to as 'mass' due to association
with Catholicism) were less frequent than nowadays, with most citizens only
attending on a few occasions during the year. Even in those churches where it
was popular, it was seldom held more than once a month. This service, however,
focused attention on the altar, more usually referred to as the communion table
(Fig. 55), with communicants kneeling at a rail to receive the sacrament. The

FIGURE 55.
St Benet Paul's
Wharf, communion
table. (*NMR*)

churches as designed had only single step platforms against the east wall for the altar tables, almost all of which were of oak, often with carved work and with turned or decorated legs. Some of the more elaborate had supporters in the form of carved figures, as at St Stephen Coleman Street. At All Hallows-the-Great the table was of marble but it too was supported by a figure of an angel.

Some of the first of the churches to be finished had the Decalogue, or Tablets of the Law, the Creed and Paternoster attached to the wall behind the altar and not assembled into a formal altar-piece, as in the later churches (Figs 56, 57).

FIGURE 56.
St Stephen
Walbrook, altar-
piece. (*NMR*)

FIGURE 57.
All Hallows-the-
Great, altar-piece
with statues of
Moses and Aaron.
(*NMR*)

These gradually developed into elaborate architectural compositions with classical columns (usually of the Corinthian order), entablatures, pediments, urns, vases, lamps, cherubim, pelicans and other carved motifs. Portraits of Moses and Aaron often flanked the Decalogue. In this, as with other fittings, the vestries tended to copy each other – once the idea of a large, classical altar-piece had been introduced, all the parishes wanted one. Churches that had earlier been fitted out without them soon took the opportunity of getting one. These included

St Mary-at-Hill, where a new altar-piece incorporating the pre-existing tablets was installed in the early years of the eighteenth century, and St Mary-le-Bow, which installed its altar-piece in 1706.

A few of the churches were built with separate chancels, presumably retained from the old church at the wish of the vestry or its incumbent at the time. The absence of any sanctuary area was in keeping with the liturgical sympathies of many of the clergy at the time of the Restoration, an attitude which was to change as the century progressed. Symptomatic of this change was the introduction of a chancel screen in St Peter Cornhill in 1681, at the instigation of the Rector, William Beveridge. This was followed in the parish of All Hallows-the-Great with a somewhat similar but more elaborate screen, now in St Margaret Lothbury.[9] The motive at All Hallows seems to have been one of following St Peter, rather than any heartfelt need for a specially sanctified area.

The use of fonts for the ceremony of baptism had been discouraged in the Reformation, their being replaced with pewter or other metal basins. Earlier in the century attempts were made to bring fonts back into use, notably by William Laud whilst Bishop of London. His visitation articles of 1631 inquired 'doth your minister baptise any children in any bason or other vessel than in the ordinary font . . .?' Matthew Wren, Bishop of Norwich, and uncle to Sir Christopher, issued an instruction for his diocese that 'the font . . . be filled with clean water and no dishes, pails or basins be used . . .'[10] Such fonts as remained in the City may have been lost in the Commonwealth, when their use was again forbidden. The 1662 Act of Uniformity and the revised Prayer Book once again required their use.[11] It is doubtful if many of the City churches had their new

FIGURE 58. St Nicholas Cole Abbey, baptismal font. (*NMR*)

fonts by 1666, when they would have been destroyed in the Great Fire. By 1670, when the churches began to be fitted out, they were once again regarded as essential items. The new fonts were classical in design, generally flat marble bowls, decorated with cherubim, festoons and acanthus leaves, usually on baluster stems, although a few examples are more chalice-shaped with carved pictorial scenes including baptism. Good examples from this period are those by Grinling Gibbons at St James Piccadilly, and another, possibly also by him, at St Margaret Lothbury. Most of the City fonts are somewhat plainer (Fig. 58). Among the earliest is that in St Martin Ludgate, dated 1670, which must have been in use in the tabernacle prior to the rebuilding of the church.[12] Font covers, or types, were also provided. Those in the City include some fine examples of carved-oak workmanship, notably at St Edmund the King, St Magnus the Martyr, St Stephen Walbrook and from Christchurch Newgate, now in St Sepulchre.

The baptism of infants generally took place close to one of the doors of the parish church. A pew, known as the christening pew, was set aside by the font with, in some churches, the area separated by rails from the rest of the church (Fig. 59). A fine example of this, although not close to a church door, remains

FIGURE 59. St Martin Ludgate, baptismal font in balustraded enclosure. (*NMR*)

at St Edmund the King. The ceremony usually employed was that of affusion, in which water was poured over the head of the infant, or of dipping, first on the right, then on the left, then of the face.[13] The fonts had therefore to be large enough for this and an open bowl was an ideal shape. The 1662 Prayer Book made provision for the baptism of 'such as are of riper years', probably because of the large numbers of adults who had not been baptised as infants during the Commonwealth. This problem may have been considered as no more than a temporary one and no special arrangements for it are known in the City churches.

In the late seventeenth century parish dead were still being interred in graveyards attached to or close by the parish church, with the more affluent citizens laid below the floor of the church, some in private vaults. Large vaults beneath the churches were becoming fashionable and many were constructed by the turn of the century. Interment in the ground below the floor of the church was not looked upon with great favour because of the disruption caused to the church, with the floors inevitably becoming uneven and the pews requiring repeated levelling, quite apart from the disturbance caused to the fabric of the building when burials took place close to the columns or walls. Wren recorded his disapproval of the practice. The ceremony of interment was a private one, but church bells were tolled to mark the passing of the citizens whose heirs or executors could afford to pay for them.

13

Past Destructive, Future Uncertain

Of the fifty-one parish churches of the City of London rebuilt by order of Parliament under the direction of Sir Christopher Wren in 1670–1717, only twenty-three – less than half – now remain as complete buildings; half of these have been substantially rebuilt. The towers and steeples of six more remain, mostly converted to secular use. The destruction of so many of these churches stems ultimately from the changing character of the City, from residential in the seventeenth century to commercial and financial in the nineteenth. It is easy to understand how the view has arisen that with virtually no resident population there is no need for parish churches. For many years the argument was that the assets of the City churches would be better employed in building and endowing new churches in the rapidly-expanding suburbs of London. In some cases other reasons were found for their demolition – they were found to be unsafe, in need of expensive repairs, or simply stood in the way of progress if their sites were needed for other purposes. The truth of the matter seems to be that the declining population no longer required and could no longer support over a hundred parishes based on the use of fifty churches.

The first of the Wren churches to disappear was St Christopher-le-Stocks. Adjacent to the church in Threadneedle Street was the house of Sir John Houblon which provided the first premises for the Bank of England. The bank then grew by acquisition of neighbouring houses within the parish until, by 1781, it had acquired it all except the church, a few houses in Princes Street and a few offices. In that year the Governors of the Bank obtained an Act of Parliament enabling them to purchase and pull down the church.[1]

This was followed by the demolition, in 1831, of St Michael Crooked Lane,[2] whose site was required in connection with a new approach road to London Bridge, rebuilt upstream of the old bridge. This was followed in turn and in rapid succession by the loss of St Bartholomew-by-the-Exchange and St Benet Fink. St Bartholomew was demolished in 1846 at the instigation of the Bank of England, to allow the widening of Bartholomew Lane to the east of the Bank. This proposal had been made in 1800 but action to acquire the church was not taken until later. Fittings from the church were used for the short-lived St Bartholomew Moor Lane, a church erected to the design of C. R. Cockerell, demolished soon after 1902. Acts of Parliament gave approval for the Corporation of the City of London to acquire and demolish the church of St Benet Fink in Threadneedle Street in 1841, as a means of improving the site adjacent to the Royal Exchange, rebuilt after a fire in 1838.

The problem of a declining population and dwindling congregations occupied the attention of both City and church throughout much of the nineteenth century.[3] In 1834 a Corporation of London Committee recommended the demolition of thirteen churches, but the scheme was not acceptable to the Bishop of London or to the Archbishop of Canterbury.[4] After an abortive attempt in 1854 to introduce legislation for the removal of churches, Parliament gave its approval to the 1855 Act for the Union of Benefices. This proved ineffective and no City closures were made under it. It was replaced by a further Union of Benefices Act in 1860.[5] Closures under this Act came slowly, largely because of opposition from parish vestries, but gradually and perhaps inevitably parishes were amalgamated and churches declared redundant. Each closure was followed by the dispersion of its fittings and funishings, and sale of its building and site. By the end of Tait's episcopate in 1868, twenty-four schemes for union had been considered 'beneficial and acceptable', although only one church – St Benet Gracechurch – had by then been demolished. Nevertheless, between 1867 and 1939, under this legislation, twenty-one of the City parish churches were lost, including the following Wren churches:

Demolished

St Benet Gracechurch	1867
St Mary Somerset	1871 (tower remains)
St Mildred Poultry	1872
St Antholin Budge Row	1875
St Michael Queenhithe	1876
All Hallows Bread Street	1877
St Dionis Backchurch	1878
St Matthew Friday Street	1885
St Olave Jewry	1887 (tower remains)
All Hallows-the-Great	1894 (tower and north aisle in 1876)
St Michael Wood Street	1897
St Michael Bassishaw	1900

St George Botolph Lane   1904
All Hallows Lombard Street   1939

In 1886 a fire in a neighbouring warehouse spread to the church of St Mary Magdalen Old Fish Street, destroying the roof of the building (Fig. 60). With the continuing drive to remove parish churches, there can have been little incentive to restore St Mary Magdalen and it too joined the procession of churches lost under the clauses of the Union of Benefices Act. The united parishes of St Mary Magdalen with St Gregory-by-St Paul's were joined to that of St Martin Ludgate, the fire-damaged church was demolished and its site sold.

FIGURE 60.
St Mary Magdalen
Old Fish Street,
showing fire
damage. (*NMR*)

A commission appointed by Bishop Creighton in 1899 recommended the demolition of another ten churches,[6] but, as a result of the Bishop's death in 1901, the report was not published and no action was taken on its recommendations. A further commission appointed in 1919 proposed a major revision of the parochial adminstration in the City of London,[7] reducing the number of parishes to four and demolishing no less than nineteen of the then remaining churches, many of which would have been from the Wren period. There was provision for the retention of some of the more important towers and steeples. The scheme met with considerable opposition, from the public and the Corporation of London, and was abandoned. An attempt to pass a new Union of Benefices and Disposal of Churches Act failed in 1926.[8]

The last victim of the Union of Benefices Act (1860) was All Hallows Lombard Street. Shops on the west side of Gracechurch Street were demolished in 1934, revealing defects in the east wall of the church, which was then declared a dangerous structure. The church was patched up but the will to undertake a major structural repair seems to have been lacking; in 1939 the opportunity was taken of demolishing the whole building. This was done in the face of much opposition, including that of the City Corporation. The church was known particularly for the wealth of its fittings; these were transferred to a new church

FIGURE 61. City of London churches proposed for demolition (1879). (*The Builder*)

of All Hallows, Twickenham. The church tower was carefully dismantled and rebuilt at Twickenham as a campanile serving the new church.

The war of 1939–45 was particularly destructive of the City's parish churches, many of which were damaged or destroyed as a result of fire-bombing (Fig. 62). In one raid, on the evening of Sunday 29 December 1940, churches destroyed or badly damaged included St Andrew-by-the-Wardrobe, St Anne and St Agnes, St Bride Fleet Street, Christchurch Newgate, St Lawrence Jewry, St Mary Aldermanbury, St Stephen Coleman Street and St Vedast Foster Lane. St Mary Woolnoth was again damaged and there was some damage to St Paul's Cathedral. In this and other raids the following churches were reduced to ruins:

Christchurch Newgate	tower and some walls remain
St Alban Wood Street	tower remains
St Andrew Holborn	restored
St Andrew-by-the-Wardrobe	restored
St Anne and St Agnes	restored
St Anne Soho	rebuilt to a new design
St Augustine Old Change	tower remains
St Bride Fleet Street	restored
St Clement Danes	restored
St Dunstan-in-the-East	tower and some walls remain
St James Garlickhithe	restored
St James Piccadilly	restored
St Lawrence Jewry	restored
St Mary Aldermanbury	reerected at Fulton, Missouri, USA
St Mary-le-Bow	restored
St Michael Paternoster Royal	restored
St Mildred Bread Street	
St Nicholas Cole Abbey	restored
St Stephen Coleman Street	
St Stephen Walbrook	restored
St Swithin London Stone	
St Vedast Foster Lane	restored

The losses of St Swithin London Stone, with its fine plasterwork, and St Mildred Bread Street, with its period fittings, are particularly regrettable.

A further Bishop's Commission reporting in 1946 recommended the re-building of ten of the badly-damaged churches, mostly but not entirely from

FIGURE 62. St Dunstan-in-the-East after wartime bombing. (*NMR*)

the Wren period.[9] All were eventually rebuilt, together with St Olave Hart Street ('restoration should not be attempted') and St Andrew-by-the-Wardrobe ('rebuilding unjustified'). In the post-war planning, a part of the sites of Christchurch Newgate, St Alban Wood Street and St Mary Somerset were taken for street widening, although the towers of all three remain. St Augustine Old Change was used as the site of a new choir school for St Paul's, although the tower was left, fitted with a new fibreglass replica of the steeple designed by Nicholas Hawksmoor.

In 1952 the City of London (Guild Churches) Act was passed. This enabled the Bishop of London to designate sixteen churches as guild churches to serve the non-resident population. The Act allowed new roles for many of the churches, with activities associated with a variety of Christian and civic groups: St Lawrence Jewry became the guild church of the Corporation of London; since 1966 St Anne and St Agnes has been a Lutheran church; St Nicholas Cole Abbey serves a Free Presbyterian congregation; St Peter Cornhill has, since 1990, been used as a Christian study centre by the Proclamation Trust· All Hallows London Wall was (but no longer is) the base of the Council for the Care of Churches; and St Michael Paternoster Royal is used by Missions to Seamen. St Benet Paul's Wharf has long been used by a Welsh-speaking congregation.

In 1970 a new commission under Sir Denys Buckley, after again reviewing the number of churches in the City of London, recommended that five parish and four guild churches should be declared redundant.[10] Seven large parishes were to be created, each served by a team ministry. No action was taken to implement his recommendations.

The establishment of guild churches did not solve the problem and in 1992 the Bishop of London established yet another commission to consider the future of Anglican worship in the capital. This commission, under Lord Templeman, reported in 1994. It is the latest in a century-long series of efforts to find a solution to the problem of too many parish and guild churches and too few worshippers.[11] He recommended the creation of four new parishes based upon St Bartholomew-the-Great, St Giles Cripplegate, St Helen Bishopgate and All Hallows-by-the-Tower. There would in addition be eight other churches, described as 'active' churches and twenty-seven 'reserve' churches, some of which would still have well-defined functions (some of the present guild churches would no doubt continue in their present roles). It is not clear whether the twenty-seven would be designated as guild churches, nor whether functions can be found for all of them.

The four churches named to serve as the new parish churches for the City of London are all medieval buildings. For the first time in 300 years, under the Templeman recommendations, there would be no parish church in the City erected under the direction of Sir Christopher Wren.[12]

The principal purpose of the commission was to review the organisation of religious life in the capital. It is therefore no surprise that Lord Templeman's report was not unduly concerned with the churches as buildings, which in the words of the report 'would have to be declared redundant or otherwise deconsecrated', and possibly 'locked up and maintained wind and water tight'. This recommendation has been roundly condemned as unacceptable. There is much support for an alternative regime to look after these buildings, whatever use is found for them. The buildings possess religious, architectural, historical and cultural values, making them of national importance. With the acknowledgement in the report that it is not the primary function of the Church of England to act as guardians of such buildings, surely the time has now come for this duty to be discharged by some other body. As usual, the root of the problem is money; fortunately, at present there seems to be adequate funding available to care for them, although much will depend upon whether the funding is syphoned off for the maintenance of churches outside the City.

Arguments based upon the spiritual and pastoral needs of a City packed with 300,000 individuals each day, but few at night or at the week-ends, lend some weight to the idea that parish churches should be retained for this and to provide 'places of spiritual calm' and places of rest and reflection for individual workers and visitors.[13] Nevertheless, it is doubtful if this use would justify the retention of all of the present churches. It has not escaped notice that the most successful churches operating as parish churches (apart from those such as St Giles Cripplegate, which has a resident population in the Barbican) do so by drawing their electoral rolls from the inner suburbs.

Whatever use is eventually found for those which are no longer required for ecclesiastical use, it has long been appreciated that due recognition must be given to the unique contribution which the Wren churches make to the City's architectural and cultural heritage. As such, their wanton destruction for the sake of exploiting their sites is no longer acceptable. Great efforts must continue to be made to find other uses for the churches that remain, either as alternatives to worship or to supplement it. This has sometimes meant the reordering of a church, as for example St Michael Paternoster Royal, where the auditorium has been reduced from five to four bays to accommodate offices at the west end, upsetting the balance of the interior. Regrettable though this may be, it is a small price to pay for its continued existence, which for so long was in doubt.

The grouping of parishes, the use of churches by congregations of other denominations (St Anne and St Agnes, St Benet Paul's Wharf and St Nicholas Cole Abbey), increased lunch-time weekday services and Sunday services for congregations who come into the City from the suburbs, and concerts, recitals and lectures, all now form the pattern of activity for the parish churches. It is recognised that there is a limit to the extent to which these buildings can be pressed into use for functions other than those for which they were designed (lack of adequate toilet facilities is but one difficulty, another is the limitations imposed by their remaining consecrated buildings). The use of many of them as guild churches has provided a temporary respite from the commercial pressures that have swept away so many, but it cannot yet be said that the future of all the twenty-three remaining Wren churches is fully assured.

The precarious existence of these Wren churches was underlined following the fire at St Mary-at-Hill on the night of 10 May 1988. The roof was badly burnt and the cupola and lantern were destroyed. The blazing timbers, descending into the body of the church, damaged the fittings. What remained of the roof was structurally unsound and had to be removed. Without insurance this church would have joined the long list of those whose sites are now occupied by offices and banks. Fortunately for the City, the decision was taken to restore the church. With a less determined Rector the outcome could so easily have been different. Its future as a parish and ward church may still not be secure.

On 26 January 1995 the Diocese of London, the City Corporation and English Heritage jointly commissioned Alan Baxter and Associates, consulting engineers, to produce a survey of the existing churches in the City of London. Their report was produced in August 1995. It relates to a total of thirty-seven Anglican churches within the City, including most of those by Sir Christopher Wren that now survive, which constitute rather more than half the total. As a result of a recent review, all of them except three were listed as Grade I buildings (the three, none of them Wren churches, were listed II*). Demolition of any of them for the recovery of their sites for 'development' is unthinkable.

The report notes that two of the churches are closed for repair or restoration; and that, of the remainder, only St Sepulchre Newgate and All Hallows London Wall are not currently used for worship. However, the extent of such usage varies greatly. There is extensive non-liturgical and secular use, in which music by way of recitals and concerts predominates. Other cultural activities which are accommodated include lectures, meetings, classes and exhibitions. Problems of flexibility, lighting and disabled access, as well as of toilet and kitchen facilities, would arise and need to be taken into account if extended additional uses of this kind were to be developed.

Alternative uses, as theatres, museums, heritage centres, restaurants and offices, might generate more income than the current additional uses, but would also probably require a greater degree of alteration to the buildings and intrusion into the sacred and architectural character of the churches. They might also require the removal of the fittings which, at the present time, would be likely to be unacceptable. Such uses are therefore unlikely to be appropriate for these Grade I listed buildings.

The report notes that those churches which are noticeably less active, or which are now closed, are not in their present state because of any fundamental lack of quality. On the contrary, their condition is more the result of short-term circumstances, mainly related to a decline in their liturgical use and a lack of resources to staff them. The fate of individual churches is less the result of their intrinsic quality than of the way each church is run. Churches which are now vibrant with activity could easily slip back into inactivity; while churches at present underused might well reawaken.

There are no clear recommendations attached to any particular church. Although it may safely be said that none is likely to be turned into a wine bar or hamburger restaurant, the problem of what to do with those that are underused, or unused, remains. An ideal solution will be difficult to find and any attempt to resolve the problem quickly should be resisted.

14

Sir Christopher Wren:
By Hooke and by Hawksmoor

Despite the claim made by his son, it can no longer be accepted that Sir Christopher Wren personally designed all the fifty-one parish churches rebuilt after the Great Fire of London. Many of those undoubtedly by him have survived, although rebuilt or extensively repaired after the war of 1939–45. The galleried basilica which evolved from its conception at St Bride Fleet Street set a pattern for the Church of England which persisted for over a century. His designs for St Mary-le-Bow and St Stephen Walbrook, although not repeated elsewhere, were individual masterpieces and extensively admired. His church, referred to here as 'St Mary-in-the-Fields', designed for a site in Lincoln's Inn Fields, would also have been a masterpiece.

Sir John Summerson commented that the parish churches were:

> built in haste, with too much participation by their craftsmen, Wren's themes are rarely developed to their full extent or with complete technical competence.[1]

Wren's work, and that of his assistants, should not be viewed so narrowly. The suggestion of craftsman participation, although often mentioned, has still to be substantiated. The view has also been expressed that much of Wren's work on some of the City churches was mundane and lacking in character and vitality; in short, that it was second-rate. I do not believe that the few examples where this description might be applied with any degree of justice relate to anything designed by Wren himself or executed under his personal control.

This study of the Wren parish churches has revealed the extent to which Wren worked in partnership with Robert Hooke and the enormous burden that the latter took from Wren's shoulders in the design of so many of the fifty-one churches. Robert Hooke was an extraordinary man – an architect, mathematician, scientist and inventor, as well as the personal friend of Wren and an influential Secretary of the Royal Society. He deserves to be remembered for more than simply Hooke's Law alone, familiar to countless students of physics. Without Hooke, or someone of his calibre, Wren could not have entertained the task of rebuilding the churches.

Time has dealt harshly with Hooke's architectural projects: his most important secular buildings have been destroyed; few houses known with certainty to be by him remain; and even his large body of City churches has been much reduced. Time is no respecter of quality and what were probably Hooke's most ingenious and spectacular designs, such as St Benet Fink, are among those which do not survive. None of Hooke's churches can be described as major master-pieces, but they deserve further study and judgement must be reserved. Who is now to say what he would have achieved had he not been under great and constant pressure from churchwardens, craftsmen and lack of money – constraints from which Wren was largely if not completely free.

In their architecture, the parish churches can now be seen to be pragmatic solutions to the problems of the time, providing few opportunities for exploiting the full potential of the classical revival. Wren's genius in creating the pattern followed by so many English parish churches for the next century has been widely acknowledged. Alongside this must now be placed the very considerable achievement of Robert Hooke, who, dealing with obstinate, recalcitrant and just plain old-fashioned parish vestries, and being forced to adopt, adapt and compromise, nevertheless produced his own gems of architecture. Nor must it be thought that the Wren period was an isolated example, a brief flowering of classicism under a man of note that faded into dull pastiche when he had gone.

Nicholas Hawksmoor, Robert Hooke's successor, was the man whose vision has dominated the London skyline for three centuries. While the churchwardens knew perfectly well that they wanted steeples resembling those destroyed in the Fire, it was Hawksmoor's imagination which clothed these thoughts from the past with the new and exciting ideas of the time. His ingenuity and inventiveness raised him from the ranks of just another British architect to that of sheer genius. It is true that he had the opportunity of producing new and revolutionary designs, but it is what he did with that opportunity that make him so special and, perhaps, the most brilliant of all English architects.

Wren's church-building programme should not be considered in isolation. The idea that parish churches could be built by public funding was to persist. A new Act, passed in 1711, set out to build fifty new churches in and around the cities of London and Westminster. The churches erected under it, generally if incorrectly known as the Queen Anne churches, were paid for from a coal tax which was a direct continuation of the tax used for the Wren churches.

Continuity with earlier church-building is seen also in the appointment of William Dickinson and Nicholas Hawksmoor as Surveyors to the Commission established under the new Act. In the matter of design this Commission received plans and models from a wider circle of architects, but in their achievements it is the churches of Nicholas Hawksmoor which dominate. If they represent his maturity, it is his steeples for Wren and the 1670 Act Commissioners which provided the work of his youth.

For nearly half a century the work of rebuilding the parish churches and adding their steeples was directed by Sir Christopher Wren. The records of the time show him obtaining what he wanted from Parliament, tacitly managing the Commissioners, convincing the parish churchwardens that he knew what they wanted, controlling the enthusiasm of the difficult Robert Hooke, and nurturing the talent of the precocious Nicholas Hawksmoor. He successfully handled large sums of money derived from the coal tax, satisfied the auditors of the propriety of his work and that of those he directed, but above all guided and directed the men who created the spectacular and familiar skyline, the skyline which was to dominate the views of London for centuries to come. Although he undertook the burden of architectural design to only a limited extent, there is clearly no reason for regarding the parish churches as anything other than his. They are and always will be the Wren parish churches.

PART II

A Gazetteer of
Wren's Churches

Introduction to Gazetteer

The City churches erected under the care and conduct of Sir Christopher Wren are here considered, church by church, in alphabetical order, beginning with All Hallows Bread Street and ending with St Vedast Foster Lane. The list includes those in the City of Westminster that are also attributed to Wren. To these have been added notes on 'St Mary-in-the-Fields' (the unbuilt design for Lincoln's Inn Fields), the French Protestant Church in the Savoy and St Thomas, Southwark, rebuilt 1700–3, largely with funding from the coal tax revenue, but not designed by Wren.

No building remains intact for long, and the adaptation of these churches for changing use continues to the present day. Some have changed more than others and none is now as designed. We know the outline plan of all the Wren churches, but with few can we be certain of the number of doors and windows given to them and the exact position of them within each church. Convenience, comfort, economy and changes in both ideology and liturgical practice have all led to changes in the fabric, changes that have not always been sympathetic, have seldom been fully documented and sometimes not even recorded. These processes of change, of alteration and amendment for the accommodation, ideas and convenience of the clergy, churchwardens and parishioners, began within the lifetime of Wren and of the Commissioners, who were pursuaded to pay for some of them. Reasons given for change included provision of increased burial space, increased number of pews (resulting in an increase of income from pew-rents), the rebuilding of adjacent property to remove party walls, installation of organs, the creating of chancels and choirs and the provision of vestries. Convenience and comfort were often uppermost in mind and the cold, draughty churches of the seventeenth century were not acceptable to the nineteenth, when provision of adequate heating and lighting became universal. It was fortunate when the changes were executed in a manner sympathetic to the building.

In some cases, changes to the original design were made while the building was being erected – the provision of extra doorways for St Martin Ludgate is an example; the building of vestibules to St Bride Fleet Street is another – which make it difficult to define what is meant by the expression 'original design'. In some cases we know neither what was built nor what was intended in the detail we would like. By the time of Clayton's recording in the nineteenth century there had been over 150 years of change, with four of the churches demolished. We are thankful that sufficient detail of the ground plans and elevations have survived to tell us what all the churches described here, erected by Wren and his associates, were like.

As in the case of all public funding, the accounts for the building campaign were audited, with great care taken to ensure the accuracy of the figures. These enabled Wren to account to Parliament for the expenditure under the Rebuilding Act. This account of the money spent was never intended as a measure of how much each church cost, although approximate figures can be obtained from a total of the craftsmen's bills. These totals invariably include the cost of materials, but miscellaneous expenditure and income (such as the sale of materials from the tabernacles which was offset against craftsmen's bills) were not, however, always brought to account for the church to which they refer. The cost of each church given here is based, in most cases, upon the manuscript copy of the building accounts in the Guildhall Library.

All Hallows Bread Street

The dedication to All Hallows, or All Saints, suggests a Saxon origin. A foundation in the ninth to eleventh centuries would seem reasonable, although nothing is known of the church or parish at this date. It was on the east side of Bread Street at its junction with Watling Street. Little is known of the medieval church. Like many of the other London parish churches, it grew by accretion; plots of land for enlarging the church being given in 1349 and 1350 and a further plot for the Salters' or Beaumont Chapel to the south of the chancel at about the same time. At one time the church had a stone steeple, but this was struck by lightning and taken down to save the cost of repair.

By the Act of 1670 the parish of St John the Evangelist Watling Street was united with All Hallows Bread Street. Even by City standards, both parishes were small. Rebuilding of the church began in 1681 and proceded rapidly with some, possibly a great deal, of the pre-Fire fabric incorporated. Work continued into 1684 when the church was completed and ready for use. The tower had been carried up to the bell-loft, but, like others at that time, it was then boarded over and left. The tower was completed and the steeple added in 1697–98.

Rebuilding the Church, 1681–84, £3348 7s. 2d.

Craftsmen: Samuel Fulkes, mason; John Longland, carpenter; William Cleere, joiner; Matthew Roberts, plumber; Richard Howe, smith; Henry Doogood and John Grove, plasterers; Richard Joyner, glazier; Edward Bird, painter; Thomas Laine, painter.

Completion of the Tower, 1697–98, £1382 16s. 4d.

Craftsmen: Samuel Fulkes, mason; John Longland, carpenter; Roger Davis, joiner; Matthew Roberts, plumber; Thomas Robinson, smith; Henry Doogood, plasterer; Matthew Permaine, glazier; William Thompson, painter.

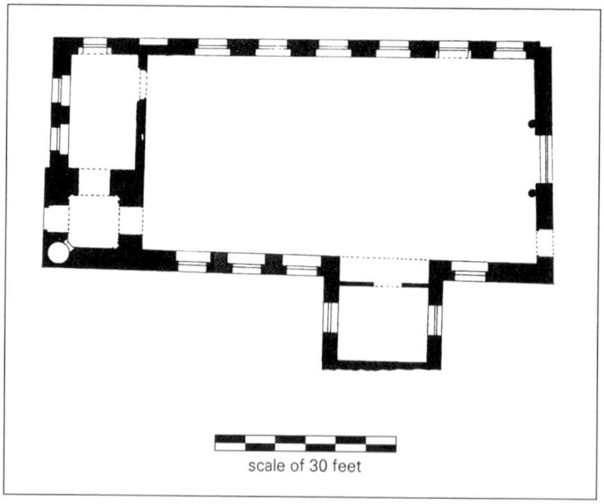

scale of 30 feet

FIGURE 63. All Hallows Bread Street, plan. (*PJ*)

The cost, including £150 paid to Roger Davis, joiner, for the refitting of pews was £4881 3s. 6d.

The church was demolished in 1877–78.

FIGURE 64.
All Hallows Bread Street, north front and tower. Drawn by W. Niven, c. 1885.

All Hallows Lombard Street

In 1053 the church of All Hallows Lombard Street, standing at the junction with Gracechurch Street, was given by a citizen of London called Brithmaer to Christchurch, Canterbury. In medieval times it occupied the whole of the corner plot, but building between the church and both streets eventually hid the church from view, hence its nickname 'the church invisible'. It was rebuilt in 1294 and a south aisle added. It was rebuilt again in 1494–1516, with the aid of the Pewterers' Company who either added or rebuilt a north aisle. The steeple was not completed until 1544 and the church acquired a porch from the dissolved Priory of St John of Jerusalem in Clerkenwell.

Malcolm reported that, following the Great Fire, the steeple was still standing in 1679, although in a very dangerous state. In February of that year complaint was made that stones were falling but, in spite of that, a bell was hung in it. On 7 August 1680 the vestry minutes contain an order for the steeple to be inspected 'to see where the defects lie', but nothing seems to have been done until just prior to the rebuilding, when John Thompson, mason, pulled down a great deal of both church and tower.

Unusually, the new church was provided with a chancel. This may have been at the insistence of the parish vestry, but could have arisen from the earlier rebuilding of a party wall. The new church included a porch with Corinthian columns, a conscious replacement of the old porch from Clerkenwell. It was rebuilt largely, if not entirely, to its old dimensions and to some extent upon its old foundations. The construction appears to have started in 1686. Work came to a halt in 1688 but was resumed in 1690. The church was completed in

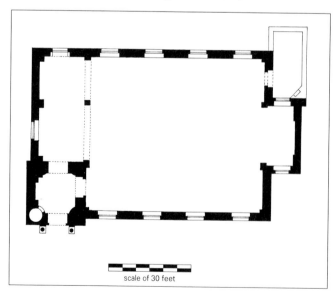

scale of 30 feet

FIGURE 65. All Hallows Lombard Street, plan. (*PJ*)

1694. By this time the tower had been raised to its full height of four stages and completed with parapet. Finally, in 1712, consideration was given to the possibility of completing the church by adding a steeple to the tower, but there are no records of any order for the work and no drawings are known to show what may have been intended.

Rebuilding of Church and Tower, 1686–88; 1690–94, £8058 15s. 6d.

Craftsmen: John Thompson, mason; John Evans, bricklayer; Charles King, bricklayer; Thomas Woodstock, carpenter; William Cleere, joiner; John Miller, carver; Edward Beard, plumber; Henry Doogood, plasterer; Humphrey and Elizabeth Clay, smiths; Francis Moor, glazier; William Thompson, painter; James Hurst, labourer and carter.

FIGURE 66. All Hallows Lombard Street, south front and tower (*Godwin and Britton*, 1835)

The general excellence of the woodwork reflected the wealth of the parish. It not only could afford a great deal of carving but for it to be of the highest quality. The church and vestry were panelled with wainscot and the doorcases elaborately carved, particularly those of the vestibule screen – which had fluted Corinthian pilasters supporting an enriched entablature with segmental pediment and figures of Death and Time respectively. The doors were carved with curtains extending partly across the upper parts, similar to those in St Michael Crooked Lane. The pulpit, hexagonal in shape, had raised panels on each side, veneered and flanked by festoons and surmounted by cherub heads and swags. The sounding-board, also hexagonal, supported richly-carved vases at the projecting angles. The joiners were William Grey and John Mitchell. The carver's name is not known. The carved oak altar-piece, or reredos, had four fluted Corinthian columns with entablature and pediment. It had seven candlesticks and a 'pelican in her piety'.

Shops in Gracechurch Street, successors to the buildings between church and street, were demolished in 1934, revealing defects in the east wall of the church. The building was declared a dangerous structure. It was patched up for a time, but the will to make a permanent repair appears to have been lacking and the opportunity was taken to demolish the whole building in 1939. This was done in the face of considerable opposition, notably from the City Corporation. The tower of All Hallows was carefully dismantled and reerected in 1940 to serve as a campanile for the new parish church of All Hallows, Twickenham, housing the ten bells from the Lombard Street church. Furnishings and fittings from the old church were also transferred, included the Renatus Harris organ of 1708, reredos, wainscoting, pulpit, sounding-board, royal arms, carved doors and doorcases.

All Hallows-the-Great

The name All Hallows-the-Great derives not from any perceived greatness of the church but from the size of the parish in comparison with that of its neighbour, All Hallows-the-Less. Both churches were on the south side of Thames Street, separated by just one block. The earliest reference to it appears to be in 1291. The church and parish had many names including All Hallows Thames Street, All Hallows-the-More, All Hallows ad Fenum, All Hallows in the Ropery, All Hallows in Parva Ropery etc. Within the parish lay the Steelyard, the headquarters in London of the Hanseatic League. The close association between the parish and the foreign, particularly north German, merchant community dates from medieval times.

On the south side, the church had a large cloister, the northern part of it being repaired as an entrance to the tabernacle, which also served the parish of All Hallows-the-Less which was united with it. Soon after the Fire, the parish recovered bell-metal from the ruins of the church and, in 1670, the vestry ordered it to be cast into a new bell; two more were ordered in 1671 and the great bell hung in 1670–71. From this it may be assumed that the tower was soon repaired, much of it having survived the Fire. As with other churches, much of the old walling remained and was incorporated in the new building, which differed little in plan from the old but had an undivided auditorium. Construction seems to have started in 1677 and continued until 1682, when the church was completed.

Although the tower had earlier been repaired sufficiently for bells to be hung, its condition cannot have been satisfactory, as William Hamond, who held the mason's contract for the church, then rebuilt it, completing it in

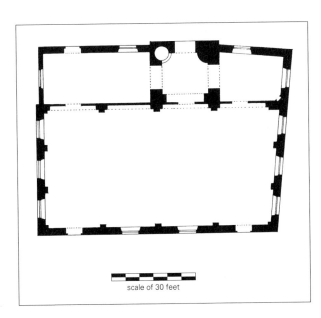

scale of 30 feet

FIGURE 67. All Hallows-the-Great, plan. (PJ)

FIGURE 68. All Hallows-the-Great, north front and tower. (*Godwin and Britton*, 1835)

FIGURE 69. All Hallows-the-Great, the great screen (now in St Margaret Lothbury). Photograph of a watercolour by John Crowther (1884) from the Chadwyck-Healey Collection. (*Guildhall Library*)

1684 with a plain, balustraded parapet. Even before it had been completed, the Commissioners wrote to Sir Christopher Wren: 'We have thought it convenient that the Tower of All Hallows-the-Great be forthwith finished with a cupolo or spire as you shall best approve of, by reason it stands conspicuous to the Thames . . .' There is no record of any further work on the tower or steeple; the cupola or spire was never built.

Rebuilding of Church and Tower, 1677–84, £5641 9s. 11d.

Craftsmen: William Hamond, mason; Thomas Horn, bricklayer; Robert Day, carpenter; William Cleere, joiner; Thomas Powell, joiner; Edward Phillips, plumber; William Smith, plumber; Henry Brookes, smith; Henry Doogood and John Grove, plasterers; John Sherwood, plasterer; Richard Charnley, glazier; Edward Bird, painter; Thomas Laine, painter; William Thompson, painter; Bartholomew Scott, labourer and carter.

Minor Repairs and Changes, 1714–16, £288 15s. 7d.

Craftsmen: Edward Strong, mason; Matthew Fortnam, bricklayer; Richard Jennings, carpenter; Thomas Robinson, smith; Chrysostom Wilkins, plasterer; Matthew Jarman, glazier; Francis Bird, painter; Joseph Thompson, painter.

Total cost, £5930 5s. 6d.

The tower and north side of the church were demolished in 1876 to permit the widening of Thames Street. The tower was then replaced by another, on the south, which was destroyed in the war of 1939–45. The church was demolished in 1894 and the fittings dispersed.

Christchurch Newgate

The church now known as Christchurch was first built in 1306–25 by Franciscans or Greyfriars. It was approximately 300 feet in length, by far the largest in London after St Paul's Cathedral, and was the burial place of nobility, including four Queens, notably Margaret, second wife of Edward I and daughter of Philip II, King of France, who died in 1317 while the church was under construction. By the sixteenth century it had many fine tombs. With the Dissolution of the Monasteries and seizure of religious houses in the reign of Henry VIII, the building was taken to serve as a warehouse. Its tombs and monuments suffered badly, many being wantonly broken and destroyed, others sold. In the last year of his reign, Henry granted the building to the City as the church of a new parish, created from those of St Ewin and St Nicholas-in-the-Shambles, whose churches were then pulled down. A part of St Sepulchre's parish within the City walls was added to the new parish, then named Christchurch.

Wren's replacement was on a much smaller scale – only 113 feet in length. Even so it was still, by City standards, a large church, built to accommodate not only the inhabitants of Christchurch and St Leonard Foster Lane parishes, but also the boys of the adjacent Christ's Hospital.

The church was one of those selected for early rebuilding but soon lost its place. The vestry minutes and churchwardens' accounts for both Christchurch and St Leonard parishes for this period have not survived and little is known of the events leading to the acceptance of a design for this church. A study of surviving drawings reveals a complex history from which only tentative conclusions can at present be drawn.

The drawings representing early designs suggest that work on it may have begun as early as 1673–74 (Fig. 70). Included among these is a set with an early plan showing a church, about 140 feet in length, with a long nave of nine bays, each fifteen to sixteen feet in width, and shorter aisles of five bays only. These would have had large galleries, supported upon the principal columns and additional pillars in the centre of the aisles. The longitudinal emphasis of the building was enhanced by a deep chancel spanning the nave and occupying two full bays. In the absence of any record, there is no explanation of what happened to this design. It is possible that building started, perhaps in 1675, but it may have been difficult or impossible to provide adequate foundations. Excavations in 1974 revealed that the medieval church had been built upon a rubbish dump

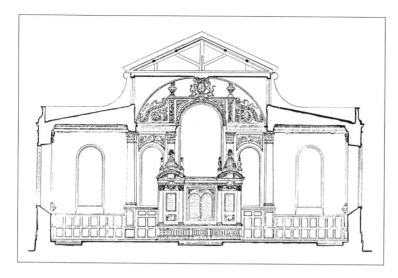

FIGURE 70.
Christchurch, New-
gate, section north–
south showing
reredos at the east
end. (*Birch*, 1896)

and that there the site consisted of poor, unconsolidated ground. These circumstances may have provided a reason or excuse for redesigning the building and
aligning the walls with those of the medieval building. This had stood for over
300 years and its foundations had presumably been taken down to solid ground.
Even so, external buttresses were provided for the new east and west walls –
uncharacteristically and uniquely among the Wren churches.

An alternative explanation, discussed in Chapter 9, is that Wren and Hooke
simply changed their minds and opted for a basilican design as more appropriate
for the parish. Construction of Christchurch to its final design had started by
the year 1677. It proceeded slowly and the building was not finished until 1687.
This long period seems to have arisen from the decision that the church was
to be built on the 'extraordinary'. The parishes succeeded in raising £1000 to
get the construction going, but this was not sufficient to employ the numbers
of craftsmen needed to make rapid progress. The tower was completed, with a
segmental pediment on all four fronts, and a steeple added in 1703–4.

Rebuilding of Church and Tower, 1677–87, £11,778 9s. 7¼ d.

Craftsmen: John Shorthose and Richard Crooke, masons; Edward Helder,
bricklayer; John How, bricklayer; John Longland, carpenter; Matthew Williams,
joiner; Thomas Browne, plumber; Matthew Roberts, plumber; Richard Howe,
smith; Henry Doogood, plasterer; Matthew Jarman, glazier; Edward Bird, painter;
John Styford, carter.

Construction of the Steeple, 1703–4, £1963 8s. 3½ d.

Craftsmen: Edward Strong junior, mason; John Longland, carpenter; Matthew and

FIGURE 71.
Christchurch
Newgate, font and
font cover. Drawn
by A. W. Bentham.
(*Birch*, 1896)

Joseph Roberts, plumbers; Thomas Robinson, smith; Jane Brewin, coppersmith; Matthew Jarman, glazier; William Thompson, painter.

Total cost, £13,741 17s. 10¼ d.

The church was destroyed by incendiary bombing on the night of 29 December 1940. A part of the site was taken for road widening in 1962. Some of the shell has been left, but the east end has been totally demolished. The tower and steeple remain, now rebuilt to include the urns that had been removed prior to 1814.

St Alban Wood Street

The dedication is to St Alban, martyred at Verulamium early in the third century. The church is reputed to have been a chapel of King Offa (d. 796), but confirmation of this is lacking. Excavations in 1961–62 showed the remains of buildings from the Roman period, but these were probably the barracks of a second-century fort. The earliest church, with nave and chancel, was of the eighth or ninth century. This grew by accretion, with chapels added to the north and south, later extended into aisles; a further chapel to the north; and a tower at the west end. Major building of 1633–34 has been attributed to Inigo Jones.

Following the Great Fire the parish was united with that of St Olave Silver Street. In 1681 Sir Christopher Wren wrote to the Commissioners:

> I have viewed the Church of St Alban Woodstreet, & although I finde an irregular peece of ground & not fit for a chargeable fabrick, yet it may be brought to a decent & useful Church, and the Tower also carried up from ye ground to the highth of the Church for ye Summe of £1850 . . .

Wren gave no hint of what he meant by 'chargeable fabrick', but it presumably implies a church in classical style. It may also have been a design with a

FIGURE 72. St Alban Wood Street, west front and tower. (*Godwin and Britton*, 1835)

more regular outline, possibly by incorporating the site of the rectory on the south-west corner, which intruded into the church. The existing nave and north and south aisles could then have been converted into a large auditorium. In the event, the Rector may not have agreed to the loss of the rectory site and the parishioners of the united parishes of St Alban and St Olave Silver Street may not have wished for such a 'chargeable fabrick'. Any idea of a church in classical style was swept aside in favour of a church restored to the former gothic, using as much as possible of the surviving walls.

The rebuilding started in 1682. The tower, on entirely new foundations, was begun but carried only as high as the roof of the building, with the mason, Samuel Fulkes, providing the mask heads that were later to serve as corbels. The roof was covered in 1684 and plaster vaults were installed in 1685. The tower was boarded over in 1687. Work on it was resumed in 1696–98.

Rebuilding the Church, 1683–87, £3165 0s. 8d.

FIGURE 73. St Alban Wood Street, interior looking east. (*Godwin and Britton*, 1835)

Craftsmen: Samuel Fulkes, mason; Matthew Banckes, carpenter; William Cleere, joiner; Peter Read, plumber; Thomas Hodgkins, smith; Henry Doogood and John Grove, plasterers; Matthew Jarman, glazier; Edward Bird, painter.

Completion of the Tower, 1697–98, £1253 10s. 11d.

Craftsmen: Samuel Fulkes, mason; Abraham Jordan, carpenter; Peter Read, plumber; Thomas Colborne, smith; Henry Doogood, plasterer; Matthew Jarman, glazier; William Thompson, painter.

Total cost, £4418 11s. 7d.

The church was destroyed by incendiary bombing in December 1940. In 1954 the walls were demolished and the tower left with roadways on all sides. It has been converted to secular use.

FIGURE 74. St Alban Wood Street, exterior showing war damage, 1941. (*NMR*)

St Andrew Holborn

Named after the Apostle, the church stands on the rising slope of Holborn Hill. In a charter of King Edgar of 959, in which he granted an estate to Westminster Abbey, there is reference to an old wooden church of St Andrew, probably St Andrew Holborn. It was replaced by the late thirteenth century with a stone building, originally perhaps no more than a nave and chancel. This church was rebuilt in 1439–47 with north and south aisles and a west tower linked to the church by an arch that can still be seen. The steeple was not 'covered, leaded nor fully finished' until 1468, but by 1526 it had to be reroofed.

The parish was densely populated and, like its neighbours St Bride Fleet Street and St Sepulchre Newgate, suffered badly in the Great Plague, with 3108 recorded deaths between May and October 1665. Unlike its neighbours, St Andrew escaped destruction in the Great Fire and, with no claim upon the coal tax, the parish rebuilt the church at its own charge. The need for a new building is generally assumed to have arisen from the decrepitude of the old, but there may have been other factors, such as the need to accommodate a large increase

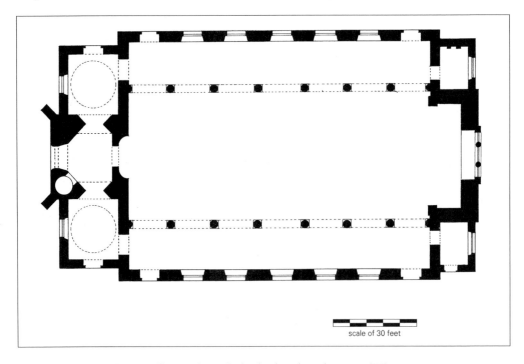

scale of 30 feet

FIGURE 75. St Andrew Holborn, plan of rebuilt church and tower. (PJ)

in parish population. Many Londoners, fleeing north when their homes were
destroyed in the Great Fire, did not wish to return to the City.

There can be no doubt of the personal involvement of Sir Christopher Wren
in the rebuilding of the church in the years 1684–86, with frequent references
to him in the accounts. There are no surviving records for the later campaign,

FIGURE 76. St Andrew Holborn, north front, 1866. (*NMR*)

FIGURE 77.
St Andrew Holborn,
upper stages of the
tower, 1995. (*NMR*)

in which the old tower was reclad with Portland stone to match the newly rebuilt church. The core of the fifteenth-century tower remains, together with its western angle butresses. It was increased in height with a new bell-loft, parapet and corner pinnacles. The design of these pinnacles and the windows of the bell-loft suggest that the author was Hawksmoor, rather than Wren. There is some uncertainty over the cost of the new building, with the church-wardens' accounts giving it as £9530 1*s*. 4*d*., including the cost of fittings and furniture. The new parsonage house may also have been included.

Craftsmen: Edward Pierce and William Stanton, masons; John Longland, carpenter; Valentine Houseman, joiner; 'Mr Pierce', carver*; Edward Tewe,

smith; Simon Money and William Wise, plumbers; Robert Dyer, plasterer;
William Price and Widdow Dutton, glaziers; William Cooke, painter;
(unnamed), locksmith;
* Edward Pierce or Pearce, mason.

The rebuilt church of St Andrew, Holborn, one hundred feet in length and
sixty-eight feet in width, was one of the largest constructed by Sir Christopher
Wren. It was erected upon the site of the old church, but on new foundations.
The provision of a chancel flanked by two small rooms at a lower height looks
forward to later designs for the 1711 Act Commissioners. These rooms were
covered with small oval domes, recalling those used by Wren at the west end
of St Clement Danes and by others in the early eighteenth century at St Luke
Old Street and St Botolph Aldgate. The double-storied exterior is faced throughout with Portland stone.

The interior of the church was altered by T. H. Good in 1818 and in 1871–72
remodelled by S. S. Teulon. It was destroyed by incendiary bombing in September 1941. The fittings from the church were lost, including a marble font
adorned with cherubim by Edward Pierce. The church was restored by Seeley
and Paget, and reopened for worship on 25 October 1961. The destroyed fittings
were replaced by those from the chapel of the old Foundling Hospital Chapel,
including an organ given to the hospital by Handel in 1750, a pulpit of 1752
and a font of 1804.

St Andrew-by-the-Wardrobe

The church of St Andrew-by-the-Wardrobe now stands in an elevated position on the north side of Queen Victoria Street but was formerly much hemmed in by housing. It owes its name to its proximity to the Great Wardrobe of King Edward III, moved from the Tower of London in 1361, the 'Wardrobe' being the department of the royal household in which the King's stores were kept.

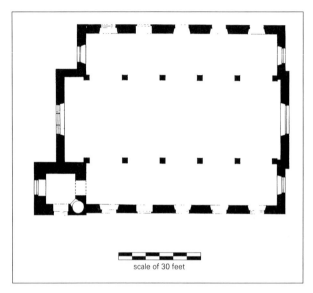

FIGURE 78. St Andrew-by-the-Wardrobe, plan of the church as built. After Noorthouck, with entrance doors in fourth bay from the east. They are now in the fifth bay. (*PJ*)

The earliest recorded date for the church appears to be 1244 as St Andrea de Castello, from the proximity of Castle Baynard.

The parish of St Andrew-by-the-Wardrobe was united with St Ann Blackfriars, these two parishes being among the poorest in the City and the cost of fittings and furniture was met by the Commissioners. The contract for the demolition of the walls of the old church then still standing is dated 29 September 1685; and work on the site must have started soon after. It continued until 1688 when, as with all other work of the Commissioners, it ceased. By that time the walls had reached their full height but the church had not been roofed. Work resumed towards the end of 1690 and payments continued to be made until 1694. St Andrew-by-the-Wardrobe was therefore one of the last of the City churches to be rebuilt.

Rebuilding the Church, 1685–88; 1690–94, £7062 14s. 10¼ d.

Craftsmen: Nicholas Young, mason; Thomas Horn, bricklayer; Israel Knowles, carpenter; John Longland, carpenter; William Cleere, joiner; Roger Davis, joiner; Jonathan Maine, carver; Peter Read, plumber; Matthew Roberts, plumber; Samuel Colbourn, smith; Henry Doogood, plasterer; Francis Moore, glazier;

FIGURE 79.
St Andrew-by-the-
Wardrobe, tower
and south front,
1962. (*NMR*)

Ann Cooke, painter; James Hurst, labourer; Bartholomew Scott, carter and
labourer.

The church is brick-built with the exterior at one time stuccoed in imitation
of stone. It has been described as a small-scale version of St Andrew Holborn,
being basilican, with nave and aisles. The galleries are supported on wainscot-
panelled piers, with the roof carried not on Corinthian columns but on further
panelled piers. The ceiling is barrel-vaulted; the aisles, groin-vaulted. The church
is double-storied, with round-headed windows above and segmental windows
below. The tower, of brick with stone quoining and banding to separate the
stages, is one of the plainest of the Wren towers to be erected in the City.

The church was restored in 1824 and again in 1838, with alterations made to
the tower and south front by T. Garner in c. 1875. It was gutted by incendiary
bombing on the night of 29 December 1940, restored by Marshall Sisson in
1959–61 and reconsecrated on 14 July 1961.

St Anne Soho

The parish of St Anne, Soho was, like its neighbour, St James Piccadilly, taken from the large and heavily populated parish of St Martin-in-the-Fields. The church was consecration on 21 March 1686. By that time the building was complete, although not all the fittings had been installed. The church was probably named in honour of St Anne as a compliment to Princess Anne, later Queen Anne, by her mentor, Henry Compton, Bishop of London.

The earliest record of the church is from 1676 when the vestry minutes of St Martin-in-the-Fields record that the Bishop of London would give £5000 towards the building. Bishop Compton knew Wren well, being a Commissioner for the rebuilding of St Paul's and the parish churches. That Wren provided such a design is evident from surviving plans for the church, comprising a section, an elevation of the east end, a plan of the church and a plan of the tower. They are described as not in his hand, but from his Office. There is no indication that Wren or his Office had any part in the construction of the church. It was begun in 1677 but progress was slow. In April 1685 Compton appointed twelve Commissioners, including Wren, to contract with William Talman for the completion of the building. The dimensions of the building as it was erected and the general plan to which it conformed, with its rectangular eastern projection, match those of the early plan, confirming that the building

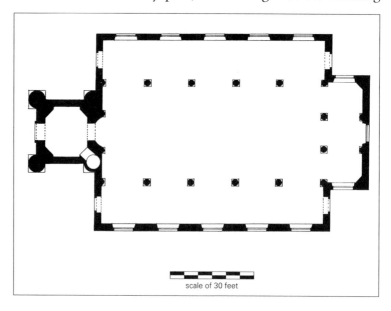

FIGURE 80.
St Anne Soho, plan.
(PJ)

scale of 30 feet

FIGURE 81.
St Anne Soho, north
front. (Maitland's
History of London,
1756)

was set out to Wren's design. It is, however, unlikely that his design would have included the apse. This was described in 1708 and must therefore have been a part of the completed building, or installed soon after, possibly by Talman.

The building completed in the seventeenth century had a tower, but no steeple. Interest in providing this revived in the early eighteenth. In 1714 Talman produced a design, but it is not known if the construction of 1718 was to it or to a design of John Meard, carpenter and resident of Soho, who was probably responsible for the building.

Accounts for the building have not survived and the only craftsmen's names that are known (from a Chancery petition) are Richard Campion, described as a carpenter but who performed 'the greatest part of the brickwork'; Alexander Williams, a bricklayer of St Giles; and Beare and Thomas, of unknown craft, who may have been involved with Campion as partners or contractors for the church.

The church was bombed in 1940 and the body of the building destroyed. The site has since been redeveloped, with a church to a new design (1989–91), known as St Anne with St Thomas and St Peter, Soho.

St Anne and St Agnes

The church is on the north side of what is now Gresham Street, formerly St Anne's Lane. It has been known at various times as St Agnes, St Anne, St Anne by Aldersgate and St Anne by the Willows. The earliest record of the church is in a mandate of Edward I to the Mayor and Sheriff of London dated 27 May 1283. Nothing is now known of the early church on the site. According to Stow, it was burnt down in the year 1548 and the building that replaced it repaired and 'richly and very worthily beautified' in 1624. The steeple was repaired soon afterwards and a new turret added for the saints' bell. It was this church that was destroyed in the Great Fire, its parish then being united with that of St John Zachary.

The Commissioners decided that the church of St Anne and St Agnes should be one of the first fifteen to be rebuilt, but this decision was rescinded and a start was not made until 1677, following further authorisation 'that the said church be begun and carried on to be built with such money as the parishioners shall advance . . .', indicating that the church was to be built on the 'extraordinary'. The decision of the Commissioners to proceed with the construction of the church was preceded in March 1676 by a site visit from Robert Hooke, recorded in his diary, probably in connection with a design for the building. The church does not feature again in Hooke's diary until 1680, by which time the construction was largely complete. Further work on the tower and steeple was undertaken in 1686–87. The lower stages of the medieval tower were retained, but the upper stages were completely rebuilt.

Rebuilding the Church, 1677–87, £2348 0s. 10d.

Craftsmen: William Hammond, mason; Robert Waters, mason; John Fitch, bricklayer; John Howard, carpenter; Ralph Cadman, joiner; Thomas Dobbins, plumber; Stephen Leaver, smith; John Sherwood, plasterer; George Peowrie, glazier; Robert Bird, coppersmith; Robert Streeter, painter; John Jay, ? slater; John Hoy, labourer; Bartholomew Scott, labourer.

The church was constructed largely in brick with brick quoins and with little stone used. It is almost square in plan, with each side of three bays. The roof is supported on four large wooden Corinthian columns on high, wainscotted pedestals. The ceiling is in the form of intersecting barrel-vaults with transverse coffered bands between the columns.

The church was repaired and restored on a number of occasions, notably by

FIGURE 82. St Anne and St Agnes, exterior from south east, 1966. (*NMR*)

Charles Tyrell in 1820 when the outside was cement rendered. This has since been removed from the south and east fronts. The south entrance, originally in red brick, was rebuilt in stone. Alterations to the interior were made by Brooks in 1838–39, when it lost many of its original fittings, and again by Christian in 1888–89. The church was severely damaged by incendiary bombing on 29 December 1940, resulting in the loss of many of the remaining fittings. The church, restored by Braddock and Martin Smith in 1963–66, now serves as St Anne's Lutheran Church.

St Antholin Budge Row

The church of St Antholin, named after St Anthony the hermit, was on the north side of Budge Row near its junction with Watling Street. It was first recorded in the year 1119 and noted subsequently with a variety of names including St Anthony, St Antony, St Antelyne, St Antolin, St Antonii, St Antonin, and St Autolyn, combined on occasions with Budge Row, Boge Rowe, Walbrook and Watling Street. The early church was rebuilt by Thomas Knowles, Lord Mayor in 1400, and again rebuilt or enlarged by John Tate, Lord Mayor in 1514. It was repaired and beautified in 1616 and a richly-decorated gallery erected in 1623–24, which was destroyed with the church in 1666.

The parish was united with that of St John the Baptist Walbrook, and a tabernacle for the use of both parishes erected on the site of St John the Baptist. The construction of the new church began in 1678 and was completed by 1684, when work stopped with the tower also more or less complete. John Longland, the carpenter, was then paid £6 for covering it with boards, indicating that the steeple had not then been added. This was done in 1687–88.

Some of the original drawings for the church have survived. Together they provide evidence for the evolution of the design which, because of the awkward shape of the plot with its south-west corner sliced away, posed particular problems. The earliest drawing is a section which also shows an early version of the tower and steeple. The body of the church is smaller than that built, indicating that it was to occupy only the eastern part of the site, with the tower at the northern part of the west end. There is also a preliminary design for the steeple, having a cupola and lantern. This was replaced by a stone steeple, no doubt inspired by that of the church destroyed in the Fire.

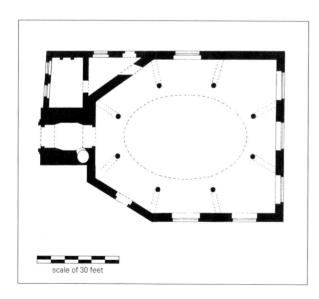

scale of 30 feet

FIGURE 83. St Antholin Budge Row, plan. (*PJ*)

FIGURE 84.
St Antholin Budge
Row, interior look-
ing east, from a
watercolour by H.
and J. D. Mathews,
1876. (*NMR*)

Rebuilding the Church and Tower, 1678–84, £4860 10s. 8¼ d.

Craftsmen: Thomas Cartwright, mason; Edward Helder, bricklayer; Thomas Horn, bricklayer; William Attwell, carpenter; John Longland, carpenter; William Cleere, joiner; Matthew Roberts, plumber; Samuel Colbourn, smith; Stephen Leaver, smith; Henry Doogood, plasterer; Francis Moore, glazier; William Woodroofe, glazier; Edward Bird, painter; Thomas Laine, painter.

Construction of the Steeple, 1687–88, £808 15s. 5½ d.

Craftsmen: Thomas Cartwright, mason; Matthew Roberts, plumber; Samuel Colbourn, smith; Robert Bird, coppersmith; William Woodroffe, glazier; Edward Bird, painter.

Total cost, including £33 4s. 0d. paid for the church's share of the party wall, £5702 10s. 1¾ d.

The church, small and plain but well-proportioned, was constructed of brick with Portland stone facing. In plan it was rectangular with its corner missing and had within it an elongated octagonal area marked with eight composite columns, with their entablatures supporting an oval cornice and dome with circular windows to each cardinal point. The dome was richly decorated with a plaster rose, festoons, scrolls, leaves and flowers.

The church was demolished in 1874 and the site, furniture and fittings sold.

St Augustine Old Change

The church of St Augustine is named after the missionary saint sent by Pope Gregory I to Britain in the year 596. Known also as St Austin's, the church was situated on the north side of Watling Street at the east corner of Old Change, close to the south-east corner of St Paul's Cathedral. It was first recorded in a deed of 1148 and there is a record of a grant of land made in 1252–53, in the reign of Henry III. Little is known of the medieval church but it must always have been one of the smaller of the City parish churches. According to Stow, it had been partly rebuilt and beautified in 1630–31. In the Great Fire the fabric of the church was largely destroyed, with the walls and steeple left in a dangerous condition. These were taken down by order of the Commissioners in 1671.

The parish of St Augustine Old Change was united with that of St Faith-under-St Paul's whose inhabitants had, since medieval times, used the crypt of St Paul's when their old church had been pulled down to extend the cathedral. In 1680 the two parishes approached the Commissioners, pleading for their new church to be put in hand, and work on it began later that year. The church and tower were complete by 1684, with the tower then boarded over.

The ground plan of the church was not completely regular, suggesting that it was rebuilt on the pre-Fire site, possibly using some of the old foundations. Post-war excavation of the site showed that the tower was originally square in section but that in the post-Fire rebuilding its width was reduced from twenty feet to seventeen to be accommodated within the width of the south aisle.

The steeple was added in 1695–96. Drawings of a preliminary design are known, neither of which represents the steeple as built. They have been identified as in the hand of Hawksmoor and the design finally built was probably by him.

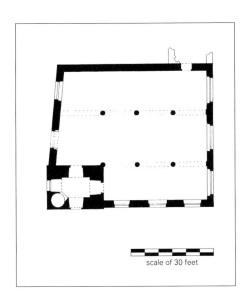

scale of 30 feet

FIGURE 85. St Augustine Old Change, plan of the rebuilt church. (*PJ*)

Rebuilding the Church and Tower, 1680–84, £3170 11s. 4d.

Craftsmen: Edward Strong, mason; Israel Knowles, carpenter; William Draper, joiner; Jonathan Maine, carver; Matthew Roberts, plumber; Thomas Hodgkins,

FIGURE 86. St Augustine Old Change, interior looking east, 1909. (*NMR*)

smith; John Combes, plasterer; Henry Doogood, plasterer; John Brewer, glazier; Thomas Young, slater; Edward Bird, painter; Thomas Laine, painter.

Construction of the Steeple, 1695–96, £1005 9s. 3d.

Craftsmen: Edward Strong, senior, mason; John Phillips, bricklayer; Thomas Denning, carpenter; Israel Knowles, carpenter; Jonathan Maine, carver; Matthew Roberts, plumber; Thomas Colbourn, smith; Thomas Brewin, coppersmith; Henry Doogood, plasterer; Francis Moore, glazier; William Thompson, painter.

Total cost, £4175 0s. 7d., including a late payment to Matthew Roberts for the supply of lead and £25 to Edward Strong by which his bill was abated.

The church was built mainly of brick but faced with Portland stone on the south and west fronts. Both the church and tower were very plain, the exterior of the building being devoid of any decorative elements. Internally, the plainness was relieved somewhat by the plasterwork of the ceiling, but the church must always have been among the least decorated of the parish churches. The tower is built of stone rubble at the lower level and brick in the upper parts, both faced with Portland ashlar. Very little, if any, of the medieval work survives, but there may be some rubble work in the tower levels of the tower.

The church was divided by six Ionic columns on high octagonal bases into four bays of nave and aisles, that to the west being larger than the others. The nave had a semicircular barrel vault with enriched bands between the bays, each bay being divided into panels. The vault contained ceiling lights, unusually without groining. The aisles had plaster, quadripartite ribbed vaults, with a plaster rose at each centre.

The upper stage of the lead-covered steeple collapsed and was removed in 1829. The church was repaired and the spire replaced by Ainger and Taylor, the replacement being a simpler spire with straight, ribbed sides on an octagonal base, which did nothing for the view against the dome of St Paul's. This steeple was destroyed in 1941 and was replaced with a fibreglass replica of the flask–shaped original, now losing its colour. The church was not rebuilt after its destruction in 1941, but the site used for a new choir school for the cathedral, with the tower attached.

St Bartholomew-by-the-Exchange

The church of St Bartholomew-by-the-Exchange was on the east side of Bartholomew Lane close to its junction with Threadneedle Street, taking its name from the nearby Royal Exchange. The church was earlier known as St Bartholomew-the-Less or St Bartholomew-the-Little to distinguish it from St Bartholomew-the-Great in Smithfield. Stow has little to say concerning its history and the earliest reference found is in 1291 as St Bartholomew Parva. The church was rebuilt in 1438 and it was probably this building that was burnt in 1666. Little was done to restore the church until 1672, when the Commissioners agreed that it could be rebuilt on the 'extraordinary'. In January 1674 Hooke surveyed the steeple and his diary for that year records the decision to pull it down. The rebuilding of the church appears to have begun in 1675. The building accounts indicate that much use was made of recovered stone, and descriptions of the church suggest that the building had much brickwork. There is no record of any new foundations and the new building was probably constructed entirely upon the old. Old walls were pulled down but some were left in place, including the vestry on the north-east corner, some of the chancel and portions of the south aisle.

The pre-Fire church had, on its south side, a chapel built by William Capel, Lord Mayor in 1509. It was later converted into a vestry. The desire to rebuild the new church in its old form can be seen not only in the retention of this chapel, but in the design of the new church with nave and aisles separated, much as they were in the old, by rows of four columns supporting a clerestory. The church was one of the few to retain a separate chancel.

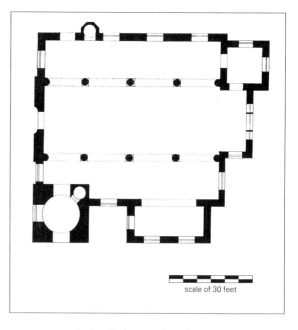

FIGURE 87. St Bartholomew-by-the Exchange, plan. (PJ)

In 1681 the vestry was concerned that encroachments by houses on its south side would prevent Sir Christopher Wren from carrying out his promise 'to add some ornament upon the Church Steeple', possibly explaining the curious appearance of the tower, with its arches seen against the sky, waiting for the ornament that never came.

Rebuilding the Church and Tower, 1675–83, £5077 1s. 1d.

Craftsmen: John Thompson, mason; Robert Browne, bricklayer; Matthew Banckes, carpenter; William Cleere, joiner; Jeffery Flexney, plumber; Matthew Roberts, plumber; Robert Bates, smith; Henry Doogood and John Grove, plasterers; John Brewer, glazier; Margaret Pearce, painter.

FIGURE 88. St Bartholomew-by-the Exchange, west front and tower. (*Godwin and Britton*, 1838)

At the instigation of the Bank of England, the church was demolished by C. R. Cockerell in 1841 to allow the widening of Bartholomew Lane. Most of the fittings from the church were transferred to the new church of St Bartholomew Moor Lane, but this was demolished in 1902 or soon after and the fittings dispersed.

St Benet Fink

St Benet Fink was on the south side of Threadneedle Street, near to its junction with Broad Street and close to the east end of the Royal Exchange. The church was recorded in 1291 as St Benedictus Fink and there is an earlier reference to it in 1216. On the evidence of a tenth- or eleventh-century grave slab from its churchyard it has been suggested that it was Saxon in origin. St Benet, or St Benedict, is generally assumed to be St Benedict, the patriarch of western monasticism, but the dedication may have been to Benedict Biscop, the bishop who played a large part in the Synod of Whitby (664), which established the supremacy of the Latin rite in England, and who founded the monasteries of Jarrow and Monkwearmouth. The name Fink is from Robert Fink (hence also the nearby Finch Lane), who is said to have rebuilt the church.

Stow reported that the church was repaired in 1433 and 'richly and very worthily beautified' at a cost of '£400 and upwards', but gave no description of the building. It had a tower and the outline on Leake's map of 1667 suggests that it was a rectangular building. The decision of the parish vestry to rebuild the church was made at some time on or before 26 April 1670, prior to the Act of 1670, when representatives were appointed to treat with workmen for the rebuilding of the church and the repairing of the steeple. In that year a parishioner, Mr George Holman, said to be a Roman Catholic, donated £1000 towards the cost. Little can have been done before the Commissioners assumed responsibility and the parish deposited £500 with the Chamber of London to gain a place in the rebuilding programme. A foundation stone was laid on 1 December 1670. Work proceeded rapidly and the construction of both the church and steeple were complete by about 1675. The old church had been aligned roughly east-north-east, but a part of the site was taken for road

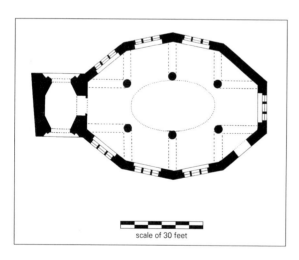

FIGURE 89. St Benet Fink, plan. (*PJ*)

scale of 30 feet

FIGURE 90. St Benet Fink, north front, tower and cupola. Drawn by G. Shepherd, etched by J. Wedgwood, for the *Architectural Series of London Churches* (1811)

widening and a new design in the shape of an elongated decagon produced which permitted an orientation east–west.

Rebuilding of Church, Tower and Steeple, 1670–75, £4129 16s. 11d.

Craftsmen: Thomas Cartwright, mason; Nicholas Wood, bricklayer; Henry Blowes, carpenter; William Cleere, joiner; Jeffrey Flaxney, plumber; James Dovey, smith; Robert Bird, coppersmith; John Grove, plasterer; John Brace and George Peowrie, glaziers; Robert Streeter, painter.

The church was constructed of brick and rubble but faced with Portland stone. For much of its life the greater part of the building was obscured by houses and a watch house. Its unusual shape and design attracted much comment, including both praise and criticism. The tower was squat, rising to about 110 feet including the steeple, but in proportion to the rest of the church.

The Royal Exchange, rebuilt after the Great Fire of 1666, was again destroyed by fire in 1838. As a means of improving the site, the Corporation obtained parliamentary approval to take a part of St Benet Fink's churchyard and to demolish the steeple. The west wall of the church, formerly the lower part of the east wall of the tower, was patched to give a new entrance to the church, but this arrangement did not last long. A further Act of Parliament empowered the Corporation to demolish the rest of the building in 1846.

St Benet Gracechurch

The church was on the east side of Gracechurch Street at its junction with Fenchurch Street. The name Gracechurch appears in a number of forms, including Graschurch, from the grass or hay market formerly held there. The earliest reference to the church is in a charter of 1053 conveying the church to Christ Church, Canterbury. According to Stow, the late medieval building was repaired and beautified between 1630 and 1633 and it was this building that was destroyed in 1666. The tower was left standing, although Malcolm indicated it was dangerous and people were prevented from passing under it. By the Act of 1670 the parish was united with that of St Leonard Eastcheap.

Work on the new church seems to have started in 1681. New foundations were provided for the tower but probably not for the church, which occupied the same area as its predecessor. The tower was completed by January 1685 and the building glazed by June of that year. The church was opened for worship in 1686, when the churchwardens' accounts record the expenditure of £1 14s. 0d. 'to wine and sweetemeats for treating the Lord Mayor at the opening of the Church'. Work on the steeple, timber and lead-covered, with its octagonal cupola, lantern and spire, continued until 1687.

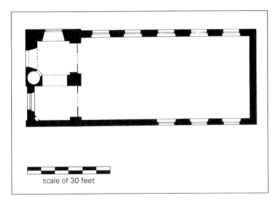

scale of 30 feet

FIGURE 91. St Benet Gracechurch Street, plan. (PJ)

The only known surviving original drawing for St Benet Gracechurch is a west elevation of the tower and steeple, not as built, although with some resemblance to it it (Fig. 40). It may well date from 1670 and be the work of Robert Hooke.

Rebuilding of Church, Tower and Steeple, 1681–87, £4583 9s. 5¾ d.

Craftsmen: Thomas Wise, mason; John Longland, carpenter; William Cleere, joiner; John George, plumber; Matthew Roberts, plumber; Samuel Colebourn, smith; Stephen Leaver, smith; Thomas Smith, smith; Robert Bird, coppersmith; Henry Doogood and John Grove, plasterers; Samuel Ranger, glazier; Edward Bird, painter.

FIGURE 92.
St Benet Grace-
church Street, north
front, tower and
steeple drawn by
W. Niven, c. 1885.

Total cost, £4599 9s. 5¾ d., including £16 by which Longland's bill was abated. The church was demolished in 1867–68 to allow the widening of Gracechurch Street.

St Benet Paul's Wharf

St Benet Paul's Wharf on Upper Thames Street, now to the south of Queen Victoria Street, was close to the medieval waterfront. The church was first recorded in the year 1111. It was known in medieval times by a bewildering variety of names, reflecting its position on the Thames, in Castle Baynard Ward and by St Paul's or Wood Wharf. The old church was the burial place of Inigo Jones (d. 1651), whose monument, erected by his executor, John Webb, was destroyed in the Great Fire. The church had a nave, aisles and a western tower. By the Act of 1670 the parish was united with that of St Peter Paul's Wharf. The church was built on the 'extraordinary', and there is an air of economy its brick-faced walls and tiled roofs. The use of expensive stone was restricted, although used for the carved decorative panels. No new foundations are recorded, and the lower parts of the present walls may incorporate old walling and reused masonry. The plan of the old church is reflected in the design of the present building, with the nave and south aisle rebuilt to give the auditorium, to which the north aisle of the old church was attached. A number of preparatory drawings for the church survive indicating that there was a proposal to give the building an attic story with oval windows.

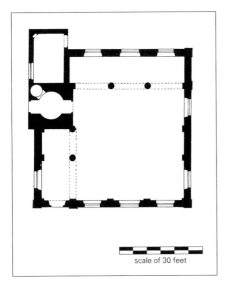

FIGURE 93. St Benet Paul's Wharf, plan. (*PJ*)

The construction of the building seems to have started in 1678 and, including the tower and steeple, was complete by 1684. The vestry, since demolished, was added in a separate campaign of 1692–93.

Rebuilding of the Church, 1678–84, £3328 18s. 10d.

Craftsmen: Edward Strong, mason; Thomas Strong, mason; Israel Knowles, carpenter; William Cleere, joiner; Matthew Roberts, plumber; Samuel Colbourn, smith; Thomas Hodgkins, smith; Stephen Leaver, smith; Robert Bird, coppersmith; Henry Doogood and John Grove, plasterers; George Peowrie, glazier; Thomas Laine, painter.

Construction of the Vestry, 1692–93, £143 3s. 1¼ d.

Craftsmen: Edward Strong, mason; Thomas Hughes, bricklayer; John Longland, carpenter; Roger Davis, joiner; Matthew Roberts, plumber; Samuel Colbourn, smith; Henry Doogood, plasterer; Francis Moor, glazier; William Thompson, painter; William Edge, labourer.

Total cost, £3472 1s. 11¼ d.

FIGURE 94.
St Benet Paul's
Wharf, from south
east. Drawn by
W. Niven, *c.* 1885.
The church is now
used for services in
the Welsh language.

*Church of S. Benedict, Paul's Wharf
Burial Place of Inigo Jones.
Built 1181   Rebuilt 1682
Disposed of 1878*

St Benet Paul's Wharf is one of the smaller of the Wren parish churches. Its appearance, with red brickwork, modillion cornice, overhanging gables and festoon decoration, is strongly reminiscent of Dutch architecture of the early seventeenth century, supporting the suggestion that it is by Robert Hooke. The brick walls are laid in English bond, with purplish-coloured headers and red stretchers giving a chequered appearance to the walls, now sadly marred by a great deal of unsympathetic repair and patching. The interior of the church is, like the exterior, somewhat plain. Corinthian columns on high bases separate the nave from the north aisle and a western aisle used as a vestry.

Many of the original fittings survive, including the hexagonal pulpit with panels flanked by carved festoons. It has been attributed to Grinling Gibbons, although no evidence for this is known to exist and the style is not convincingly his.

In 1877 St Benet Paul's Wharf was one of nineteen of the City parish churches proposed for demolition. Instead, it was handed to the Welsh Episcopalian Church in 1879 and is still used for services in the Welsh language.

St Bride Fleet Street

St Bride's was a large and important parish extending northwards from the Thames. Its size may be judged from the fact that over 2000 people from the parish died in the Great Plague of 1665–66. It was known variously as St Bride, St Bridget, St Brigid without Ludgate, St Brigid the Virgin of Fleet Street etc. The parish, astride the road from the City of London to the Palace of Westminster, was formerly the residence of wealthy citizens and affluent artisans but had many indigent poor.

St Bride, or St Bridget, a saint from Kildare, Ireland, was born in 453. She is credited with a number of worthy but unlikely acts, including changing water into beer. She has always been a popular saint with the Irish and there is a suggestion that the first church or chapel on this site may have been built in Saxon times for an Irish community. St Bridget is first mentioned in connection with the church on this hill in the time of Henry II, but excavations have revealed the remains of a Saxon church and, beneath that, a Roman building of some kind.

The church was destroyed in the Great Fire, although the north porch remained and was used as a vestry. The tower was repaired to prevent its collapse. In all the parish raised a total of £4500, the size of the loan reflecting the determination of the parish that the construction of their new church should not falter. The first contract for the church, to Joshua Marshall, mason, for the taking down

FIGURE 95.
St Bride Fleet Street, plan, as originally designed without galleries and the western vestibules. (PJ)

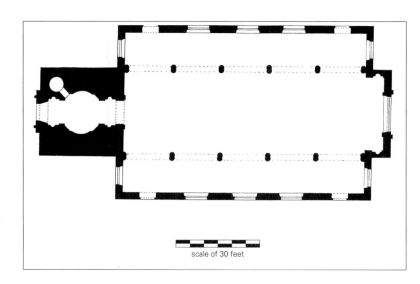

scale of 30 feet

FIGURE 96. St Bridge's Fleet Street, in 1940. (*A. F. Kersting*)

what remained of the walls of the old church, is dated 25 February 1671. The first measurement of new work, also by Joshua Marshall, was on 16 January 1672, by which time the building of the east, north and south walls, with the returns to the tower, had been raised to a height of eleven feet. The shell of the church was essentially complete by 1674. The tower was taken to its full height by the time of Marshall's death in April 1678, although some work remained for Samuel Fulkes, who took over the mason's contract. The church was opened for worship on 19 December 1675.

A surviving drawing indicates the proposal for a steeple in the form of a domical cap resting upon its own pedestal, rising above the balustrade and the bell-loft stage of the tower (Fig. 47). It is marked 'St Brides offer', presumably indicating that it was to have been constructed by contract. In 1678, with the moratorium upon completion of towers and steeples, work on St Bride stopped with the tower at its full height but without the ballustrade.

Nothing more is heard of the steeple until 1681, when the Commissioners gave their approval for it to be built. This was, however, a statement of principle rather than an instruction to proceed and the parish had to wait until early in the eighteenth century for their steeple. The first stone was laid on 6 October 1701 and it was probably complete towards the end of 1703.

FIGURE 97. St Bride Fleet Street, west end, tower and steeple. Drawn by John Clayton.

Reconstruction of Church and Tower, 1671–78, £11,389 14*s*. 3*d*.

Craftsmen: Samuel Fulkes, mason; Joshua Marshall, mason; John Longland, carpenter; William Cleere, joiner; Charles Atherton, plumber; John Cale, plumber; George Drew, smith; Stephen Leaver, smith; John Grove, plasterer; Hannah Brace, glazier; Edward Bird, painter; Robert Streeter, painter.

Construction of the Steeple, 1701–3, £3773 7*s*. 7¼*d*.

Craftsmen: Samuel Fulkes, mason; John Longland, carpenter; Abraham Goodwin, plumber; Thomas Robinson, smith; Thomas Brewin, coppersmith; Matthew Jarman, glazier; William Thompson, painter.

Total cost, £15,163 1*s*. 10¾*d*.

St Bride is divided into nave and aisles by a series of Doric pillars, each composed of two back-to-back three-quarter columns. The nave is barrel-vaulted with openings to the clerestory windows, semicircular plaster panelled and decorated strips across the nave marking the bay divisions. The chancel occupies the full width of the nave but extends eastward only by a few feet. A large, round-headed east window, divided by mullions into three vertical sections, the inner of which is round-headed, originally illuminated the space before the altar. Both north and south aisles and the western part of the nave had wooden galleries, but these have now gone.

The tower and steeple is, at 226 feet, the tallest of the City. The spire was struck by lightning in 1764, inflicting considerable damage and requiring the rebuilding of much of the upper part by Sir William Staines, credited with having reduced the height by eight feet from its original 234 feet. The steeple was struck again by lighning in 1803, when the damage was much less. In effecting repairs, the opportunity was taken to remove the urns from the upper part of the spire, immediately below the obelisk. It is time they were replaced.

On the night of 29 December 1940 the church was once again destroyed by fire, in this case by incendiary bombing. It was restored by Godfrey Allen and reopened for worship on 19 December 1957. The seating is now collegiate in arrangement. The fittings are new, ranging from a reredos freely copied from that of the Chapel Royal at Hampton Court to large carved figures of St Bridget and St Paul by David McFall at the end of the nave looking down towards the altar.

St Christopher-le-Stocks

The church of St Christopher-le-Stocks was on the north side of Threadneedle Street, taking its name from the nearby Stocks Market, which, after the Great Fire, was moved to the site of St Mary Woolchurch Haw, later used for the Mansion House. Stowe recorded a fifteenth-century rebuilding in 1462, with the steeple being finished in 1506, thanks to a donation from Richard Shore, Sheriff of London.

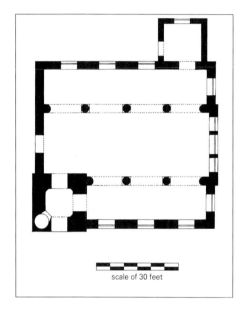

scale of 30 feet

FIGURE 98. St Christopher-le-Stocks, plan. (*PJ*)

The walls of the church were, apparently, still standing after the Great Fire, as was also the tower in the south-west corner. A parish committee was appointed on 1 November 1667 to consider an estimate for repairing it. Work on clearing the site had begun by 1669 and in restoring the church by 1670. The responsibility for it was assumed by the Commissioners later that year, by which time the work of rebuilding was well under way.

By 23 November 1670 the vestry minutes record 'that the taking down of the East End of the Church been freely left to the Judgement and consideration of ye Lords Commissioners and the Surveyors to act as they shall think convenient'. This statement can be compared with the Commissioners' minute, dated 26 November, which provides an explanation:

> Whereas the Surveigher and Parishioners of St Christophers have both represented to us the convenience of making the East end of St Christophers Church to range even with the Isle, to make better passage into the Churchyard, and for the better conveighance of the water, It is heerby ordered that the Parish be heerin complyed with . . .

That this order was carried out can be seen from the bill submitted by the carpenter, Matthew Banckes, who charged for 'three squares of the Roofe of the middle Isle, being laid aside, by reason the Church was cut shorter than it

FIGURE 99. St Christopher-le-Stocks, showing tower and south front adjacent to the Bank of England. (*Bank of England*)

was first intended, the Roofe being all framed and brought to the place'. Only a few of the parish churches built at this time were constructed with separate chancels, St Christopher-le-Stocks setting the pattern to be followed by most of the others.

The appearance of the building does not seem to have been recorded in any detail. Those parts of the church that remained from before the Great Fire were described as of 'the gothick order', with pointed windows on at least the south front and probably also on the north, with two more in the east. Like the tower, the church was battlemented. The walls were of brick and stone, with the interior rendered.

The condition of the restored church soon gave rise to concern. In 1685 the churchwardens approached both Wren and the Bishop of London in an un-successful attempt to get repairs undertaken at public charge. In April 1703 the churchwardens were ordered to consult John Oliver or some other surveyor concerning repairs to the steeple. On 4 May 1703 the vestry again decided to appeal to the Commissioners. Finally, work began under the care of William Dickinson in 1711/12. The upper part of the tower was pulled down, the battlements on north and south fronts removed, together with with the upper parts of the side walls. The east returns were similarly removed, together with their gothic windows. New round-headed windows with large key-stones were provided for the north and south fronts and two circular windows for the east. The tower was completed by 1712 and the remainder by 1714.

Repairs to Church and Tower, 1669–71, £1622 0s. 4d.

Craftsmen: John Thompson, mason; Matthew Banckes, carpenter; William Emmet, carver; Joseph Franklin, plumber; Robert Todd, glazier; Matthew Holland, smith; John Grove, plasterer; Robert Streeter, painter.

Reconstruction of Church and Tower, 1711–14, £4321 10s. 0¼d.

Craftsmen: Edward Strong, junior, mason; Matthew Fortnam, bricklayer; Richard Jennings, carpenter; William Knight, plumber; Thomas Robinson, smith; Andrew Niblett, coppersmith; Matthew Jarman, glazier; Chrysostom Wilkins, plasterer; Joseph Thompson, painter.

Total cost, £6420 2s. 7¼d., including £476 12s. 3d. to the churchwardens, reimbursing them for early work on the site.

Adjacent to the church was the house of Sir John Houblon, the first Governor of the Bank of England. The house became the Bank, which then grew by acquiring adjacent property, pulling it down and rebuilding. Further acquisition took in most of the parish which by 1781 it was in possession of all except the church and a few houses and offices. In 1780 the Bank was threatened by the Gordon rioters. This so alarmed the Governor that, in 1781, he obtained an Act to purchase and pull down the church to prevent future attacks on the Bank using the church tower as vantage-point. As the Bank argued, since it then owned virtually all the parish, there was no longer any need for the church and its site could therefore be made available for their future expansion. The church was demolished in 1782–84.

St Clement Danes

The first church on the site may have been founded in Saxon times by a Danish Christian community. It was on the north side of the Strand, which formed the highway between the cities of London and Westminster.

The rebuilding of the church in the seventeenth century is usually attributed to decrepitude. It began with a reconstruction of the tower. The old steeple was taken down and rebuilt upon the old foundations in 1668–70. The order for demolition includes the instruction 'to build a new Steeple from the foundations according to a plottforme now produced'. This instruction was addressed to Joshua Marshall and Stephen Switzer, suggesting that the new tower may have been to their design. It was to have been constructed to a contract price of £1700.

The building was completed in 1670, when Marshall was paid £120 as the last installment of his bill 'in full satisfaction of all demands for masons work about the steeple and church'. The work done is not described in detail. The costs seem to have escalated well above those originally suggested, possibly due to additional work at the west end of the church, where a new west wall was provided and vestibules with flat roofs added to the north and south of the tower.

Rebuilding of the Church and West End, 1668–70, £3696 6s. 1d.

Craftsmen: Joshua Marshall, mason; Stephen Switzer, mason; James Ham, bricklayer; Porter*, bricklayer; Henry Sherborne and Henry Pearson, carpenters; *Blake, plumber; Gibbons*, smith; John Masters, plasterer; Lewis Prothers, paviour.
* No Christian name entered.

The names of the glazier and painter and their bills are not recorded.

The rebuilding of the body of the church took place in 1679–85. An early version of the design for the church is known from a surviving drawing which indicates the limitations imposed by the awkward shape of the site, particularly on the south-east corner. The church could not be resited further west without abandoning the newly-built tower and west end. Wren's design, with the north and south walls of the nave curving at the east end and a semicircular chancel beyond, can be seen as a sensible solution to the problems imposed by the site.

Wren's design included a steeple in the form of an octagonal dome surmounted by a small lantern and panelled spire. The west front was to be given a tetrastyle Ionic temple front and the tower raised in height by adding a further story for

FIGURE 100.
St Clement
Danes, plan of
late medieval
church (but
with tower of
1668–72),
based on
Ogilby's map
of 1676. (PJ)

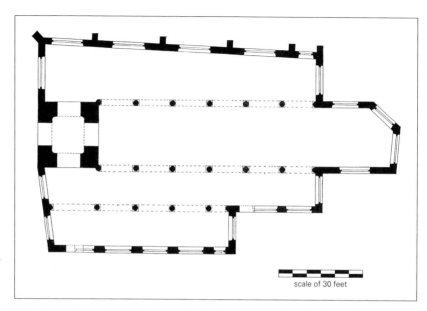

FIGURE 101.
St Clement
Danes, plan for
proposed
church. (PJ)

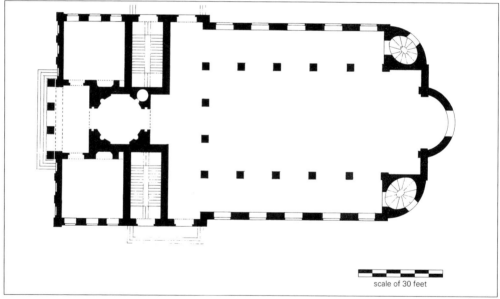

the bell-loft. This story would have had three round-headed windows, arranged side-by-side, a design used for the steeple of St Peter Cornhill. The construction of a steeple was left to a later date and the portico was never built.

Rebuilding of the Church, 1679–85.

Craftsmen: Edward Pearce and John Shorthose, masons; Howett* and Prince*, bricklayers; Pearson* and Green*, carpenters; Bratton*, joiner; John Smith, joiner;

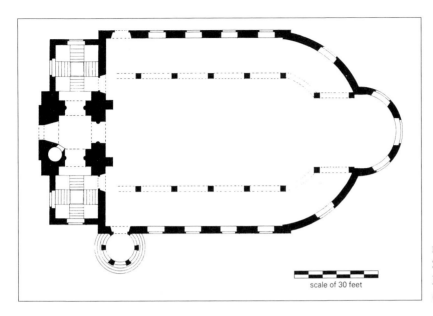

FIGURE 102.
St Clement
Danes, as built.
(*PJ*)

scale of 30 feet

John Symms, joiner; Morse* and Butler*, plumbers; Chesheire*, smith; Disney*, smith; Fox*, smith; Hunt*, smith; Ringrose*, smith; Sabine*, smith; ? John Sherman, smith; Powell* and Gouge*, plasterers; Edward Pearce, carver (in part); Phillips*, turner; Ragdall* and Wilson*, glaziers; Newman*, painter; Weaver*, painter.
* No Christian name entered.

The total cost, given as £9568 13*s*. 0*d*., includes sums paid to other individuals, not now identified, as well as payment for some of the materials.

The idea of raising the height of the tower and adding a steeple to it was not forgotten. The churchwardens' accounts record expenditure when 'Mr Hawkesmore and others' viewed the church in February 1714. This was followed nine days later by a further visit by Hawksmoor. There is no record of his further involvement with the church and the vestry minutes are silent as to the purpose of his visits, but they may well have been in connection with a design for the steeple. If so, the designs have been lost and any parish consideration of them is unrecorded.

The construction of the neighbouring church of St Mary-le-Strand may have encouraged the vestry to think again about a new steeple. The decision was made that it would include the addition story and that this would be built by John Townesend, mason, to a contract price of £1650, payable in five instalments. It was completed in 1719–20. The vestry minutes do not record the name of the architect, known to have been James Gibbs.

The church was destroyed by fire-bombing on the night of 10 May 1941, leaving the tower and the fire-scarred walls still standing. The church was restored by Anthony Lloyd and reconsecrated on 19 October 1958. It now serves as the central church and shrine of remembrance of the Royal Air Force.

FIGURE 103.
St Clement Danes,
from the south west.
Drawn by J. Coney,
etched by J. Skelton,
for the *Architectural
Series of London
Churches* (1818).

St Clement East Cheap

The dedication is probably to St Clement, Pope at the end of the first century, who was venerated as a martyr, suffering death (it is said) by being lashed to an anchor and thrown into the sea. The church is on the east side of Clements Lane, now close to its junction with King William Street. It was first mentioned in the time of Henry III, but a confirmation of a grant to Westminster Abbey by William I in 1067 records a church of St Clement, probably this one. The foundation may therefore well be Saxon. It was known also as St Clement by Kandelwikstrete, St Clement in Lumbard Street and St Clement the Little, possibly in comparison with St Clement Danes. By the Act of 1670 the parish was united with that of St Martin Orgar.

Work on the rebuilding of the church, after its destruction in the Great Fire, should have started in 1671, when the vestry gave instructions that the foundations of the old church were to be cleared and the new building set out, but this may have been optimism on their part, anxious that their church should be included in the building programme. An order of the Commissioners dated 22 June 1674 names St Clement Eastcheap and St Peter Cornhill as the next two churches to be put in hand, 'as the parishioners . . . deposit money into the Chamber the said money shall be immediately expended', but there is no record of St Clement's parish making any such deposit and therefore, not surprisingly, no indication that the rebuilding of the church began at this date.

Although not a major thoroughfare, Clements Lane was widened after the Fire. A narrow strip of land was taken from the west of the church, with the new building set back from the pre-Fire frontage. Little seems to have been done until 1683, when the foundations of the old west wall were dug up and new foundations provided. There is no record of any new foundations for the north and south walls, suggesting that those of the old

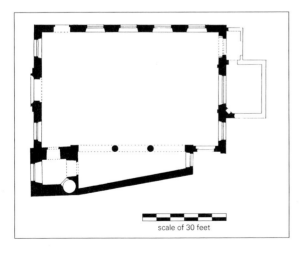

scale of 30 feet

FIGURE 104. St Clement Eastcheap, plan. (PJ)

FIGURE 105.
St Clement
Eastcheap, interior,
1941. (NMR)

church were reused. Construction of the church was in hand in 1684, but the
parish was in dispute with the Commissioners over the size of the new church
which, it claimed, would be too small for the families of both parishes. This
was resolved when the Commissioners agreed to add a further fourteen feet to
the east end of the church, ground previously a part of the churchyard. The
shell of the church, including the new east end of the building, was completed
in 1685. The church was roofed in that year and the roof covered with lead
early in 1686. Work on the tower, a burial-vault, gallery and vestry continued
into 1687.

Rebuilding of Church and Tower, 1683–87, £4365 3s. 5d.

Craftsmen: Edward Strong, mason; Israel Knowles, carpenter; William Grey, joiner; Thomas Dobbins, plumber; Matthew Roberts, plumber; Humphrey Clay, smith; Henry Doogood and John Grove, plasterers; James Thompson, glazier; Thomas Thompson?, glazier; William Thompson, painter; Bartholomew Scott, carter and labourer.

The church is constructed of stone rubble with brick facing and stone quoining but now covered with stucco. The tower, on the south-west corner, is somewhat plain. It is of rubble masonry with brick facing and has rustic quoins. The interior of the church is a single auditorium with a tapering south aisle separated by two giant pillars of the Composite order. There is much evidence of alteration to the windows.

The church was extensively restored by Butterfield in 1872. The reredos was split into three parts, each placed on a separate wall. They were later reassembled by Ninian Comper and decorated in his characteristic colours of blue and gold. The church was damaged by bombing on 9 September 1940. It was restored, redecorated and reopened in 1968.

St Dionis Backchurch

The church may have been dedicated to St Dionis the Areopagite, baptised by St Paul; or, perhaps more likely, to the bishop and martyr, beheaded on Montmartre and (after carrying his head for two miles) buried at Saint-Denis. The name Backchurch may be derived from the position of the church, standing

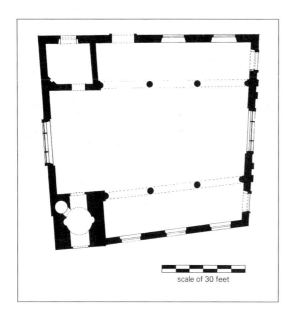

FIGURE 106. St Dionis Backchurch, plan. (*PJ*)

back from the main line of Fenchurch Street, but it is perhaps more likely from the name Godwin Bac – the man who gave the church to Christ Church, Canterbury. The church was on the west side of Lime Street, north of its junction with Fenchurch Street. It was first recorded between 1198 and 1214. The middle aisle was new laid in 1629 and the steeple repaired and a new turret added in 1632.

The exact dates of rebuilding following destruction in the Great Fire have not been recorded, and few of the craftsmen's bills are dated. Those that are suggest rebuilding in 1670–74. In 1678 the vestry approached the Commisioners to get the tower completed and a steeple added, pleading that their tower had been left unfinished because of the needs of other churches. The work was carried out in 1681–86.

Rebuilding the Church, 1670–74, £4340 2s. 8d.

Craftsmen: John Thompson, mason; John Longland, carpenter; William Taylor, carpenter; William Cleere, joiner; William Bonnick, plumber; John Lingard, plumber; George Drew, smith; Stephen Heath, smith; Walter Clement, anchorsmith; John Grove, plasterer; John Holden, glazier; Robert Streeter, painter.

Construction of the Tower, 1681–86, £1385 7s. 2d.

Craftsmen: John Thompson, mason; George Turnley, mason; William Attwell, carpenter; Richard Reading, carpenter; John George, plumber; Henry Brooks,

FIGURE 107. St Dionis Backchurch, exterior largely obscured by shops on Fenchurch Street. Drawn by G. Shepherd, etched by W. Wise, for the *Architectural Series of London Churches* (1818).

FIGURE 108. St Dionis Backchurch, proposed remodelling by G. E. Street, *c.* 1858.

smith; Robert Bird, coppersmith; Henry Doogood and John Grove, plasterers; Francis Moor, glazier; Edward Bird, painter; Robert Streeter, painter.

Total cost, £5737 9s. 10d., including a payment of £12 for stone brought from St Paul's.

The church was the most irregular in shape of all the City churches, no two walls being at right angles to each other. This suggests that the building occupied the same site as its predecessor. It had nave and aisles, with the tower occupying the south-west corner, and a vestry on the north west. Being hidden by other buildings, there are few good recorded views of the church. Only the most decorated east side had a frontage to the street.

In 1857 G. E. Street surveyed the church and produced a detailed plan to transform it into a gothic building. In view of the Bishop's attempts to reduce the number of City churches, nothing was done. The scheme was abandoned, the church closed and the building demolished in 1878.

St Dunstan-in-the-East

The church and parish were dedicated to Dunstan, the Saxon Archbishop of Canterbury (d. 988), suggesting the possibility of a Saxon foundation, although the earliest mention of the church seems to be in 1271–72. It occupied a site stretching between Idol (or Idle) Lane and St Dunstan's Hill, and between Thames Street to the south and Tower Street to the north. The medieval building was enlarged in 1382. Stow described it as 'a fair and large church within a large church yard'. It possessed a tall, fine spire and had a college of priests, a choir school and a grammar school. The church was repaired in the year 1633, only to be destroyed in 1666.

St Dunstan-in-the-East was fortunate in receiving from Lady Dyonis Williamson the sum of £4000 towards its rebuilding, including £1000 to be spent on bells, font and organ. It is uncertain when work on the repairing of the church began but it must have been soon after the Fire, as it had been substantially completed by November 1670, when an approach was made to the Commissioners. By then the cost had exceeded the sum provided by Lady Williamson. The Commissioners ordered Wren and Hooke to audit the churchwardens' accounts. Of the total expenditure, excluding that on bells, font and organ, of £4029 8s. 2d., the Commissioners paid £1029 8s. 2d., with the costs of other minor works then still to be completed.

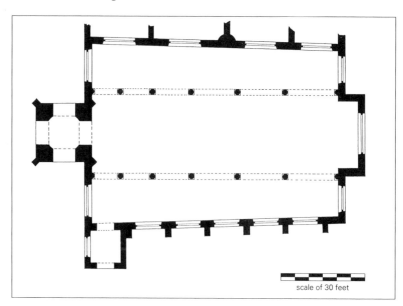

FIGURE 109.
St Dunstan-in-
the-East, plan of
church as rebuilt
(?1668–70), based
on Ogilby's map
of 1676. (*PJ*)

scale of 30 feet

FIGURE 110.
St Dunstan-in-the-East, tower and steeple. Drawn by John Clayton.

There is no record of what was done to the church, but the work was clearly no more than a repair and reconstruction of the damaged building, undertaken by workmen who contracted directly with the vestry. Except for audit and repayment, neither Wren nor Hooke was involved.

At St Dunstan-in-the-East, as in other places, defects were later to become manifest. In 1693 the vestry reported that church and steeple were defective and anticipated that they would be rebuilt at public charge. The order for this has not been preserved, but Hooke's diary records his visit to the church. The Commissioners apparently approved the rebuilding of tower and steeple, construction of a new vestry, insertion of some new columns in the church, repairs to the butresses, parapet and battlements, and the building of a new churchyard wall. Work began in 1695 and the new tower was complete with its corner pinnacles early in 1698. The spire, supported on four arches, was undertaken to a contract price of £400 and complete early in 1701. The idea of a spire carried upon arches or flying buttresses was not new. The pre-Fire church of St Mary-le-Bow had a lantern similarly carried on 'bows' or arches.

Construction of Tower, Steeple etc., 1695–1701, £8286 17s. 11½ d.

Craftsmen: Ephraim Beauchamp, mason; Francis Stockley, bricklayer; Thomas Denning, carpenter; Roger Davis, joiner; Jonathan Maine, carver; Matthew Roberts, plumber; Thomas Colbourn, smith; Richard Howes, smith; Thomas Brewin, coppersmith; Henry Doogood, plasterer; Francis Moore, glazier; William Thompson, painter; John Mist, paviour; James Hurst, labourer.

In the early years of the nineteenth century the walls of the church were reported as moving outward and, in 1810, tie-bars were inserted to halt this. This was unsuccessful and the building was then demolished and replaced by another in gothic style to the design of David Laing, consecrated on 14 January 1821. The tower and spire of 1695–1701 were attached to the new church. The church was destroyed in 1941. The tower and steeple remain, with the ruins of the church laid out as a garden.

St Edmund the King

The dedication is to Edmund, King of the East Angles, killed by Danes in 870 and long revered as St Edmund King and Martyr. The dedication suggests a Saxon origin. It is located on the north side of Lombard Street. The early church may, like the present building, have been aligned north-south. By the Act of 1670 the parish was united with that of St Nicholas Acons.

The offer by the parish to loan money to the Commissioners ensured an early start with the rebuilding of the church. Work began in 1670 with the demolition of the remaining walls of the old church and the emplacement of new foundations. Those for the tower were laid on 'squared pieces of heart of oake of about 10 inches square', suggesting not only that the ground was poor at this point but that the tower was being erected on a new site. Construction of the church, tower and steeple was complete by 1674.

There is a surviving drawing which shows the façade of the church in Hooke's hand. It is inscribed 'With his Maties Approbation' and carries Wren's initials in the tympanum of the pediment (Fig. 22). There can have been few designs that were shown to His Majesty, this being one. The inscription is usually taken as implying approval of the design by both Wren and Charles II.

By 1683 the vestry reported the need to repair the steeple, although no details were given. In 1701 the lead and timber structure were described as defective and, in 1702, repairs were made. By September 1705 the decision had been taken to install a new spire or steeple. This was done in 1706-7. The work included removing the festoons from the wings of the tower, together with the stone balls decorating the balustrade and the balusters themselves. They were replaced with a solid parapet and a new steeple, timber-built and lead-covered. It was decorated with lead-covered urns

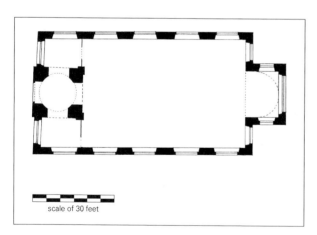

scale of 30 feet

FIGURE 111. St Edmund the King, plan. (*PJ*)

FIGURE 112.
St Edmund the
King, exterior view
from the south east.
(*NMR*)

turned from elm wood. The parapet had stone urns at the corners and pineapples in the centre of each side.

Rebuilding Church, Tower and Steeple, 1670–74, £5207 11s. 0d.

Craftsmen: Abraham Story, mason; Roberts Waters, mason; Morris Emnett the younger, bricklayer; George Clisby and Henry Wilkins, carpenters; Thomas Whyting, joiner; Peter Brent, plumber; William Smith, plumber; Edmund Smith, smith; Daniell Morris and John Sherwood, plasterers; Ian Morris, plasterer; John Brace, glazier; Robert Streeter, painter; John Hoy, carter; Thomas Praise, labourer; John Simpson, labourer.

Rebuilding the Steeple, 1706–7, £1216 12*s.* 7½*d.*

Craftsmen: William Klempster, mason; Richard Jennings, carpenter; Joseph Roberts, plumber; Thomas Robinson, smith; Jane Brewin, coppersmith; Henry Doogood, plasterer; James Thompson, glazier; William Thompson, painter.

Total cost, £6424 2*s.* 7½*d.*

The interior of the church is somewhat sparse, with a simple box-shaped auditorium, a chancel to the north and tower, with galleries on either side, intruding to the south. The ceiling is flat and coved to the walls. A remarkable feature of the church as built in 1670–74 was the semi-circular lantern or clerestory over the chancel. This was removed, possibly in the restoration of 1832–33.

The church was restored by Butterfield in 1864 and again in 1880. It was damaged in 1917 when a bomb fell on its roof and there was further damage, although not serious, in 1941 by incendiary bombing. The urns from the steeple were removed *c.* 1908.

St George Botolph Lane

The dedication is to St George of Cappadocia, a reputed martyr of the third to fourth century. The church was first recorded in the time of Henry II (1154–89) as St George Estchepe. It was known also as St George Botolph, St George in Podynge Lane and St George the Martyr. It was situated on the west side of Botolph Lane at its junction with George Lane. The medieval church was repaired in 1360, repaired again and beautified in 1627, and destroyed in 1666. The parish was united, by the Act of 1670, with that of St Botolph Billingsgate.

The Commissioners agreed to put the rebuilding of the church in hand in May 1671. Some of the foundations were dug up and new ones provided. The use of timber in these new foundations suggests that the site was originally low-lying, although in the rebuilding the level was raised with chalk and stone rubble brought to St George from Old St Paul's and from the sites of other churches. Stone, presumably ragstone, was brought from St Botolph to St George for the new walls.

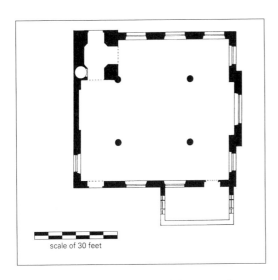

scale of 30 feet

FIGURE 113. St George Botolph Lane, plan. (PJ)

The first dated mason's bill is for work measured on 12 November 1674. By that time the walls of the church had reached their full height, the tower had been raised to just below the main cornice level and the columns inside the church were in place. The size of the plumber's bill in the period 20 October 1673 to 31 July 1674 confirms that the church had been roofed and probably leaded by then. Work on the church was complete by mid 1676, including the parapet of the tower supporting four urns with flames and paving of the interior.

Rebuilding of Church and Tower, 1671–76, £4466 7s. 11d.

Craftsmen: Nicholas Young, mason; Thomas Horn, bricklayer; Robert Day, carpenter; William Cleere, joiner; William Bonnick, plumber; Thomas Dobbins,

FIGURE 114. St George Botolph Lane, interior looking west, c. 1890. (NMR)

plumber; John Peachman, smith; John Grove, plasterer; John Odell, glazier; Robert Streeter, painter; Thomas Gammon, carter.

The church of St George Botolph Lane was constructed of brick and stone rubble, but with Portland stone dressings. It was rectangular in shape and raised upon an impressive stylobate. The tower occupied the north-west corner and the vestry was added to the south front at its east end. The tower was exceedingly plain, terminating with a main cornice and parapet with corner plinths supporting urns with flames.

The east front, facing Botolph Lane, was of three bays with the central bay, somewhat wider than the outer bays, quoined and broken forward. Hatton

FIGURE 115. St George Botolph Lane, exterior from north east. (*Godwin and Britton*, 1835)

reported that it was decorated with a cherub and festoon but this is not shown in engravings. Did this church, like St Mary-at-Hill, lose its east-end carving at the hand of an improver?

The interior of the church was divided into nave and aisles by four Composite columns (described by some authors as Ionic, by others as Corinthian. Nicholas Young, the mason who installed them, described them as Composite), which supported the barrel-vaulted plaster ceiling of the nave and the flat ceiling of the aisles. The church, then said to be in a dangerous condition, was closed in 1899 and pulled down in 1904.

St James Garlickhithe

St James is the Apostle, also known as St James the Great and St James of Compostela; Garlickhithe refers to the 'hithe', or haven, on the Thames where garlic was landed and sold. The earliest record of the church is in 1196, when it was referred to as St James apud Viniteriam. It was also known as St James in the Vintry (the parish is in the ward of Vintry), St James Comyns, St James apud Tamisyam, St James-by-the-Thames and probably also as St James super Ripam. The church is now on Thames Street but was formerly separated from it by a small strip of land occupied by housing.

The early church was, according to Stow, rebuilt in 1326, probably by Richard Rothing, Sheriff of London. It had a chancel, cloister and many altars; in 1481 it was served by seven chantry priests. The chancel was repaired in 1621 and the north aisle rebuilt in 1624. Twenty years later a gallery was added and further repairs were undertaken.

The orders of the Commissioners do not record the decision to rebuild the church, but in 1678 it was listed as one of those begun since 1673. It was also one of those built upon the extraordinary. A plaque in the vestibule beneath the tower records the laying of a foundation stone for the new church in 1676. The shell of the building was complete by 1678, it was roofed in 1679 and the roof covered by 1680. The plastering was complete by 1682 and the church opened for worship on 10 December of that year. Work then stopped with the tower incomplete: it was finished in 1684.

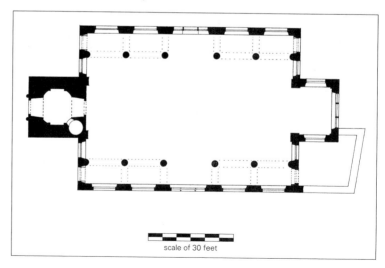

FIGURE 116.
St James Garlick-
hithe, plan. (PJ)

scale of 30 feet

FIGURE 117. St James Garlickhithe, interior looking east. (*NMR*)

Some pulling down of the old walls is recorded, including those dividing the old nave from the aisles, which was done by the parishioners in 1675–76. The accounts record payment to labourers for searching the foundations of the old tower for the piles upon which to rebuild the tower, indicating that the replacement was on the site of the old.

The church is built of Kentish rag, including stone rubble from the old building and brick, much of which is now covered with cement stucco. The tower has mostly been refaced with Portland stone, a repair following wartime fire damage of 1941. As completed, the tower was without its steeple. The building accounts show that this was then built by Edward Strong junior to a contract price of £1200. There was a further agreement with Edward Strong for 'vauses and ornaments about the spire and the parrapett wall . . .' Work on the steeple was completed by 1717.

This is one of the few churches to be erected with a separate chancel, i.e. structurally separate from the rest of the building. Its retention at St James Garlickhithe must surely be due to the insistence of the parish vestry.

Rebuilding the Church and Tower, 1676–84, £5357 12s. 10d.

Craftsmen: Christopher Kempster, mason; Thomas Warren, bricklayer; Israel Knowles, carpenter; William Cleere, joiner; Sarah Freeman, plumber; Henry Brooks, smith; Henry Doogood and John Grove, plasterers; Elizabeth Peowrie, glazier; Edward Bird, painter; John Veare, painter.

Construction of Steeple, 1715–17, £1872 13s. 8d.

Craftsmen: Edward Strong Junior, mason; Richard Jennings, carpenter; Joseph Roberts, plumber; Thomas Robinson, smith; Andrew Niblett, coppersmith; Chrysostom Wilkins, plasterer; Matthew Jarman, glazier; Joseph Thompson, painter.

Total cost, £7230 6s. 6d.

The church has nave and aisles separated by eight Ionic columns and four half columns supporting an entablature with clerestory windows containing segmental-headed windows. The spacing of the columns is equal except in the centre of the church, where the entablature is broken and turned to the outside walls. This gives a strong north-south axis to the building, reinforced by the large round-headed windows in the centre of both the north and south fronts (now replaced by large circular windows), and by the major entrance to the building in the centre of the north front. This has now been removed. The church has been referred to as 'Wren's Lantern' on account of the light admitted through the large number of windows.

The church was fortunate to survive the 1939–45 war, as a high explosive bomb pierced the roof in May 1941. It tore away the cornice and buried itself below the floor of the south aisle without exploding. It was removed a few days later. The church also suffered from fire damage, losing the twin dials of the bracket of the Tompion turret-clock, with its statue of St James, positioned over the west door. These have since been replaced. Damage from death-watch beetle closed the church in 1954 for an extensive restoration. It was opened for worship on 3 October 1963. The church was closed again in 1991, following damage from a crane falling across Thames Street with the jib embedded in the centre of the south wall of the church.

St James Piccadilly

The western part of the parish of St Martin-in-the-Fields, including the area known as St James, was developed in the seventeenth century. The parish church of St Martin was then quite inadequate to serve the needs of the area and, at some time before 1674, a site for a new church, churchyard and minister's house was offered by the Earl of St Albans. It was between Piccadilly and Jermyn Street, a part of the estate held on lease from the Crown. The Earl was the principal subscriber to the cost of erecting the church. There are no building accounts and the cost is known only to have been about £7000. Of the craftsmen who built it, only the names of Hobson, bricklayer, Storey (presumably Abraham Storey), and John Barratt, masons, and John Cock, plumber, are known with certainty. There is circumstantial evidence to suggest that Cleare (presumably William Cleere), joiner, Anthony Hart senior, bricklayer, Richard Hayburne, carpenter, and Jonathan Wilcox, carpenter, were also present.

The foundation stone of the church was laid on 3 April 1676 but the building history is unrecorded. The timber roof was probably covered with lead in 1682, when John Cock, plumber, later claimed that he had done work, suggesting that the building was completed by 1683–84. Shortly before his death in 1684, the Earl of St Albans (again) petitioned the Crown for the freehold of the site,

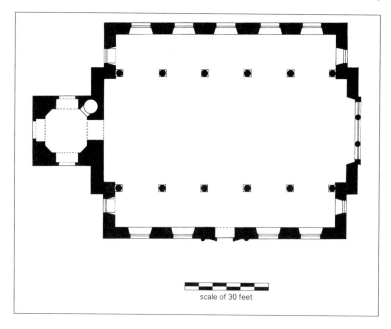

FIGURE 118.
St James Piccadilly,
plan. (PJ)

scale of 30 feet

FIGURE 119.
St James Piccadilly,
south front, tower
and steeple. Drawn
by J. Coney, etched
by J. Skelton, for the
Ecclesiastical Architecture of London.

which was granted on 31 May; enabling the church to be consecrated by Henry Compton, Bishop of London, on 13 July 1684. The church was made parochial in 1685.

Wren's name is closely associated with the building of this church and, although there are no records of any decision to approach him, there can be little doubt as to his authorship of the design. The tower also seems to have been started to Wren's design but, with the involvement of the newly-appointed parish vestry, there is some uncertainty over its completion and also over the addition of the steeple. Wren's design for the latter was, apparently, rejected in favour of a design by Wilcox, possibly Jonathan Wilcox, and the contract for its construction was given to his son, Edward Wilcox. By 1687, however, the tower had developed a leaning to the west, taking with it a part of the west end of the new church. This was attributed to bad workmanship, particularly in the laying of the foundations, said to have been on wet clay. The steeple was taken down, but plans to reduce the height of the tower were abandoned when no further leaning or cracking was observed. In 1699 Edward Wilcox was asked to give a design for a new spire, but there is no evidence to confirm that the new spire was by him. It may have come from Wren's Office.

The church is a five-bay galleried basilica, double-storied and brick-built, but with stone dressings and quoining. The rounded windows have stone architraves and keystones, the latter mostly with scrolls, but with cherub heads over the centre windows of both north and south fronts. It has a nave and aisles separated by Doric piers supporting the north, south and west galleries, and with Corinthian columns rising from these galleries to support the barrel-vault of the nave.

The church was repaired on several occasions in the eighteenth century and major alterations were made in 1803–4, with the north doorway replaced by a window. In 1856 the south doorway was also replaced by a window and vestibules were added the north and south of the tower. The rectory and vestry were destroyed by a high explosive bomb which fell on 14 October 1940. This severely damaged the east end and the north wall of the church. It was then gutted by fire following incendiary bombing. It was restored in 1947–54 by Sir Albert Richardson and rededicated on 19 June 1954. The restoration of the tower and steeple was completed in 1968 using a fibreglass spire.

The font, reredos and organ case escaped damage in the general destruction of 1940. The font, by Grinling Gibbons, shows the tree of life with a serpent coiled around it, and with figures of Adam and Eve. The bowl has three bas-reliefs, including Noah's Ark and the baptism of Christ.

St Lawrence Jewry

St Lawrence Jewry stands on the north side of Gresham (formerly Cateaton) Street, near its junction with Aldermanbury. It stood in its own churchyard but none of that now remains. It is named after a third-century saint, treasurer to the Christian church, who was martyred with or soon after Pope Sixtus II in 258 for his failure to surrender the 'treasures of the church' to the Emperor Valerian. He was, according to tradition, flayed alive before being slowly roasted on a grid iron. This part of the City is known as Jewry or Old Jewry, from the Jews who lived in the area until their expulsion in the time of Edward I. The church was first recorded in 1197, although the date 1136 has been given by some authors.

By medieval times it was a wealthy church in an affluent parish, although little is known of the history of the building. It was repaired and beautified in 1618 and again in 1631 before its destruction in 1666. A plan of it, drawn after the Fire, survives, showing that it had a nave and both north and south aisles, with a tower on the west front. The general outline was therefore similar to that of the present building, except for the encroachment of Guildhall Yard on the north-east corner. By the Act of 1670 the parish of St Mary Magdalen Milk Street was united with that of St Lawrence.

A vestry minute of 8 April 1670 records the appointment of a parish committee to oversee the rebuilding of the church; and another of 13 April records that the steeple was to be repaired by Thomas Cartwright, mason. Neither the churchwardens' accounts nor the church rebuilding accounts contain a record of payment to him, suggesting that little if any work can then have been done. With the passage of the 1670 Act the churchwardens of St Lawrence lost no time in arranging a meeting with the 'surveyors . . . to get a model and have the work begun'.

In the meantime, the Commissioners, at their meeting held on 13 June 1670, decided that St Lawrence Jewry should be one of the first fifteen of the churches to be rebuilt, a decision soon abandoned. The churchwardens were quick to grasp the idea that, by depositing loan money with the Chamber of London, they could obtain a place on the rebuilding programme. Their first deposit was made on 21 October 1670. The first contract for the church is dated 2 March 1671 and was awarded to Edward Pearce for taking down the walls of the church, together with what remained of the tower. Delays in building were caused partly by money problems, partly by a dispute over the north-east corner of the church. Problems with the foundations are also recorded in the building accounts. Edward Pearce, the mason, was paid for '22 days labour of pumping and carrying out wet soyle in tubbs in the east foundation'; and John Longland, the carpenter, for piling, also at the east end. He made two frames measuring four feet by five into which thirty iron-shod piles were driven. The heads of the piles were then close-wedged, levelled and planked over.

Although the first stone of the new church was laid on 12 April 1671, little construction work can have been undertaken until 1673. From this time the progress seems to have been fairly rapid, at least until 1676 when the shell of the building was reasonably complete. There are records of further deposits of money by the parish in the years 1676 and 1677 (in all a total of £4000) and these were probably associated specifically with the building of the tower and

FIGURE 120.
St Lawrence Jewry,
from the south east.
(*NMR*)

steeple. This would explain why, when the general embargo on tower and steeple building was imposed in 1677, the tower of St Lawrence Jewry was excluded from it. The building was reopened for worship in 1677. Work on the tower and steeple seems to have been completed by 1680. This included 'raising the spire 10 ft higher than contract', indicating that design changes were made as the building progressed.

Construction of Church, Tower and Steeple, 1671–80, £11,870 1s. 9d.

Craftsmen: Edward Pearce, mason; Thomas Newman, bricklayer; John Longland, carpenter; William Cleere, joiner; Charles Atherton, plumber; Stephen Leaver, smith; Thomas Smith, smith; Taylor and Bissell, smiths; Robert Bird, coppersmith; Thomas Meade, plasterer; William Browne, glazier; Abraham Harris, glazier; George Peowrie, glazier; Thomas Lane, painter; Margaret Pearce, painter.

The west front of the church, with the tower and steeple, is now visible from much of the western part of Gresham Street. It was not intended to have been seen in this way, but with the tower and steeple visible above the neighbouring houses. By contrast, the south front has always been exposed and is treated with greater detail and decoration. The east is the most decorated. It is of five bays externally, separated by engaged Corinthian columns and square corner pilasters, all on a high podium and supporting an enriched entablature. The three centre bays project forward and capping them, above the cornice, is a triangular pediment enclosing a round window. The centre and outer bays have round-headed niches and the intermediate bays round-headed windows. Above the heads of the windows and niches are carved festoons of fruit and flowers. The side fronting Guildhall Yard is the only one faced with ragstone.

The west end of the church remained much as it had been, with the tower curiously aligned to the west wall of the building – although the steeple above it was aligned to the south wall. The tower retained the irregular shape of its predecessor, simple and elegant but uninspiring and lacking in charm.

Noteworthy about the interior is the regularity of the auditorium, achieved despite the irregularity of the site by varying the thickness of the east wall from end to end; and by the arrangement of the west end, with the irregularity there being confined to the tower, vestibule and vestry.

The church was gutted by firebombing on the night of 29 December 1940, leaving only the tower and shell of the building. It was restored by Cecil Brown in 1954–57, much in the style of the old church. Most of the fittings are modern. It is now the guild church of the Corporation of London.

St Magnus the Martyr

There is some doubt as to which of the several St Magnuses the church was originally dedicated, but it is now ascribed to St Magnus of Orkney, killed in 1116 on the island of Egilsay. The earliest reference to the church is in 1067. The church has been known at various times as St Magnus towards London Bridge, St Magnus de Brugestrat and Sanctus Magnus ad Pontem, all indicating its position by Old London Bridge.

At the time of the Conquest the church, unusually, was of stone. In 1234 a grant of land was made for enlarging it. It was repaired in 1623–25 and 'richly beautified' in 1629, but destroyed early in the Great Fire which started in the neighbouring parish. By the Act of 1670 the parish was united with that of St Margaret New Fish Street. A slice of land, seventy-three feet in length and from seven and a half to fifteen feet in width, was taken from the church for the widening of Thames Street after the Fire.

There is no evidence from the vestry minutes of when the rebuilding began. A mason's bill of 16 May 1669 records the laying of foundations for the north wall and raising it to a height of seven feet eight inches. This was probably done in 1668, two years before the Commissioners assumed resposibility. There are, however, no craftsmen's bills for 1670 or early 1671, suggesting that work on the building had slowed, or even stopped, before the passage of the 1670 Act.

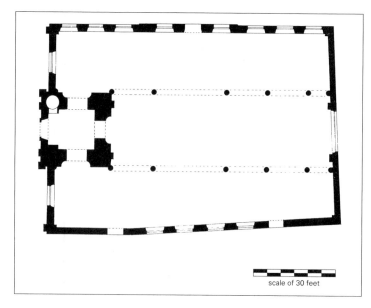

FIGURE 121. St Magnus the Martyr, plan. (PJ)

scale of 30 feet

A surviving drawing shows the building as it may have been intended (Fig. 33). The south wall of the medieval church, with its turret stair, was to be retained; the tower and north walls were to be new and the roof was to have been supported upon twelve columns. These had slightly irregular intercolumniation, possibly reflecting the position of the columns or piers of the pre-Fire church. This drawing has a number of pencil and crayon marks indicating possible alterations to the design. In the rebuilding, the design was changed little, retaining its nave and aisles and seemingly the south wall of the pre-Fire church. It was however given an interesting cross-axis, emphasised by a rebuilding of the north door (in 1675) to a greater height and by a fresh arrangement of the columns

FIGURE 122.
St Magnus the
Martyr, interior
looking east, 1965.
(NMR)

with a greater intercolumniation opposite this north door. The chancel was removed.

The masons had resumed work on the tower on its present site by 1674 and on the north wall by 1675. Much of the church was rebuilt with ragstone, some from the old building and some brought from St Mary Abchurch. Work continued until 1678, when the church was essentially complete. Work on the tower had stopped at a height of about sixty feet but, in March 1680, the Commissioners ordered that it should be carried on. Work on it restarted later that year and continued until 1684, when Matthew Banckes, carpenter, boarded up the roof. The intention was to add a spire: in 1684, the mason, John Thompson, was paid £5 14s. 0d. for a model of it. Construction began in 1703 and continued until 1706.

Work Undertaken by the Churchwardens, 1668–69, £390 4s. 4d.

Craftsmen: George Downeswell, mason; John Thompson, mason.

Construction of the Church and Tower. 1674–78; 1680–84, £9189 15s. 6d.

Craftsmen: John Thompson, mason; Matthew Banckes, carpenter; Thomas Lock, carpenter; William Cleere, joiner; Charles Atherton, plumber; Thomas Dobbins, plumber; Henry Brookes, smith; Henry Doogood and John Grove, plasterers; James Goodchild, glazier; Thomas Knight, glazier; Edward Bird, painter; Widow Pearce (Margaret), painter.

Construction of the Steeple, 1703–6, £2545 11s. 1½d.

Craftsmen: Samuel Fulkes, mason; Abraham Jordan, carpenter; Joseph Roberts, plumber; Thomas Robinson, smith; Jane Brewin, coppersmith; Henry Doogood, plasterer; James Goodchild, glazier; William Thompson, painter.

Total cost, £12,125 10s. 11½d.

The church of St Magnus the Martyr is approximately rectangular in shape, with the tower at the centre of the west end and the north and south aisles originally continued to the western front, which had an applied tetrastyle Ionic portico. In the interior are eight Ionic columns, fluted, reeded and on tall hexagonal bases, together with half columns at the east and three-quarter columns at the west, supporting an entablature with an attic storey in the nave. The east window is now blocked.

The church was damaged by fire in 1760, with the loss of the roof and the vestry on the south-east corner. In 1762, in a scheme for widening the approaches to the Old London Bridge, the new vestry, which had only just been completed, was removed and the west ends of the north and south aisles set back to enable pedestrians to use a passageway beneath the tower. This arrangement was changed again in the 1830s with the construction of the new London Bridge upstream of the old, with a new approach road further west which no longer passed beneath the tower of St Magnus.

There have been many later changes to this church, including the blocking of the north door. This made nonsense of the internal arrangements. In 1827 the round-headed windows of the north front were replaced by circular ones and the south aisle partly rebuilt. In 1924 the intercolumniation was made more uniform by inserting an additional pair of columns. The church was damaged in the war of 1939–45 and restored in 1951. It was damaged again by a fire on 4 November 1995.

St Margaret Lothbury

The dedication is to St Margaret of Antioch, a saint and virgin martyr who, in the time of Diocletian, is reputed to have suffered a series of horrifying ordeals before being beheaded. The church is on the north side of Lothbury in a position now opposite the Bank of England. It was first recorded in 1197 or

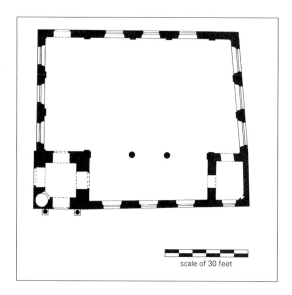

FIGURE 123. St Margaret Lothbury, plan. (*PJ*)

scale of 30 feet

possibly in 1181. The church was enlarged and partly rebuilt by Robert Large, Lord Mayor in 1440. It was repaired and beautified in 1621 before its destruction in 1666.

The rebuilding of the church seems to have started about 1683, although the first of the craftsmen's bills was not met until 1686. John Longland, carpenter, was paid for timber planking in the foundations at the west end, indicating some renewal, but the mason's accounts do not suggest any major reworking of the foundations. There is no account of any reusing of the old walls but, equally, no account of any clearing of the site before work began. The church may therefore have been reconstructed from what remained of the old building.

The church was roofed and covered in 1687, with work continuing into 1688. Here, as elsewhere, it then came to a halt with the church apparently usable but unfinished. Work resumed in 1689 or 1690 and the church itself was completed by 1692, but with the tower still incomplete and the steeple unbuilt. These were left until 1698, when work again resumed, to be completed in 1700.

Construction of the Church, 1683–88, 1689–92, £5340 8s. 1¼ d.

Craftsmen: Samuel Fulkes, mason; John Longland, carpenter; William Cleere, joiner; Matthew Roberts, plumber; Richard Howes, smith; Henry Doogood, plasterer; Francis Moore, glazier; Nicholas Sheppard, painter; Bartholomew Scott, carter and labourer.

Completion of the Tower and Steeple, 1698–1700, £1059 0s. 7d.

Cratfsmen: Samuel Fulkes, mason; John
Longland, carpenter; William Knight,
plumber; Thomas Robinson, smith; Thomas
Brewin, coppersmith; Matthew Jarman,
glazier; William Thompson, painter.

Total cost, £6399 8s. 8d.

St Margaret Lothbury has an auditorium,
rectangular except for the east wall which is
at an angle to the remaining walls, separated
from the south aisle by two Corinthian columns and now by a screen. The tower
occupies the south-west corner of the building
and provides the principal entrance through a
doorway with Corinthian columns. At one
time there was a second entrance from Lothbury, in a position closer to the south-east
corner, but this has long since been removed.
The church is still well-lit but formerly had
round-headed windows on all four sides, including the east wall where they are now
blocked.

FIGURE 124. St Margaret Lothbury,
south front, tower and steeple.
Drawn by J. Clayton.

The church is rich in its fittings, many derived from other churches. The altar
screen is from All Hallows-the-Great; it is one of only two such screens to
survive in the City (the other is in St Peter Cornhill) and may always have been
one of the most magnificent. The screen separating the auditorium from the
chapel now in the south aisle is of alternate wood and iron uprights, and is by
Bodley of 1891. At the lower level it incorporates woodwork from the altar rails
of St Olave Jewry. The reredos of the main altar belongs to St Margaret but the
paintings of Moses and Aaron on either side of it are from St Christopher-le-
Stocks. The pulpit was commissioned for St Margaret but its sounding-board,
with elaboratedly carved detail, is from All Hallows-the-Great.

The marble font has a square bowl with cherub heads at the four corners.
The sides are carved in low relief with scenes from the Garden of Eden, Noah's
Ark, the Baptism of Christ and St Philip baptising the eunuch. It was commis-
sioned for the church and is said to be by Grinling Gibbons. There is no
documentary evidence for this, but its resemblance to the font in St James
Piccadilly suggests that it may be correct.

St Margaret Pattens

The dedication is to St Margaret of Antioch of blessed memory but doubtful story. The church is first recorded in 1067 as a small wooden building and may therefore be of Saxon origin. It is referred to as St Margaret-near-the-Tower and also St Margaret Patyns, possibly from the patten-makers who were said to have lived in the area. The name Pattens may equally well be from the family name 'Patin' or 'Patynz'. The wooden building was replaced with one of stone in the early medieval period. This replacement was taken down and rebuilt in 1538, partly from offerings made at the cross set up in the churchyard. This cross, or rood, gave name to Rood Lane at the west of the church and also to the church as St Margaret Rood or Rood Church. It was known also as St Margaret East Cheap and St Margaret Little Tower Street. The late medieval church was destroyed in 1666. The parish was united with that of St Gabriel Fenchurch.

Little was done to secure rebuilding of the church until 1682 when the churchwardens made repeated calls upon Sir Christopher Wren to 'put him in mind of building the church'. The Commissioners gave approval in May 1682 and, in February 1683, the Lord Mayor (probably in response to pressure from the parish) reminded Wren that, although an order for building had been issued, 'the same is not yet begun, nor contracted for'.

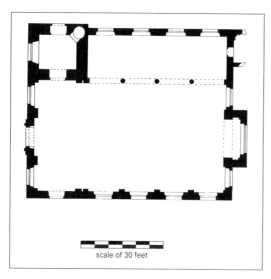

scale of 30 feet

FIGURE 125. St Margaret Pattens, plan. (PJ)

The first measurement of work done was in July 1684, when Samuel Fulkes, mason, recorded the laying of stone from the top of the foundation to the top of the window sills round the church. He also claimed for taking down 825 yards of old walling and for the digging of 369 yards of new foundation. The church was roofed and covered with lead by the end of 1685 and the main body of the church completed with its western gallery by 1687 or early 1688. Work on the building then ceased with the tower only partly

FIGURE 126.
St Margaret
Pattens, south
front, tower and
spire. Drawn by
W. Niven,
c. 1885.

built. Work did not resume again until 1698, with the completion of the tower with its parapet, pinnacles and lead-covered timber spire in 1702. Further work on the spire of St Margaret Pattens was undertaken by the Commissioners in 1712–14. This may have been largely repairs.

Construction of the Church and Tower, 1684–87, £4986 18s. 8¼d.

Craftsmen: Samuel Fulkes, mason; John Evans, bricklayer; Thomas Woodstock, carpenter; William Cleere, joiner; Thomas Poultrey, joiner; James Dobbins and Stephen Smart, plumbers; Humphrey Clay, smith; Edmund Smith, smith; Henry Doogood and John Grove, plasterers; Samuel Rainger, glazier; William Thompsom, painter; Bartholomew Scot, carter and labourer.

Completion of the Tower and Spire, 1698–1702, £2496 12s. 8d.

Craftsmen: Samuel Fulkes, mason; Abraham Jordan, carpenter; Jonathan Maine, carver; Matthew Roberts, plumber; Thomas Colbourn, smith; Thomas Brewin, coppersmith; Henry Doogood, plasterer; Sarah Rainger, glazier; William Thompson, painter.

Repairs to the Church and Steeple, 1712–14, £244 15s. 9½d.

Craftsmen: William Kempster, mason; Richard Jennings, carpenter; Joseph Roberts, plumber; Thomas Robinson, smith; Matthew Jarman, glazier; Joseph Thompson, painter; Andrew Niblett, coppersmith.

Total cost, £7748 7s. 1¼d., including £20 by which the bill of Thomas Woodstock was abated.

The church is rectangular in shape but with the tower intruding into the north-west corner. The main auditorium is separated from the north aisle by three columns of the Corinthian order. The ceiling is flat, with a large central panel, coved to the walls and groined to the round windows of the clerestory.

The square tower, faced with Portland stone, has corner pilasters, rising the full height of the tower to an entablature with triglyphs immediately below the main cornice. The balustrated parapet has pedestals to the corners, each supporting a square, panelled obelisk, enriched at the base and terminating with a ball and spike. The octagonal panelled spire is timber-framed and lead-covered; it rises to a height of about 200 feet above the ground. When built it was decorated with lead-covered urns, but these have since been removed.

St Martin Ludgate

St Martin Ludgate, known also as St Martin Ludgate Hill (and earlier as St Martin-the-Little and St Martin-the-Less to distinguish it from St Martin-le-Grand), is on the north side of Ludgate Hill, inside the Ludgate of the City Wall. The first church on this site was said to have been founded by Cadwallo (d. 677), but the earliest record of the church is in 1189. In 1425 a lease was granted for ground at the west end of the church, to build a tower and belfry. The church itself was substantially repaired or rebuilt in 1437. The steeple fell in 1561, in the same storm that wrecked the spire of St Paul's Cathedral.

The medieval church of St Martin had its major dimension, and was probably also liturgically orientated, north-south. Destroyed in 1666, its ruins lay until 1673, when Robert Hooke authorised their clearance. A strip of land is said to have been taken from the church for widening Ludgate Hill. No payment for this has been traced and no evidence found to confirm the story. A plot of land occupied by the vestry to the west of Ludgate was taken but it cannot have adjoined the church. The new church occupied the same site as its predecessor, probably with the same slight irregularity in the east wall marking the pre-Fire boundary.

The Commissioners approved the re-building of St Martin on 20 September 1676. A surviving elevation drawing shows the façade to Ludgate Hill broadly as built (Fig. 19). It has the faint outline of a taller spire, much as built. The earliest bills for work on the church site are dated 1679 but, since these include a payment to Henry Blowes, carpenter, for the roofing of the building, construction must have started much earlier, probably in 1677. The construction of the tower followed and continued to 1682. By that time the tower had reached just over eighty-two feet, at which height it was covered and left. Work resumed in 1684 and was essentially, if not fully, completed by the end of 1686.

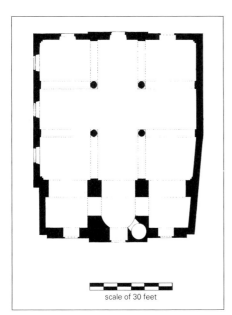

scale of 30 feet

FIGURE 127. St Martin Ludgate, plan. (PJ)

FIGURE 128. St Martin Ludgate, interior looking south. (*NMR*)

Construction of Church, Tower and Steeple, 1677–82, 1684–86, £5378 10s. 3d.

Craftsmen: Nicholas Young, mason; Thomas Horne, bricklayer; Alan Garway, bricklayer; Robert Day, carpenter; Henry Blowes, carpenter; Matthew Banckes, carpenter; William Draper, joiner; William Emmet, carver; Stephen Leaver, smith; Samuel Colbourn, smith; John Talbot, plumber; Peter Read, plumber; John Grove and Henry Doogood, plasterers; Richard Bowler, glazier; Richard Pinder, glazier; Robert Bird, coppersmith; Edward Bird and Thomas Lane, painters; John Styford, labourer.

Only the façade of the church is exposed to view. The most imposing feature is the tower and steeple. The octagonal, lead-covered cupola supports a railed platform or balcony above which is a lantern carrying the slender lead-covered spire, complete with ball and vane.

All three entrances to the church from Ludgate Hill lead into vestibules separated from the main auditorium by massive arches with coffered soffits, each containing a plaster rose. The auditorium itself is a Greek cross within a square. The roof is supported on four large columns with Composite capitals. The ceiling is barrel-vaulted with a large plaster rose marking the groined intersection. The church is noted for the quality of its carved woodwork, particularly the screens occupying the arches between the vestibules and the auditorium. The reredos, altar-table, rails and pulpit were gifts to the church; no accounts for them are known, and the craftsmen's names are not recorded. The pews were remade from the old box pews in 1894.

Although repaired and restored on a number of occasions, the church is still largely as it was built, although the altar and choir are now on a platform raised in 1894–95 and there has been much rearrangement of the furniture. The church escaped all but minor damage in the war of 1939–45. It has recently been restored and redecorated.

St Mary Abchurch

St Mary Abchurch, on the west side of Abchurch Lane, was one of more than a dozen churches in the City of London dedicated to the Blessed Virgin Mary. The origin of 'Abchurch' is obscure. The earliest mention of the church is in 1198–99. It was was restored and beautified in 1611 and destroyed in 1666. By the Act of 1670 the parish was united with that of Laurence Pountney.

In 1670 the vestry minutes record discussion about covering one of the aisles to make a place for assembly until such time as the church was rebuilt. Payments to a carpenter and a bricklayer suggest that some work was done, but it cannot have been much. In that year the vestry appointed a committee to consider the rebuilding of the church, discussing the form of it with Robert Hooke. These discussions may relate to a large building, about seventy-five feet square, for which drawings survive. It was to have had a dome supported on six columns, two three-quarter and four pilasters, in an arrangement that recalls St Stephen Walbrook. Notwithstanding this early interest, little was done until 1681 when construction began. What remained of the old walls of the tower and vestry was taken down and the foundations opened. The church was roofed in 1683 and covered with Delabole slates in 1684. This covering may not have been entirely satisfactory, as in 1687 the slating was replaced with a covering of lead for which the parish agreed to reimburse the Commissioners with a proportion of the cost. The rebuilding was complete in 1686 or early in 1687.

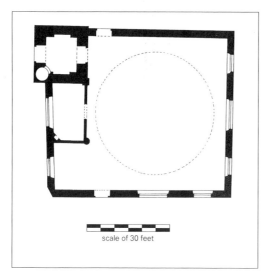

scale of 30 feet

FIGURE 129. St Mary Abchurch, plan. (*PJ*)

Construction of the Church, Tower and Steeple, 1681–86, £4922 2s. 5½d.

Craftsmen: Christopher Kempster, mason; John Bridges, bricklayer; John Evans, bricklayer; Thomas Woodstock, carpenter; William Grey, joiner; Thomas Dobbins, plumber; Sarah Freeman, plumber; Henry Brooks, smith; Thomas

Hodgkins, smith; Stephen Leaver, smith; William Newton, slater; Robert Bird, coppersmith; Henry Doogood and John Grove, plasterers; Henry Bray, glazier; Edward Bird, painter; William Thompson, painter; Bartholomew Scott, carter and labourer.

Total cost, £4974 2s. 5½d., including a number of minor items not in the craftsmen's bills.

The church of St Mary Abchurch is a brick building with stone quoining and dressings. It has a brick tower on the north-west corner with a timber-framed cupola, lantern and lead-covered spire. At its rebuilding it was given a gilded copper pelican in its piety as weather vane, but this was removed in 1764 and is now kept in the church.

The church has a dome carried on eight arches and pendentives springing

FIGURE 130.
St Mary Abchurch,
exterior from the
south east. (*NMR*)

from corbels with Corinthian capitals. It is painted with eight female allegorical figures representing virtues. It was formerly attributed to Thornhill but is now known to have been painted by William Stone. It was badly damaged in 1940 and extensively restored in 1945–52.

The fittings of this church are particularly fine. The carving of the reredos is documented as the work of Grinling Gibbons. The pulpit was by William Grey, with the carving for it possibly by William Newman or William Emmett. William Kempster, brother of the mason Christopher Kempster, supplied the font, an octagonal bowl of white marble.

The church was badly damaged in the war of 1939–45 and restored by Godfrey Allen in 1948–53.

FIGURE 131.
St Mary Abchurch, interior showing altar-piece with carving by Grinling Gibbons. (NMR)

St Mary Aldermanbury

The church was on the west side of the street known as Aldermanbury, at its junction with Love Lane. It is first recorded in an inquisition of 1181, but its position close to the south-east gate of the Roman fort at Cripplegate suggests that the site may have been occupied by a church in Saxon times. The tower was, according to Stow, rebuilt in 1437. This building was repaired and beautified in 1633 before destruction in 1666. The church of St Mary Aldermanbury was not to be rebuilt, but the churchwardens of St Mary petitioned the Lord Mayor and the Bishop of London and obtained a reprieve, recorded in the Act of 1670.

By an agreement of 2 March 1671 Joshua Marshall was to take down all the walls of the church and tower. This does not seem to have been carried out in its entirety, as some of the late medieval tower remained into the twentieth century. The construction of the new building started in 1671. Some of the old foundations were used but new ones were provided for the columns and at the south-east corner. The church was roofed, probably early in 1673, and the roof covered with lead by the end of that year. The windows were glazed in 1674. The plasterer was not paid until 1677, but most of his work must have been done in 1675. The steeple was constructed in 1680–81.

Construction of Church and Tower, 1671–75, £4943 8s. 10d.

Craftsmen: Joshua Marshall, mason; Matthew Banckes, carpenter; Robert Day, carpenter; William Cleere, joiner; John Talbot, plumber; Thomas Hodgkins, smith; Grace Smith, smith; John Grove, plasterer; Daniel Davis, glazier; Robert Streeter, painter.

Construction of the Steeple, 1680–81, £256 11s. 4d.

Craftsmen: Samuel Fulkes, mason; Matthew Banckes, carpenter; Thomas Hodgkins, smith; Robert Bird, coppersmith; John Slaughter, plumber; John Talbot, plumber; William

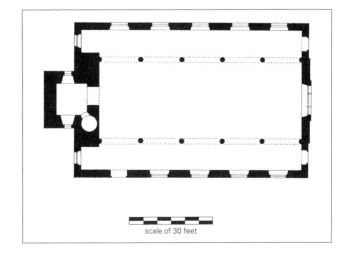

scale of 30 feet

FIGURE 132. St Mary Aldermanbury, plan. (*PJ*)

FIGURE 133.
St Mary Alderman-
bury, south front and
tower. (*NMR*)

Cocker, supplier of lead, Robert Streeter, painter.

Total cost £5237 3s. 6d. including £12 paid to St Paul's for stone and a
payment to the churchwardens for work done.

St Mary Aldermary was built largely of stone rubble and brick, with Portland
stone facing to the south and east. The tower was centrally placed at the west
end, intruding into the nave. The most decorated front was the east, with the
central of three bays broken forward. It had a large round-headed window
supported by carved stone scrolls. The parapets were completed with carved
stone pineapples at either end, duplicated at the west end of the building.

The church was repaired and restored on a number of occasions. It was
destroyed by fire-bombing in December 1940, leaving little except the fire-scared
walls and the tower. What remained was dismantled in 1965 and reassembled
at Westminster College, Fulton, Missouri, USA, as a memorial to Sir Winston
Churchill.

FIGURE 134. St Mary Aldermanbury cleared after war damage. The church was reerected in Fulton, Missouri, USA. (*NMR*)

St Mary Aldermary

St Mary Aldermary, on the east side of Bow Lane, was said to be the oldest of the City churches dedicated to the Virgin Mary. It was first mentioned about 1080 and a Saxon origin therefore seems likely. The church was rebuilt about 1511 with Sir Henry Keeble or Kibbel, Lord Mayor, a benefactor. When he died in 1518 the tower was incomplete; it remained as a stump until 1626 when it was finished according to 'its ancient pattern'. The church was repaired in 1632 and severely damaged in the Fire of 1666. By the Act of 1670 the parish was united with that of St Thomas the Apostle.

Much of the old fabric remained, and the parish intended that it should be repaired and reroofed, rather than be rebuilt in its entirety. The Commissioners' orders contain no reference to the church until 1675, when it was agreed that the churchwardens would be reimbursed the cost of repairing and reroofing the tower, amounting to £74 9s. 6d.

In 1677–78 the position changed dramatically. A Mr Henry Rogers, resident of Westminster with property in Cannington, Somerset, had made a will directing that the residue of his estate should be disposed of by his niece, Anne Rogers, in such a manner as he had directed her. This, she disclosed, was towards the rebuilding of one of the City churches. After a law suit in Chancery, brought

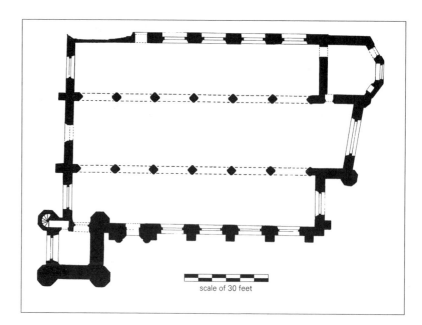

FIGURE 135.
St Mary Alder-
mary, plan. (PJ)

scale of 30 feet

by her against her fellow executors, she emerged on 6 November 1677 with an order for the money to be paid into court. A sum of £5000 was eventually paid from the court into the Chamber of London and out again in payments to workmen as authorised by her. What is not known is how her choice was made in favour of St Mary Aldermary, nor whether she was counselled in making that choice; and if so by whom.

Nearly £500 had been expended by November 1679, indicating that the work had begun. It seems to have been finished in 1682, when the church was

FIGURE 136.
St Mary Aldermary,
exterior from the
south east, c. 1870.
(NMR)

reopened for worship. Although the record of payments gives the names of some of the craftsmen involved, the architect is not identified. The work was under the direction of John Oliver but this may indicate no more than that the work was controlled from Wren's Office. As far as the Office was concerned, it was probably no more than one of the churches to be rebuilt with money channelled through the Chamber. The craftsmen were all men who had other contracts for the City churches, as one might expect when appointed by Wren's Office, rather than a more local selection made by the parish.

The church appears to be a repair and reconstruction of the late medieval building, as intended by the church vestry, using as much as possible of what

FIGURE 137.
St Mary Aldermary,
interior looking
north east. (*NMR*)

remained after the Fire. The dismantling of the parapet on the south side suggests that this wall may have been standing more or less complete, but what remained of the east end of the church was apparently demolished. The general design of the present building suggests that the foundations of the pre-Fire building were reused and the existence of fire-damaged traceried heads of windows tends to confirm that a great deal of the old masonry was reused in the new building.

It has generally been supposed that, in the repairs to the tower undertaken up to 1674, it was left without parapet and pinnacles and that these were supplied in 1701–4. In fact the building accounts for 1701–4 show that the tower was extensively rebuilt at that time. The tower of St Mary Aldermary, like others at that time, was then showing structural defects necessitating complete reconstruction. The work was under the supervision of William Dickinson. The design of the tower seems generally to have followed that of the pre-Fire tower.

Repair of the Tower, 1674.

Restoration of the Church, 1679–82.

Craftsmen: Samuel Fulkes, mason; John Longland, carpenter; Jonathan Maine, carver; Matthew Roberts, plumber; Stephen Leaver, smith; Henry Doogood, plasterer.

Rebuilding of the Tower, 1701–4, £6352 13s. 8d.

Craftsmen: John Clarke, mason; Abraham Jordan, carpenter; Matthew and John Roberts, plumbers; Thomas Colbourn, smith; Thomas Brewin, coppersmith; Henry Doogood, plasterer; Isaac Fryer, glazier; William Thompson, painter.

The church is approximately rectangular in shape, but with the east wall at an angle. It is perpendicular in style with six bays of nave and aisles separated by slim four-shafted piers and four-centred arches. The aisles and clerestory have perpendicular three-light windows, with larger windows at both east and west ends. The crowning glory of the church is its plaster fan-vaulted ceiling with rosettes in shallow saucer-shaped domes. It is an early example of Gothic Revival in London.

Most of the original fittings were disposed of in the restoration of 1876–77, being replaced with others of a more gothic character. A doorcase from St Antholin survives together with a pulpit from the Wren period, a fine carved wooden sword-case and a font of 1682. The pinnacles of the tower were renewed in 1876 and finally taken down in about 1927. New finials of fibreglass were erected in May 1962. The church was badly damaged in 1939–45 and has since been restored.

St Mary-le-Bow

St Mary-le-Bow was known in early medieval times also as St Mary atte Bowe, St Mary Arcubus, Our Lady of the Arches and Our Lady of the Bow – names derived, so it is said, from the bows or arches of the Norman crypt to the church. It stands towards the northern end of Bow Lane with its tower and steeple now fronting Cheapside. The church was the seat of the Archbishop's Court of Arches, the court of ecclesiastical appeal.

The date of foundation of the church is not known. The remains of a crypt beneath the present church are part of the Norman building of which no other trace now survives. It gave way to a medieval building, smaller than the present church. It had a tower on the southern part of the west front, where its foundations and the base of a circular stair can be seen from the crypt. The tower fell in 1270–71. It was rebuilt on a site further north but was not complete with its steeple until 1512. The steeple of this tower had, by this time, assumed the outline shown on a parish seal, with a central lantern carried on arches and four smaller lanterns on the corners of the parapet. It was rebuilt in the early part of the seventeenth century but destroyed with the tower and church in 1666. The parish of St Mary-le-Bow was united with those of All Hallows Honey Lane and St Pancras Soper Lane.

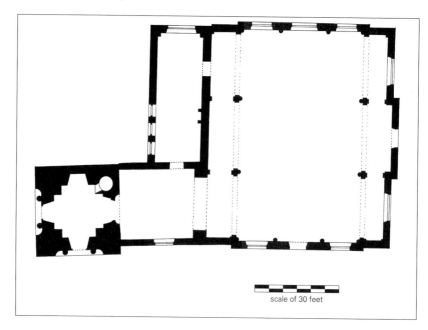

FIGURE 138. St Mary-le-Bow, plan of the rebuilt church and tower. (PJ)

scale of 30 feet

The restoration of the tower began, in 1668 or 1669, with work to a value of £340 undertaken by Thomas Cartwright, mason, and £300 by William Cleere, joiner. There may have been other payments of which there is now no record, the vestry minutes for the period immediately following the Fire being lost. There is no hint of any involvement of Sir Christopher Wren prior to June 1670.

One of the earliest of the Commissioners' decisions was that the church should be enlarged and made into 'a regular Square forme' by purchasing ground on the south-west corner. Also taken into the body of the church was the ground

FIGURE 139. St Mary-le-Bow, design for the church with a loggia projected for Cheapside. Drawn by Nicholas Hawksmoor. (*Conway Library*)

on the south adjoining Bow Lane which had, prior to the Fire, been used at various times as a vestry and school. An order dated 28 June 1670 allocated £3500 to the building of the church, estimated to be about one half of what would be required; a further unspecified amount was put aside in October of that year, with which it was hoped to complete the rebuilding.

Work started with digging the new foundations, where they were required, and pulling down the old walls. Work continued on the restoration of the tower, for which a number of contracts were issued. Its condition gave rise to increasing concern: the last contract for it, dated 28 March 1671, was to Walter Clements, described as an anchorsmith, for the supply of bars and cramps of iron, including two braces of 'good Spanish Iron', by or before 20 April 1671. Apparently even these failed to hold the tower, as on 13 May 1671 the Commissioners commented:

> since it was taken into our Care, our Officers represented to us, that they were not out of hopes of making it Firme, notwithstanding they have lately informed us that the Cracks are farther opened, and that new discovery is made that the foundacons are naught, and the Core of the Wall so Crushed and weakened that in all judicious men's Opinions, who have viewed it of late, the Tower will be very dangerous . . .

The Commissioners then ordered that a new tower should be begun, either on the same foundations (which in view of their observation that the foundations were naught is perhaps surprising) or on 'a more convenient situation adjoining' upon ground to be bought by the City.

The more convenient situation adjoining was on Cheapside, where the tower and steeple now stand. This land was owned by the Dean and Chapter of Canterbury but leased to a Mr Bartholomew Layton. It might have been expected that, following the decision to use the site, the lease for it would have been acquired by the Commissioners, using funds from the coal tax provided by Parliament for the rebuilding of the parish churches, but this apparently was not done. Instead it was acquired by the City of London, using funding from the coal tax intended for improvements to the City. A sum of £1300 was paid to Mr Layton by an order dated 24 May 1671, described in the coal duty account book as 'for the Enlargement of Bowe Church & for the Ornament of ye said Streete'. This purchase included not only the land upon which the church tower was to stand but a strip of land to the west, to provide a better access to the parish churchyard, and land to the east, presumably earmarked for the 'ornament of the street'. This site would have formed the greater part of that needed for the construction of the loggia shown in a drawing by Nicholas Hawksmoor, engraved by Hulsbergh and described 'as originally intended by Sir Christopher Wren'. It is shown as a two-bay open arcaded structure of the Doric order, with balustrade and full-length figures over. The idea of the loggia seems to have been abandoned by October 1672, when the City relet the plot. The loggia may have been a gleam in the eyes of one Lord Mayor but not in those of his successor. It would not have been an appropriate charge against the coal tax fund for the rebuilding of the parochial churches. There was a separate fund for improvements to the City, also derived from the tax on coal, but administered by the City. This was for specific projects authorised in the Act of 1670, such

FIGURE 140.
St Mary-le-Bow,
tower and steeple
from Cheapside.
(*NMR*)

as for street widening, the building of quays and the providing of off-street markets, not for such visions as the loggia. The project may therefore have disappeared simply from want of funding.

The decision to build the new tower of St Mary-le-Bow was taken between 20 April 1671 (when Walter Clements was told to use his clamps to hold the old tower) and 13 May (when the Commissioners approved the new site). It is from this period that a drawing in the hand of Edward Woodroffe must date. It represents the first known ideas for a replacement tower, probably upon the old site. It is for a tower and steeple shorter than the tower as built and has a width of only twenty-five feet, as against thirty-two as built. In its design it forms the prototype of the present tower, but the added steeple is completely different. The doorway is flanked by two engaged Doric columns with an entablature and plain triangular pediment. The frieze has metopes with roundels and the pediment is surmounted by a circular window. The bell-loft stage is decorated at the corners with overlapping Ionic pilasters and the capitals have ornate carved drops.

This pen-and-ink drawing is inscribed with a number of pencil additions, including a horizontal section of the tower, pineapples on the corners of the balustrade and a third entrance to the space beneath the tower, which is sketched upon the plan. These changes mark the first changes to the design; others were to come. The third entance is consistent with the change of site to Cheapside, while the pineapples mark the positions later occupied by the bowed pinnacles.

This elevation and ground plan may be read in conjunction with a site plan which shows the area to the north of the church, with the tower in the position now occupied by the vestibule, and a somewhat smaller vestibule to the east of this giving access to the north side of the church with a passageway from Cheapside. This gives no details of the design of tower, but it would have needed an entrance from the churchyard to the west and another from from Cheapside. The Woodroffe drawing, as amended, shows the tower to have just such entrances, suggesting that the amendments were drawn for this new site.

On 20 May 1671 Thomas Cartwright, mason, was given a contract for the demolition of the old tower and for laying the foundations of the new. The new design for the tower may not have been finalised but some decisions had been made. The foundations, for example, required a hole to be dug thirty-eight feet square and to a depth of twenty feet, indicating the the new tower was to be a great deal taller or more massive than either its predecessor or the Woodroffe design.

The story, given in *Parentalia*, is that on digging the foundations for the new tower Wren found, to his surprise, that at about eighteen feet below the surface there was a Roman causeway of rough stone, well rammed, with Roman brick and rubbish at the bottom, all firmly cemented. This causeway was four feet thick and overlay the London clay which extended to a depth of at least forty feet.

The earliest known drawing for the tower and steeple in the form that was to be built is in the King's Topographical Collection. It has some resemblance to the Woodroffe drawing but there are many differences. A new story has been added and the bell-loft has been heightened with a new section. The doorway is still framed by engaged Doric columns supporting an entablature, but the frieze of the latter has lost the roundels of the metopes. The pediment has disappeared and the circular window has been replaced with an oval one. At the bell-loft stage the Ionic pilasters are paired, and no longer overlapping, and the drops are missing. The greatest change, however, is the replacement of the small dome and spire with the steeple.

The building accounts record changes made to the design as it was built. The bell-loft was erected with swags between the volutes. The metopes of the doorways, enriched with cherub heads and cherubim, linked with festoons, were added to the sill above the entablature. The design can be seen to have been derived from Mansart's Hôtel de Conti.

Although the contract for the construction of the lower stage of the tower was signed by Thomas Cartwright and John Thompson on 3 March 1672, there is no indication of when the work began, the earliest bills being undated. The next contract, that for the second stage, was not signed until 22 September 1676, which suggests that there may have been some delay. The work was not completed until June 1680.

Construction of the Church, 1670–75, £8071 18s. 1d.

Craftsmen: Thomas Cartright, mason; Anthony Tanner, bricklayer; Matthew Banckes, carpenter; Robert Day, carpenter; William Cleere, joiner; Thomas Whyte (or Whiting), joiner; Thomas Aldworth, plumber; John Baxter, smith; John Grove, plasterer; John Grove, junior, plasterer; John Oliver, glazier; Robert Streeter, painter; William Cooke, carter; John Simpson, labourer.

Construction of the Tower and Steeple, 1668–80, £7388 8s. 7¼d.

Craftsmen: Thomas Cartwright and John Thompson, masons; Thomas Horn, bricklayer; Matthew Banckes, carpenter; William Cleere, joiner; Thomas Aldworth, plumber; Thomas Freeman, plumber; Matthew Roberts, plumber;

John Baxter, smith; Stephen Leaver, smith; Walter Clement, anchorsmith; Robert Bird, coppersmith; Henry Doogood and John Grove, plasterers; Samuel Oliver, glazier; Thomas Lane, painter; William Grey, joiner, for a model; Edward Pearce, mason for carving.

Total cost, £15,645 18s. 2¼d., including a number of minor payments.

The church of St Mary-le-Bow is of brick construction with Portland stone dressings. It has a a nave and aisles separated by piers with engaged half-round Corinthian columns. The roof is an elliptical barrel-vault, with the side aisles each having a transverse, plain, arched cross-vault. A south door, now visible only on the exterior, is no longer used and is all that remains of the cross-axis that gave also to the Court of Arches on the north side of the building. The principal entrance is from the west, with a further entrance from the base of the tower.

The steeple was repaired by George Gwilt in 1818–20. The upper part, badly damaged from corrosion of the iron cramps used to hold the stone work together, was taken down and rebuilt. Gwilt shortened the spire and renewed the Portland stone upper columns with Aberdeen granite. Subjected to incendiary bombing, the church was once again destroyed by fire in May 1941. The tower, steeple, crypt and outer walls of the church survived. The church was rebuilt in 1956–64 by Laurence King with new fittings.

St Mary-at-Hill

St Mary-at-Hill is the church on the hill above Billingsgate, known also as St Mary de Hull, St Mary de la Hulle and Sancta Maria ad Montem. The earliest references to it are in the time of King John (1199–1216). It was rebuilt in 1487–1501 and repaired and beautified in 1616. The tower, at the west end of the church, intruded into the nave. There were doors in the centres of both north and south fronts, marking the position of what were described as transepts, giving the church a prominent cross-axis. Although severely damaged in the Great Fire, the church was not totally destroyed. By the Act of 1670 the parish was united with that of St Andrew Hubbard.

On 7 August 1669 the churchwardens of the parish were authorised to get Edward Jarman, the City Surveyor, and other 'able workmen' to view the church. As a result a committee was appointed to 'contract and bargain with Workmen to secure the Steeple and Walls'. Little had, however, been done by 1670 other than the clearing of the rubbish from the ruins.

St Mary-at-Hill was, in July 1670, the first parish to make a deposit of £500 in the Chamber of London, a claim for early consideration by the Commissioners. The first contract, with Joshua Marshall, mason, is dated 1 November 1670. It was for him to rebuild the frontispiece, or east wall, with new foundations, a rubble wall, ashlar pilasters, mouldings and cornice, 'according to a design given to him'. For the four capitals, three festoons and two urns Marshall was to receive £40. Thomas Lock, carpenter, received his contract on 3 December 1670. This provided for a new roof of 'good oaken timber, according to a design and Modell'. The design was roughly sketched in the book of contracts and shows that the roof was to be supported upon four columns with the main timber beams laid across them. A further contract to Thomas Lock, dated 24 June 1671, provided for the building of a 'lanthorn upon the middle of St Mary Hill'. The rebuilding of the church began in 1670 and continued until 1674.

An examination of the fabric shows that in the rebuilding the existing north and south walls were retained, although increased in height. The tower was also retained but repaired. A new west wall was provided to the east of the tower, as well as the new east wall noted in Marshall's contract. His bill shows payment for the capitals and festoons but not for urns, which presumably by then were no longer included. The construction included the four columns supporting the roof, and a shallow saucer-shaped dome with lantern.

FIGURE 141. St Mary-at-Hill, east front, built 1670–74. Reconstruction by Richard Lea, 1996.

The design of the capitals has given rise to much comment. Hatton in his *A New View of London*, described those of the east window as being of the 'workman's own invention', a remark repeated elsewhere and taken to support the view that Wren left such design details to his craftsmen. They are, however, capitals of a Composite order described by Serlio and, as such, would have been known to both Hooke and Wren. Similar capitals are used on the steeple of St Mary-le-Bow.

A vestry minute of 23 November 1694 records that the church was 'under repair at the Public Charge', but no detail is given of what was being done or why. The building accounts record work on the steeple, including a lanthorn, i.e. a lantern, carrying a copper vane, and repairs to the church roof. Matthew Roberts, plumber, was paid for 'covering the timber work of the two lanthornes', suggesting that the lead covering of the shallow dome was repaired at this time.

Repairs, 1668–1670, £223 15s. 0d.

Craftsmen: James Florey, mason; Thomas Norfolke, bricklayer; Robert Harris, carpenter; Anthony Ives, smith; John Dawson, labourer.

Reconstruction of the Church and Tower, 1670–74, £3756 17s. 3d.

Craftsmen: Joshua Marshall, mason; Thomas Lock, carpenter; William Cleere, joiner; John George, plumber; George Drew, smith; John Grove, plasterer; John Ayliffe, glazier; Margaret Pearce, painter.

Repairs to Church, Tower and Steeple, 1694–95, £1143 10s. 5d.

Craftsmen: Christopher Kempster, mason; Abraham Wilkins, carpenter; Matthew Roberts, plumber; Thomas Colbourn, smith; Robert Rowland, coppersmith; Henry Doogood, plasterer; John Ayliffe, glazier; William Thompson, painter.

Total cost, £5137 2s. 8d., including £13 by which Kempster's bill was abated.

The body of the church is approximately square, but with the east wall on the street, known confusingly also as St Mary-at-Hill, at an angle to the north and south sides. The entrances on the north and south fronts continued in use following the seventeenth-century reconstruction, but have since been replaced by others in the vestibules to the north and south of the tower. The perpendicular windows of the north and south fronts have been replaced with round-headed windows. The extensive rebuilding of the upper parts of the church since Wren's time makes it difficult to be sure of how it was left, but the intersecting barrel-vaulting with semicircular dome, described in some books as by Wren, was by Savage.

The church was rebuilt largely of stone rubble, but with ashlar facing at the east end. It includes a Venetian window, now blocked, and round-headed windows to the north and south. These were originally decorated with the festoons recorded in Marshall's contract and in his bill. Above the windows is now a broken cornice and a broken pediment with semi-circular window, now blocked. This is a part of the reconstruction by Savage.

The first impression of the interior, before the fire of 1988, that this church preserved its late seventeenth-century fittings, is misleading. Much of what could then be seen is the work of William Gibbs Rogers in seventeenth-century style. This includes the pulpit with its sounding-board dated 1849. The lectern with lion and unicorn has the same date and the letters V. R. It is uncertain how much of the reredos is from the seventeenth century. It is of three bays, that in the middle flanked by Corinthian columns supporting an enriched entablature and round arch enclosing round-headed panels. It is much decorated with foliage, fruit, flowers and a crown. Above the arch is a segmental pediment with cherub heads and a book in the tympanum. The octagonal font, of white marble with a domed ogee cover, is probably that supplied in 1680–81 for the use of the united parishes. (At the time of writing the furniture and fittings have yet to be returned to the church following its reconstruction after the fire.)

Major changes were made to the west end of the church by George Gwilt

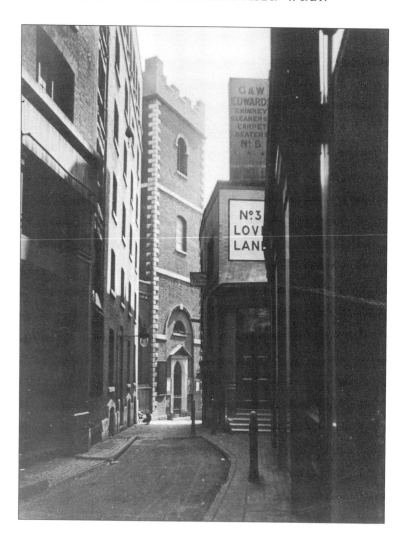

FIGURE 142.
St Mary-at-Hill,
tower viewed from
Lovat Lane. (*NMR*)

in 1787–89. The tower was rebuilt in brick, losing its octagonal turret. The west walls of the church were also rebuilt of brick and the late gothic windows replaced by round-headed ones. In 1827–28 James Savage rebuilt both the north and south walls of the church and replaced the roof to the present design. He undertook further restoration in 1848–49. The church escaped serious damage in the war of 1939–45 and was restored by Seely and Paget in 1967–68. A serious fire in May 1988 again resulted in the closure of the church. The dome was again destroyed and there was serious damage to the roof and to the pewing. The church has been restored by The Conservation Practice, architect John Barnes.

St Mary Somerset

St Mary Somerset was on the north side of Upper Thames Street on the corner of Old Fish Street Hill (or Labour-in-Vain) Hill. The title 'Somerset' is said to derive from Summer's Hithe – a small port or haven. The earliest mention seems to have been in the reign of Richard I (1189–99). A plan of the old church, drawn from the ruins, almost certainly by Christopher Kempster, shows it as somewhat larger than the building which replaced it, with its tower on the north side. By the Act of 1670 the parish was united with that of St Mary Mounthaw.

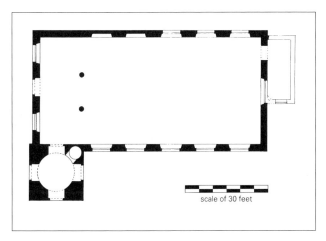

FIGURE 143. St Mary Somerset, plan. (*PJ*)

scale of 30 feet

There is no further record of the church or parish in the Commissioners' orders. It must be concluded that the vestries of the two very poor parishes were not active in seeking an early rebuilding. The vestry minutes have not survived, but the churchwardens' accounts of St Mary Somerset suggest that, other than pull down the old steeple in 1668 or 1669, nothing was done until 1685, when some of the parishioners went to see Sir Christopher Wren. There was minor expenditure with 'Kemsell the the mason' (Christopher Kempster), who came to view the church prior to beginning work. The first measurement was on 22 July 1686, by which time a great deal had been done, including pulling down old walls and digging new foundations for the tower to a depth of eighteen feet into wet ground.

The site of the tower was moved from its pre-Fire position against the north wall to the south-west corner, fronting both Old Fish Street Hill and, more importantly, Thames Street, improving the appearance of the building. A strip of land had already been taken by the City to widen Thames Street, reducing the width available for the church. Work on the church continued until 1688 and then ceased. By that time the roof had been installed and covered with lead

FIGURE 144.
St Mary Somerset, tower
viewed from Thames
Street. Drawn by
W. Niven, *c.* 1885.

and the ceilings plastered. Christopher Kempster resumed work in 1689 and the church was finished in 1694. The parish was, apparently, unable to meet the costs of fitting and furnishing and, as with St Andrew-by-the-Wardrobe, these were met by the Commissioners.

Reconstruction of the Church and Tower, 1685–88; 1689–94, £6579 18s. 1¼d.

Craftsmen: Christopher Kempster, mason; John Evans, bricklayer; James Grove, carpenter; William Cleere, joiner; Charles Hobson, joiner; Matthew Roberts, plumber; Thomas Hodgkins, smith; Henry Doogood, plasterer; Matthew Jarman, glazier; Edward Bird, painter; Bartholomew Scott, labourer and carter; James Hurst, labourer.

The interior of the church was quite plain, with two columns at the west end supporting a gallery with a panelled front, in the centre of which were the royal arms, framed on canvas. The ceiling was flat, coved at the sides and groined to the windows. The tower, with pinnacles rising to a height of 120 feet, is faced with Portland stone. The bell-loft windows are round-headed, with keystones carved as masks. The tower is completed with an entablature and plain parapet supporting eight panelled pedestals. Those at the angles have tall vases, those in the centre of each side have tall obelisks, each with enriched bands and a ball finial.

The church of St Mary Somerset was demolished in 1671, leaving the tower free-standing.

St Mary Woolnoth

The name Woolnoth may be related to the church's proximity to the wool-market, but is generally supposed to be that of its builder or benefactor. It now occupies a prominent site in the City, at the junction of Lombard and King William Streets, but in medieval times it was largely hemmed in, with its north front to Lombard Street and its west end facing a small courtyard. The earliest record is from the twelfth century. The church was rebuilt about 1438 and a chapel and steeple added in 1485. The church was either rebuilt or extensively renovated and restored in 1620.

St Mary Woolnoth, although severely damaged in the Great Fire, was not completely destroyed. Some at least of the walls seemingly remained intact, enabling an early start to be made on the reconstruction. The records of this have been lost, although the orders of the Commissioners indicate that the rebuilding was undertaken by Sir Robert Vyner, a prominent citizen of the parish, goldsmith and later Lord Mayor of London. From time to time sums were impressed to him from the coal tax fund to a total of £3202 7s. 2d. The full amount had been spent by 1674. The craftsmen's names are not recorded, nor the work described.

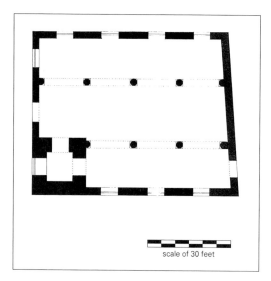

scale of 30 feet

FIGURE 145. St Mary Woolnoth, plan of the church as completed in 1674, based on Ogilby's map of 1676. (PJ)

No detailed or exact plan has been found to show the church, but in its structural features it must have followed the design of the church as restored in 1620. It was not completely rectangular but had its east wall aligned to a lane which separated the church from Sir Robert Vyner's own house. The south-east corner of the church was occupied by a chapel containing Vyner tombs, with a Vyner vault below. The reconstruction of the plan of the church (Fig. 145) is based upon Ogilby's map of 1677, which shows the disposition of the columns and the tower on the south-west corner. Hatton described the church as mostly of stone, with the new front to Lombard Street of freestone. The new work on the church was said to be of the Tuscan order, with the rest of the building remaining in the gothic style. The flat ceiling was supported by columns, of which the two middle were enriched with vines – doubtless in honour of Sir Robert Vyner. There were galleries on the south and west sides.

It was not long before it became apparent that the reconstruction of the church was unsatisfactory. Repairs were necessary in 1690–91, but by 1703 the vestry was again considering a rebuilding of the steeple. They approached the House of Commons and, after a number of abortive attempts, succeeded in getting a clause added to a Bill to enable the Commissioners appointed under the Fifty New Churches Act of 1711 to rebuild the whole church. The rebuilding was undertaken in 1716–27 to the design of Nicholas Hawksmoor.

St Mary Magdalen Old Fish Street

The church of St Mary Magdalen was situated on Old Fish Street (or Knightrider Street), at its junction with Old Change. The earliest mention seems to have been in 1162 and there are early references to it as St Mary Magdalen apud Sanctum Paulum and St Mary Magdalen in Piscaria. Stow reported that it was repaired and beautified in 1630. In the Act of 1670 the parish was united with that of St Gregory-by-St-Paul's.

It was not until the end of 1682 that the Commissioners indicated that the rebuilding of St Mary Magdalen should be then put in hand and carried on 'as far as the accounts will beare'. The church-wardens' accounts record minor expenditure in 1683 in going to Sir Christopher Wren. It seems that the church was put in hand at some time in that year. The mason's bills indicate that some of the old foundations were excavated and new ones provided, notably for the tower and the north wall adjoining. Some of the old foundations were reused, however, and possibly also some of the old masonry walls. The shell of the building was completed in 1685 and the building itself by 1687, including the steeple, a vault at the east end and a gallery.

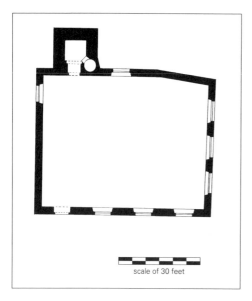

FIGURE 146. St Mary Magdalen Old Fish Street, plan. (*PJ*)

scale of 30 feet

Construction of Church, Tower and Steeple, 1683–87, £4315 12s. 10d.

Craftsmen: Edward Strong, mason; Israel Knowles, carpenter; Richard Kedge, joiner; Jonathan Maine, carver; Matthew Roberts, plumber; John Winckles, plumber; Thomas Hodgkins, smith; Robert Bird, coppersmith; Henry Doogood, plasterer; Job Claridge, glazier; Edward Bird, painter; Bartholomew Scott, carter and labourer.

This was an average-sized church, rectangular in shape, with the tower and steeple close to the north-west angle. It was constructed of stone rubble, with Portland stone facings on the south and east fronts towards Old Change and

Old Fish Street. The tower was stone-faced, and the steeple above it also of stone in the form of an octagonal pyramid of five stone steps to give a platform for the octagonal lantern above which was a short, concave, stone steeple. This was capped with a finial in the form of an urn, presumably St Mary Magdalen's unguent pot.

On 2 December 1886 the church was severely damaged by a fire that broke out in a neighbouring warehouse. Although insured and reparable, the opportunity was taken to close the building and unite the parish with St Martin Ludgate. The site was sold in 1892 and the ruined church demolished the following year.

FIGURE 147.
St Mary Magdalen
Old Fish Street,
from the south east.
(*The Builder*, 1886)

St Matthew Friday Street

The church was on the west side of Friday Street, not far from its junction with Cheapside. It was first recorded about the year 1261. The late medieval church was repaired and beautified in 1632–33 and destroyed in the Fire of 1666. By the Act of 1670 the parish was united with that of St Peter Cheap.

The Commissioners noted that they had hopes of obtaining a clause in an Act of Parliament for changing the place to some more convenient situation. No details of any firm proposals have been found. The situation was resolved in March 1682 when the vestry agreed to add to the site a piece of parish land to enable a larger church to be built. Work then seems to have begun, probably in 1682, and to have been finished by 1685.

Construction of the Church and Tower, 1682–85, £2309 8s. 2d.

Craftsmen: Edward Pearce, mason; Thomas Horn, bricklayer; John Longland, carpenter; William Cleere, joiner; Matthew Roberts, plumber; Samuel Colbourn, smith; Stephen Leaver, smith; Henry Doogood and James Grove, plasterers; Elizabeth Peowrie, glazier; Edward Bird, painter.

The church was slightly irregular in shape but roughly rectangular. It was among the cheapest of the churches to be erected at the time, being built largely of rubble and lacking much by way of decorative features. Only the east wall, facing Friday Street, was faced with stone. This had five round-headed windows with cherub-headed keystones, separated by flat pilasters of the Doric order, and raised above a plain stylobate occupying the full length of the east front. Entrance to the church was from alley ways to the north and south. The tower, of brick, had no steeple or decoration of any kind. It was the plainest of all the City church towers, commensurate perhaps with the observation that there was nowhere from which it could be seen. The church was demolished in 1886.

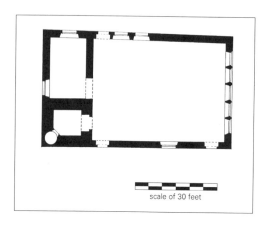

scale of 30 feet

FIGURE 148. St Matthew Friday Street, plan. (*PJ*)

FIGURE 149. St Matthew Friday Street, from the south east. Drawn by J. Coney, etched by
J. Skelton, for the *Architectural Series of London* (1814)

St Michael Bassishaw

After St Mary, St Michael was the most popular of all the City dedications, with no fewer than seven of the pre-Fire churches named in his honour. All were destroyed in the Great Fire and all but St Michael-le-Quern were rebuilt. The church of St Michael Bassishaw was on the west side of Basinghall Street. The name Bassishaw is probably derived from the Basing family, prominent in the City in the thirteenth and fourteenth centuries. The church was first recorded in 1196: the remains of this church were identified in late nineteenth-century excavations, although its form was not then established. Further excavations in 1965 revealed the eastern end of this church with an apsidal chancel. The north wall had been built over earlier Roman and medieval rubbish pits: the presence of two piers adjacent to it suggests that at some time subsidence had taken place and the wall had been strengthened with buttresses. The twelfth-century church was rebuilt in the fifteenth century and repaired and beautified in 1630 before its destruction in 1666.

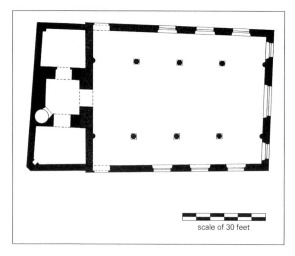

scale of 30 feet

FIGURE 150. St Michael Bassishaw, plan. (PJ)

St Michael, as all churches added to the building programme in 1675, was built 'upon the extraordinary'. A contract was signed for the work to be done by John Fitch, a bricklayer by trade but who here seems to have acted as general contractor. The intention was to rebuild the church upon its old foundations. The nineteenth-century excavations revealed, however, that at the east end Fitch must have encountered problems with these. He removed them and piled the ground. There is a suspicion that Fitch's work may not have been all of the quality expected. Some of it certainly had to be redone. The Corinthian columns supporting the roof were later described as 'specimens of . . . jerry-building . . . made up of several sorts of materials and plastered over'.

This was undoubtedly a 'utility' or 'economy' church, with little money spent

FIGURE 151. St Michael Bassishaw, east front. (*NMR*)

upon decoration or embellishment. Not only were the walls faced with brick instead of stone, it was covered with Padstow slates instead of lead. It was glazed and plastered by early 1679 and completed later that year.

In 1700 the parish reported the roof to be unsatisfactory – it may have had too low a pitch for a slate roof. Work on the church started again in 1712 and continued into 1713. The upper part of the tower was pulled down and rebuilt. It was then given its balustrade with pineapples and a lead-covered timber steeple and lantern. William Knight, plumber, replaced the slating, covering the roof with lead.

Construction of the Church and Tower, 1676–79, £2822 17s. 1d.

Craftsmen: John Fitch, contractor; James Flory, mason; Thomas Dobbins, plumber; Thomas Hodgkins, smith; Richard Howes, smith; John Sherwood, plasterer; George Peowrie, glazier; Mary Eden (Grimes), painter.

Repairs and Construction of the Steeple, 1712–14, £2830 12s. 3¼ d.

Craftsmen: William Kempster, mason; Matthew Fortnam, bricklayer; Richard Jennings, carpenter; William Knight, plumber; Thomas Robinson, smith; Andrew Niblett, coppersmith; Chrysostom Wilkins, plasterer; Matthew Jarman, glazier; Joseph Thompson, painter.

Total cost £5703 9s. 4¼ d.

Architecturally the exterior was undistinguished except for the tower, steeple and east end. The steeple consisted of an octagonal drum supporting a lantern which had a short, concave, pyramidal spire rising to a ball and vane. The interior was also quite plain, with six Corinthian columns dividing the church into nave and aisles. The church was closed for repairs on 27 April 1892 but concern for the safety of the building led to its permanent closure and to its demolition in 1899.

St Michael Cornhill

The church is on the south side of Cornhill, hidden behind a façade of shops. St Michael's Alley leads past the west end of the church, where a Victorian porch now provides the principal entrance. The recorded gift of the church to the Abbey of Evesham about the year 1055 provides evidence of a Saxon foundation. The medieval church was one of the more important in London, with a cloister and preaching cross, said to be similar to that at St Paul's. The tower was a prominent City landmark. with a spire and tall pinnacles. The tower was burnt or fell down in the year 1421 and was rebuilt in somewhat similar form, but without the spire. The church was repaired in 1618–20 and again in 1633.

The church was destroyed in the Great Fire but the walls of the tower remained standing. The timber flooring and roofing had burnt, and the bells had melted, but the walls remaining could, it was thought, be restored. On 3 October 1667 the vestry ordered that Mr Shorthose and Mr Cartwright, masons, together with some of the parishioners 'who are willing to go up into the Steeple', should view it and that an effort should be made to preserve it from 'weather and falling'. Early in 1668 the vestry contracted with a Mr Miller for the carpentry work to restore the tower and a 'Mr Flaxmore' (Flaxney) was employed to cover the roof with lead. Also in 1668 John Partridge was paid

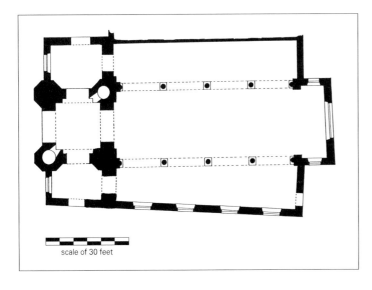

scale of 30 feet

FIGURE 152.
St Michael Cornhill, plan.
(*PJ*)

£5 10s. 0d. for making a new vane and trimming two others to complete the restoration of the tower with its four pinnacles.

With its tower completed, the vestry turned to the rebuilding of its church. In 1669 the Rector, Dr Meriton, was to advise with skilful workmen concerning the work to be done and a 'model or design' was to be procured. This model was apparently available by November of that year, when Nicholas Young signed an agreement to perform the mason's work according to the model then shown to him. Further agreements were signed with William Miller, carpenter, Floyden, bricklayer, and Jeffrey Flaxney, plumber. In May 1670 Nicholas Young agreed to provide three columns, two half columns and four arches for the south side of the building, to match those that he had already provided for the north side; while in June Jeffrey Flaxney, plumber, agreed to cover the north aisle with lead. Work on the building continued, apparently without a break, and the church was in its essentials completed by 1672.

The repairs to the tower and the rebuilding of the church had been undertaken with the aid of subscriptions from the parishioners and from donations received. It was directed by the churchwardens, assisted by the Rector. At no time does Sir Christopher Wren appear to have been consulted and the vestry minutes contain no reference to him or to any of his officers. It was not until June 1670 that the Commissioners became involved and then only to the extent of allocating a sum of £2500 for the church, a figure estimated to be about half of what would be required. A further sum was set aside in October of that year. By this time the design of the church had long been established and most of it built. Neither Wren nor Hooke can have had any impact upon this design.

The rebuilt church was apparently sound but, by the end of the century, the tower was found to be suffering from structural faults. In 1703 the vestry petitioned the Commissioners for it to be rebuilt and secured an order for it to be done. The parishioners soon complained that they could not get the order complied with. There were competing demands upon the residue of the coal tax fund and St Michael Cornhill had no claim on priority. As a result of an appeal to the Lord Chancellor, 'whose Ancistors ly interr'd in the Cloyster of our Church', work on the tower began under William Dickinson. By December 1717 the churchwardens reported that 'the workmen had left off going on with the steeple'. The money from the coal tax, levied for the rebuilding of the City churches after the Great Fire, had finally run out.

In 1718 the vestry petitioned the House of Commons and, supported by the Lord Chancellor, obtained a new Act to enable the tower to be completed by the Commissioners appointed under the 1711 Fifty New Churches Act. Work resumed soon after and, after a break in 1719–20 due to financial difficulties of the Commissioners, it was again resumed and completed in 1722. While the known documentary sources contain no reference to the authorship if the design, there can be little doubt that the upper parts are by Hawksmoor, the lower by Dickinson.

Reconstruction of the Church and Tower, 1669–72, £4686 10s. 4d.

Craftsmen: Nicholas Young, mason; Anthony Tanner, bricklayer; Robert Day, carpenter; Thomas Gammon, carpenter; William Cleere, joiner; Jeffrey Flexney, plumber; Walter Clements, smith; George Drew, smith; John Grove, plasterer; John Odell, glazier; Robert Streeter, painter; Henry Russell, labourer.

Demolition and Initial Work on the New Tower, 1715–17, £1723 10s. 7d.

Craftsman: Edward Strong junior, mason.

Completion of the Tower, 1718–22, £6451 9s. 9d.

Craftsmen: Edward Strong, mason; Henry Hester, bricklayer; John Grove, carpenter; John Brooks, carpenter; Joseph Wade, carver; John Cleave, smith; John Robins, smith; Richard Marples, plumber; George Osmond, plumber; Henry Savage, plumber; Chrysostom Wilkins, plasterer; Joseph Goodchild, glazier; James Preedy, painter.

Total cost of pulling down the old tower and rebuilding the new £12,861 10s. 8d.

The church of St Michael Cornhill is an irregular rectangle, divided into nave and aisles by six Doric columns supporting round arches. It has a plain, groined ceiling. The south wall now has gothic windows, formerly round-headed, as was the east window.

FIGURE 153. St Michael Cornhill, south front and tower. Drawn by R. W. Billings and engraved by J. le Keux. (*Godwin and Britton*, 1838)

The tower, completed in Portland stone, is both massive and stately, rising on four giant legs forming tall, elegant arches, of which that to the east is open to the church. The plainness of the lower stories contrasts markedly with the rich detailing of the upper stages. The panelled corner turrets extend through the belfry for a further story before terminating in crocketed pinnacles. The panelling at the belfry stage is decorated with carved heads, alternating young and old.

The church was restored in 1790; and again in 1858–60 by Sir Gilbert Scott, with much additional carving by William Gibb Rogers. The church was once again restored in 1960.

St Michael Crooked Lane

The earliest recorded date appears to be 1291, when the church was noted as St Michaelis de Candelwik, taking its name from Candelwick Street – the modern Cannon Street. It was on the east side of Miles's Lane, later Crooked Lane. The first church was probably quite small and was replaced by a larger building with nave, choir and aisles at some time between 1366 and 1368. It was altered and enlarged in 1381 or soon after by William Walworth, Lord Mayor of London, who added a further south aisle and a chapel dedicated to St Peter, known as the Fishmongers' Chapel. He also made the church collegiate: the college and the parish existed side by side until 1548, when the college was suppressed.

After the destruction in the fire of 1666, the shell of the church remained together with the tower. The first move towards a rebuilding seems to have been in 1682, when the churchwardens approached the Commissioners. Work began in 1685 and continued to 1688, when it stopped with the ceiling plastered, the windows glazed and the body of the church apparently structurally finished. The tower was then incomplete, lacking the bell-loft and the upper parts of the structure. Work resumed in 1697 and the church was completed in 1698.

At that time the tower, rising to a height of about a hundred feet, was crowned with a parapet having open stonework with, at the four corners, stone pyramids two feet six inches in height and one foot six inches square at the base. These were topped with urns or vases with flames. The vases did not last long, being damaged in a severe storm on the night of 27 November 1703, then removed. In 1711 work began again with the removal of stonework from the top of the tower to give an access-point for the new steeple which was completed in 1714.

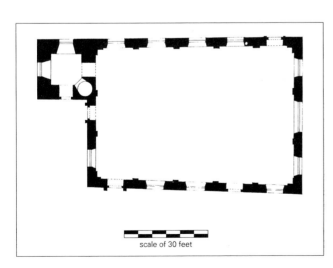

scale of 30 feet

FIGURE 154. St Michael Crooked Lane, plan. (*PJ*)

FIGURE 155. St Michael Crooked Lane. (*Guildhall Library*)

Reconstruction of the Church, 1685–88, £4541 5*s.* 11*d.*

Craftsmen: William Hammond, mason; John Evans, bricklayer; Robert Day, carpenter; Matthew Bankes, carpenter; Thomas Denning, carpenter; James Grove, carpenter; William Cleere, joiner; Henry Brooks, smith; Elizabeth Clay, smith; Edward Phillips, plumber; James Thompson, glazier; Henry Doogood and John Grove, plasterers; Bartholomew Scott, labourer and carter.

Completion of the Tower, 1697–98, £1494 4*s.* 3½*d.*

Craftsmen: John Clarke, mason; Abraham Jordan, carpenter; Thomas Denning, carpenter; Jonathan Maine, carver; Thomas Colbourn, smith; Matthew Roberts, plumber; James Thompson, glazier; Henry Doogood, plasterer; William Thompson, painter.

Construction of the Steeple, 1711–14, £2035 14*s.* 2½*d.*

Craftsmen: Edward Strong junior, mason; Matthew Portman, bricklayer; Richard Jennings, carpenter; Thomas Robinson, smith; Andrew Niblet, coppersmith;

FIGURE 156.
St Michael Crooked
Lane, south front,
tower and steeple,
1831. (*NMR*)

Joseph Roberts, plumber; Chrysostom Wilkins, plasterer; Joseph Thompson, painter.

Total cost, £8086 4s. 5d., including £15 to Bartholomew Scott for materials.

The building was slightly irregular in outline, suggesting that the old foundations were probably reused. The auditorium was undivided and the ceiling flat, coved to the walls and groined to the windows. The building, inside and out, had a somewhat plain appearance, although additional plasterwork in the form of a large expanded flower was added to the ceiling in 1775.

The steeple rose from the tower in four stages; the first three as drums with diminishing diameter, supporting the fourth stage, in the form of a flask or onion with elongated neck, mounted on three steps. The construction was of timber, lead-covered. The steeple was decorated with a series of wooden urns, turned from elm but again lead-covered. The mason, Edward Strong, provided four stone 'octangular' vases six feet two inches in height for the corners of the parapet, occupying the former positions of the pinnacles.

The decision of the Corporation of London to rebuild London Bridge up-river from the old bridge required the construction of a new approach road from the north. This in turn required the destruction of much property in the parish, including the church and churchyard. After considerable opposition to the plan, the churchwardens surrendered the church to the Corporation on 22 March 1831 and it was pulled down shortly afterwards.

St Michael Paternoster Royal

Paternoster is said to derive from the former Paternoster Lane, probably from the paternoster or rosary makers who lived there. Royal is derived from Riole or Reole, a small town near Bordeaux, a reminder of the former wine trade in this Vintry Ward of the City. The earliest mention of the church is in 1241–42. In 1409 a part of a vacant plot in the street called 'le Ryole' was granted for the rebuilding of the parish church. The most famous citizen of the parish, Richard Whittington, four times Lord Mayor of the City, founded a college here, suppressed in 1548. The church is on the east side of College Hill. Following destruction in 1666, the parish was united with that of St Martin Vintry.

The church was one of the last of the City to be rebuilt. Edward Strong senior, mason, began in 1685 with the demolition of the tower and what then remained of the walls. New foundations were provided at the east end of the church, and a vestry built behind the east window of the church attached to the middle of the east wall. This may have occupied the position of the late medieval chancel. Work continued to 1688 but then ceased, with Edward Strong covering what had then been built of the walls of both church and tower. Work began again in 1689 and continued until the church was finished in 1694. The tower had by then been completed with an open-work parapet but lacked its steeple. This was added in 1713–17 by Edward Strong junior at a contract price of £1050, with a further £70 for vases added to it.

Construction of the Church and Tower, 1685–88; 1689–94, £7455 7s. 10¼d.

Craftsmen: Edward Strong, senior, mason; Thomas Denning, carpenter; William Cleere, joiner; Thomas Dobbins, plumber; Henry Brooks, smith; Humphrey Clay, smith; Henry Doogood, plasterer; Samuel Rainger, glazier; Edward Bird, painter;

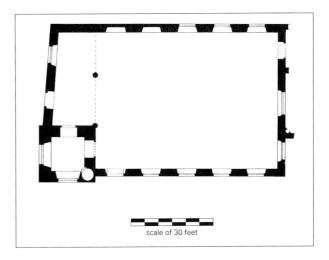

scale of 30 feet

FIGURE 157. St Michael Paternoster Royal, plan. (*PJ*)

FIGURE 158. St Michael Paternoster Royal, south front, tower and steeple, 1962. (*NMR*)

William Thompson, painter; James Hurst, carter and labourer.

Construction of the Steeple, 1713–17, £1403 4s. 0d.

Craftsmen: Edward Strong, junior, mason; Richard Jennings, carpenter; Thomas Robinson, smith; Andrew Niblett, coppersmith; Joseph Roberts, plumber; Joseph Thompson, painter.

Payments were made also for minor work in the church to Thomas Robinson, smith; Matthew Jarman, glazier; Christopher Wilkins, plasterer; and Joseph Thompson, painter.

Total cost £8937 1s. 0¼ d.

The south front of the church has five round-headed windows, with cherub heads as keystones. A cherub keystone is used also for the segmental-headed doorway on the south side, formerly blocked but now used as the main entrance to the building. The interior of the church is also plain, the principal decoration being the plasterwork of the ceiling planels. The stone statues of Moses and Aaron now in the church are from the altar-piece of All Hallows-the-Great. The figure of charity below the lectern is also from All Hallows.

The church was severely damaged in 1944, although the tower and steeple remained. In the reconstruction the number of bays has been reduced from five to four, with the west end of the church converted to office accommodation.

St Michael Queenhithe

The church is named Queenhithe from the hithe or haven by the river. The earliest record of the church is in the twelfth century as St Michael de Aedredshud. Other names include St Michael de Quenhith, St Michael in Huda, St Michael de Hutha Regina, St Michael super Ripam Regine and St Michael upon Thames. It was situated on the north side of Thames Street. Following the destruction of the church in 1666, the parish was united with that of Holy Trinity-the-Less.

The building accounts indicate that by 1676 walls of the church and the tower were being demolished and the stone recovered ready for rebuilding. By this time the Commissioners had given their approval for the church to be rebuilt on the extraordinary. Construction of the new building started with James Flory, mason, paid for '23 rodd of rubble in the foundations of the church and steeple'. These were provided for the new south wall, which was set back from the line of the demolished medieval south wall, and for the tower. This too may have been set back. The north and east walls of the church were probably constructed upon the old foundations and utilised some at least of the old walling. This was noted when the church was finally demolished. The church was completed by 1686.

Construction of the Church, Tower and Steeple, 1676–86, £4375 10s. 0¾d.

Craftsmen: James Flory, mason; Samuel Fulkes, mason; John Bridges, bricklayer; Thomas Warren, bricklayer and tiler; Matthew Banckes, carpenter; Robert Layton, joiner; Sarah Freeman, plumber; Matthew Roberts, plumber; Samuel Colbourn, smith; Stephen Leaver, smith; Robert Bird, coppersmith; Henry Doogood and John Grove, plasterers; Edward Jarman, glazier; Samuel Oliver, glazier; Edward Bird, painter; Thomas Laine, painter; Edward Hide and John Pledge, labourers*; John Hoy and Joseph Simpson, labourers.

*and others, unnamed.

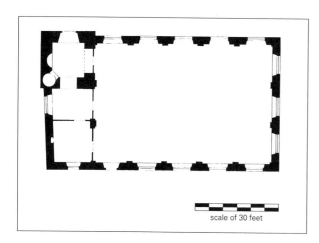

scale of 30 feet

FIGURE 159. St Michael Queenhithe, plan. *(PJ)*

The church had five bays to the north and south with three to the east. The fenestration included round-headed windows in the lower tier with circular windows over, separated by swags or festoons of flowers and fruit carved in stone. The interior had no columns or arches and the roof was flat, forming a single panel separated from the coving by an ornamental band. In the angle between the church and the tower was a vestibule and entrance lobby at a lower level than the church, giving access from Thames Street.

The tower had round-headed windows with simple moulded architraves but otherwise devoid of decoration. The steeple consisted of an ascent of four steps to a panelled pedestal supporting a panelled obelisk with ball finial. The whole of the steeple was of timber, lead-covered. The spire was topped with a vane in the form of a three-masted barque, fully rigged, in gilded copper. The church was demolished in 1876.

FIGURE 160. St Michael Queenhithe, south front, tower and steeple. Drawn by W. Niven.

St Michael Wood Street

St Michael Wood Street was on the west side of the street, close to its junction with what is now Gresham Street. The church was first recorded about 1225 as St Michael de Wodestrate but known also as St Michael Hoggenelane. The church was repaired about 1394, and repaired again and beautified in 1620. Following the Great Fire the parish was united with that of St Mary Staining.

In November 1670 the Commissioners granted the sum of £150 which, together with the £500 deposited by the parish with the Chamber of London, was used to provide a new roof for what remained of the old building. The work was completed by February 1671 but it soon became apparent that further repairs would be needed. In May 1671 a contract was given to Thomas Wise, mason, 'to take down the walls of the East and South Side[s] to the Ground and a foot and a half if necessary within ground . . .' New walls were constructed of stone rubble, mostly taken from the old walls but supplemented with seventy-two tons from

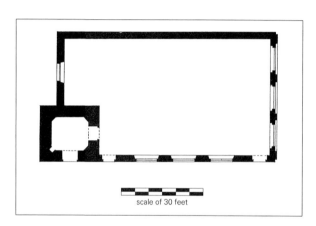

scale of 30 feet

FIGURE 161. St Michael Wood Street, plan. (PJ)

St Paul's Cathedral. Work continued until 1675 and included the renewal of the top of the tower and the construction of battlements. Further work on the tower in 1686–87 included the provision of a new lantern.

Reroofing the Church and Repairs, 1670–75, £2301 10s. 1½ d.

Craftsmen: Thomas Wise, mason; Richard Cobett, bricklayer; Samuel Lynn, carpenter; Richard Lens, joiner; Nathaniel Cham, plumber; Tohn Talbot, plumber; Joseph Wheatley, smith; Joseph Sherwood and Daniel Morrice, plasterers; William Browne, glazier; Robert Streeter, painter.

Repairs to Tower and Lantern, 1686–87, £238 14s. 9d.

Craftsmen: John Hayward, carpenter; John Longland, carpenter; John Talbot, plumber; Samuel Colebourn, smith; Robert Bird, coppersmith; Edward Bird, painter.

Total cost £2554 12s. 10½d., including £14 8s. 0d. for the stone rubble from St Paul's.

The church was not quite square, with the east end wider than the west. The tower on the south-west corner intruded partly into the church, but also projected beyond the west wall. The interior was described as very plain with a flat ceiling coved to the north and south walls. The lantern and cupola seem to have been lost at the end of the eighteenth century, when the spire was added. The church was demolished as redundant in 1897.

FIGURE 162.
St Michael Wood Street, from the south east. Drawn by J. Coney, etched by J. Skelton, for the *Architectural Series of London Churches* (1814)

St Mildred Bread Street

St Mildred, on the east side of Bread Street, was dedicated to St Mildred the Virgin, abbess of a convent at Minster in Thanet, Kent, who died about the year 700. The earliest reference to it is in 1170. The stone spire of the late medieval church was struck by lightening in 1559 and taken down. The body of the church was repaired and beautified in 1628, when a new, painted, five-light east window was added and paid for by Sir Nicholas Crisp, a citizen then living in Bread Street. This church had a nave with side aisles separated by columns and arches. It was destroyed in 1666 and the parish united with that of St Margaret Moses.

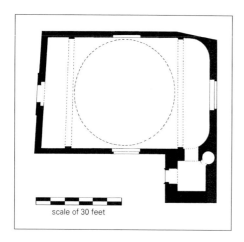

FIGURE 163. St Mildred Bread Street, plan. (*PJ*)

Although the church had been destroyed, the walls were apparently still standing. A roof, probably only a temporary structure, was thrown over these, and pews and a pulpit installed to enable services to continue. This seems to have been organised by the vestry although the cost was met by the Commissioners. By December 1671, however, the building had become dangerous. The walls were then repaired and the building continued in use for a further ten years. In 1680 the vestry decided to approach the Commissioners to press for a rebuilding and, in 1681, the work was put in hand, continuing until 1687. New foundations were provided for the tower, the eastern corners and for the west front. The building accounts record that rubble was brought to St Mildred from the old church of St Peter Cornhill (more probably from St Peter Cheap), and this may have been used for the new foundations.

The choice of a domed ceiling can hardly have been obvious for a rectangular building. Were the churchwardens so impressed with St Stephen Walbrook, with its domed interior, that they wanted something of the kind for St Mildred?

Construction of the Church, Tower and Steeple, 1681–87, £3705 13s. 6d.

Craftsmen: Edward Strong, mason; Thomas Horne, bricklayer; Israel Knowles, carpenter; Thomas Woodstock, carpenter; William Cleere, joiner; Matthew

FIGURE 164. St Mildred Bread Street, interior looking west. (*NMR*)

Roberts, plumber; Samuel Colebourn, smith; Stephen Leaver, smith; Robert Bird, coppersmith; Henry Doogood and John Grove, plasterers; Francis Moor, glazier; Elizabeth Peowrie, glazier; Edward Bird, painter; Bartholomew Scott, labourer and carter.

FIGURE 165. St Mildred Bread Street, south front, tower and steeple. Drawn by J. Coney, etched by J. Skelton, for the *Architectural Series of London Churches* (1812).

The church and tower were constructed largely of brick, but the west front, the only part of the building that could be seen from the street, was faced with Portland stone. It was tall and elegant, reminiscent of a Dutch gable end. The brick, four-stage tower of the church, scarcely visible from the street, was very plain. It was of timber construction, lead-covered. It had a spire in the form of an obelisk with ball-ornaments at the base and vane at the top carrying the monogram MB and the Crisp arms.

The church, with its fittings which had survived with little of no alteration from the late seventeenth century, was destroyed by bombing in 1941.

St Mildred Poultry

St Mildred Poultry, named after the Kentish virgin, was on the north side of Poultry, almost opposite the Mansion House. The earliest surviving record is from 1175 as St Mildrithe. It has also been called St Mildred the Virgin in the Poultry, St Mildred in Poletria, St Mildred de Walbroc and St Mildred near Conhop – a reference to the nearby Conyhope Lane and St Mary Conyhope, a chapel suppressed in the time of Henry VIII. An early church, then in a decayed condition, was pulled down in 1456. According to Stow, the east end of the new church was then built over the Walbrook. It was extensively repaired in 1626 and destroyed in the fire of 1666. The parish was united with that of St Mary Colechurch.

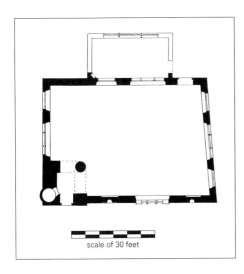

FIGURE 166. St Mildred Poultry, plan. (PJ)

scale of 30 feet

Some work towards restoring the church had been done before the Commissioners took over responsibility for the church in 1670, but it cannot have been much more than clearing the site. Work on the new church began in 1671. It is not known how much of the old walling was retained. As there is no payment for new foundations, it may be assumed there were none. Work on the fabric of the church seems to have been completed by the end of 1674.

Construction of the Church and Tower, 1671–74, £4654 0s. 4¾ d.

Craftsmen: Jaspar Latham, mason; Maurice Emmett, bricklayer; Robert Day, carpenter; Thomas Lock, carpenter; William Cleere, joiner; Charles Atherton, plumber; Nathaniel Cham, plumber; Edmund Smith, smith; William Wells, smith; Henry Doogood and John Grove, plasterers; James Tompion, glazier; Robert Streeter, painter.

The church was built largely of stone rubble with ashlar quoining and Portland stone facings. The north front was stuccoed, probably at a later date. In 1828 Allen reported that the central window of the south front had been blocked and those to either side had been converted into aedicules or niches. This may

FIGURE 167. St Mildred Poultry, south front and tower. Drawn by W. Niven, *c.* 1885.

have been done to reduce street noise from the busy Poultry. The interior of the church was very plain. Its most conspicuous feature was the Ionic column supporting the north-east corner of the tower, located within the body of the church. The flat ceiling of the church was coved to the windows. It was decorated with a large square of husks and a circle composed of fruit with flowers within it.

The tower was small and plain. It was completed with a small cage and a spike that carried a vane in the form of a ship in full sail – the pulpit had a similar motif, its significance now lost. In view of the plainness of the tower, it is not surprising that the churchwardens would have liked a steeple of some sort to complete the design. In 1718 the vestry appealed to the House of Commons. The petition was referred to a Committee of the House, but consequent upon the early rise of the House, the Committee did not report. The vestry minutes record that the consideration of the new spire was adjourned to another opportunity. This, apparently, never came and the spire was never built. Nor is it known if a design was prepared.

The church was demolished in 1872.

St Nicholas Cole Abbey

The church is dedicated to St Nicholas of Bari, a fourth-century bishop of Myra in Lycia. He is the patron saint of children, fishermen, sailors and pawnbrokers; little is known about him, although much appears in legend. The church fronted Old Fish Street, later Knightrider Street, at its junction with Old Fish Street Hill (known also as Labour-in-Vain Hill), but it now stands prominently on the north side of Queen Victoria Street. The earliest references to the church are from 1241–59, when it was called St Nicholas Cold Abbey, possibly a corruption of 'Cold Harbour', i.e. a cold shelter or shelter for travellers. In 1352 a plot of land to the south west of the building was acquired, for use as a churchyard, and in 1377 a further strip along the south side, enabling a south aisle to be added to the church. The tower and steeple were built or rebuilt at that time and new battlements added in 1628. The building was repaired and beautified in 1630. It was destroyed in 1666.

In the 1667 proposals for the grouping of the London parishes, the church of St Nicholas Cole Abbey was not one of those scheduled for rebuilding; instead the parish was to be united with St Mary Magdalen Old Fish Street and St Mary Mounthaw, all three using the church of St Mary Magdalen. In the light of this, and by right of Crown patronage, King Charles II promised the site of St Nicholas to a Lutheran community. It is doubtful if the parishioners were consulted about it and the subsequent reversal of this decision may have been as a result of their diplomatic efforts. A new site was found for the Lutherans and the parish united with that of St Nicholas Olave.

The design of the church seems to have been settled in 1671 or 1672; the work of demolition of the walls and tower probably began soon after. Much of the old walling was then left and was probably used for the rebuilding. The church was roofed and the roof covered with lead in 1676. The plasterwork and glazing were done in

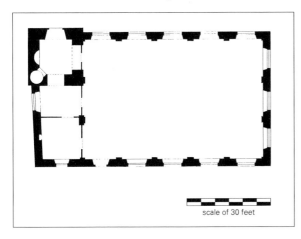

FIGURE 168. St Nicholas Cole Abbey, plan. (*PJ*)

scale of 30 feet

FIGURE 169.
St Nicholas Cole
Abbey, north front,
tower and steeple.
Drawn by
W. Coney, etched
by J. Skelton, for the
*Architectural Series of
London Churches*
(1828)

1677 and the building probably completed in 1678. When the Commissioners introduced their moratorium on the building of towers and steeples, St Nicholas was nearing completion and was specifically excluded. It was probably finished in 1678.

Construction of Church, Tower and Steeple, 1672–78, £5042 6s. 11d.

Craftsmen: Thomas Wise, mason; Matthew Banckes, carpenter; Henry Blowes, carpenter; John Longland, carpenter; William Cleere, joiner; Charles Atherton, plumber; William Savage, plumber; George Drew, smith; Stephen Leaver, smith; Robert Bird, coppersmith; Edward Martin and John Sherwood, plasterers; Richard Bowdler, glazier; Margaret Pearce, painter.

St Nicholas Cole Abbey is a medium-sized church with an open auditorium. The tower is in the north-west corner. A conspicuous feature is the triple-arch arrangement at the west end, with openings to the church at the gallery level. The principal entrance to the church was through a doorway at the base of the tower in Old Fish Street. A further doorway gave access to the churchyard to the south.

The steeple forms the frustum of a cone, constructed of timber, lead-covered with eight concave faces. A small railed gallery is surmounted by an ogee-roof and the finial, originally a gilt ball and vane, but now including a ship in full sail from the demolished church of St Michael Queenhithe.

The construction of Queen Victoria Street in the nineteenth century altered the street pattern of the area, requiring changes to the church. These included a new approach from the south and a remodelling of the interior. By the end of the century, the deterioration of the lead covering of the steeple, and the consequent decay of the timber of which it was constructed, required the rebuilding of the upper part of the tower and the steeple. The church was destroyed by incendiary bombing in May 1941. It was restored from the burnt-out shell by Arthur Bailey and reconsecrated on 10 May 1962. The upper part of the tower was again rebuilt. The church now serves a Presbyterian congregation.

St Olave Jewry

St Olave Jewry was one of a number of City churches dedicated to Olave or Olaf, King of Norway, killed in battle but venerated as a martyr. The church was on the west side of the street called Old Jewry. The earliest record of the church is in an inquisition of 1181, but a St Olave, probably this one, is mentioned in a manuscript of about 1130. There are references to the church as St Olave in Colchirchlane and St Olave Upwell in the Jewry, possibly recalling a well on the north-east corner of the church. The church was repaired in 1608 and again in 1628; it was destroyed in 1666. By the Act of 1670 the parish was united with that of St Martin Pomeroy.

In 1669 the churchwardens considered what should be done about their church and labourers were paid for pulling down the pillars of the old building. In 1670 Cartwright was paid for 'amending the steeple' – probably for making it safe. The rubble was cleared but there is no indication of any rebuilding.

In November 1670 the Commissioners allocated £500 for work on the church, although the rebuilding had not then been agreed. There is no record of any deposit in the Chamber of London, but approval to start the work of rebuilding must have been given early in 1671. Problems were soon encountered with the foundations at the east and west ends, but they were not serious enough to warrant piling. Excavations to a depth of sixteen feet for the tower were either drained or pumped to enable Matthew Banckes to lay a timber raft upon which John Shorthose, mason, could lay his rubble foundation. There was a further problem with water at the north-east corner – the site of the 'Upwell'.

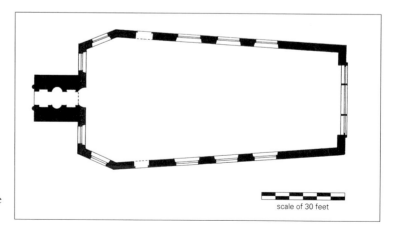

FIGURE 170. St Olave Jewry, plan. (PJ)

scale of 30 feet

The church was roofed and covered by mid 1673 and completed for use by 1675. At that stage the tower had been raised to a height roughly equal with that of the church, before being covered and left. Work resumed again in 1677 with the completion of the tower with its simple parapet and corner pinnacles.

Construction of the Church, 1671–75, £4892 17s. 4d.

Craftsmen: John Shorthose, mason; Edward Ballance, bricklayer; Matthew Banckes, carpenter; John Longland, carpenter; Valentine Housman, joiner; Thomas Whyting, joiner; Richard Cleere, carver; Richard Howes, smith; Thomas Aldworth, plumber; John Talbot, plumber; Samuel Tanner, plumber; Mary Tipton, glazier; John Grove, plasterer; Robert Streeter, painter.

FIGURE 171. St Olave Jewry, from the south west. Drawn by J. Coney, etched by W. Wise, for the *Architectural Series of London Churches* (1828).

Completion of the Tower, 1677–79, £679 7s. 6d.

Craftsmen: John Shorthose, mason; Robert Day, carpenter; Thomas Aldworth, plumber.

Total cost £5580 4s. 10d., including £10 0s. 0d. to St Paul's for stone rubble.

St Olave was a long but narrow church. Its curious coffin-shape would always have been more apparent in plan than it would have been from either the inside or outside the building. The walls of the west front and the tower, which are all that now remain of the church, are faced with Portland stone. The door on the west of the tower is square-headed, flanked with engaged Doric columns, each with a separate entablature, but with a segmental pediment over. The vane now on the tower of a ship in full sail is from St Mildred, Poultry.

The church was demolished in 1887. The tower remains.

St Peter Cornhill

The church of St Peter is on the west side of Gracechurch Street with its north porch on Cornhill. A former churchyard to the south remains as an open space. The church is on a site which has been used for Christian worship since antiquity. An early claim that it was founded by a (mythical) King Lucius in 179 would give the church the distinction of being the oldest in London. There may indeed have been Christian worship on this site in Roman times, but there is no evidence for it. The earliest recorded date is 1040. The pre-Fire building, with nave and aisles, occupied the area of the present church but extended eastwards. Its steeple was repaired in 1628–29 and the church in 1632–33.

In 1667 the vestry began to make preparations for a rebuilding. The foundations were to be cleared and a decision was made to procure a surveyor who would submit a model and an estimate of its cost. In April 1668 Edward Jerman or Jarman, City Surveyor, was appointed surveyor to the parish; he was paid for providing plans and drawings. The vestry also gave approval for the building of a new east wall for the church to a height of at least thirty feet. On the death of Jerman in 1669, John Oliver was appointed in his place, but there is no record of any construction by him. A number of the original drawings for the church survive, suggesting that the church was rebuilt along the lines of the pre-Fire building and, except for the east end, probably making use of much of the old foundations. The arrangement of columns, dividing the church into

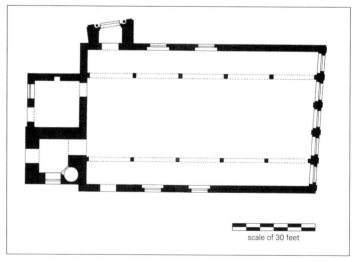

FIGURE 172.
St Peter Cornhill, plan. (*PJ*)

scale of 30 feet

FIGURE 173.
St Peter Cornhill,
interior looking east,
showing pulpit and
chancel screen, 1941.
(*NMR*)

nave and aisles, derives also from the medieval building. A drawing, now in poor condition, shows an elevation of the east end. It differs from the east end as it now exists in having pineapples above the corner pilasters and urns above the corner pilasters of the attic story. The wings to the attic story are also shown decorated with the fruit and foliage provided by Joshua Marshall, mason. The drawing has a strong stylistic resemblance to the drawing for St Edmund the King attributed to Robert Hooke, and some resemblance to the east front of St Mary-at-Hill and an early design for St Mary Abchurch, both of which are probably also by Hooke.

Although the Commissioners gave approval for the rebuilding of the church on 22 June 1674, the mason's contract was not signed by Joshua Marshall until 31 October 1677, with work on site beginning soon after. By 1678 the new east wall had been rebuilt, together with the south side and the lower courses of the tower. On the death of Marshall, in April 1678, his contract was taken over by Abraham Story, en-abling Thomas Woodstock, carpenter, to roof the building in 1680. It was covered with lead by 1681 and the glazing and plaster work completed later that year. Work continued on the tower and steeple which were completed in 1684.

Construction of the Church, Tower and Steeple, 1677–84, £5647 8s. 2d.

Craftsmen: Thomas Humphrey, mason; Joshua Marshall, mason; Abraham Story, mason; Thomas Warren, bricklayer; Thomas Woodstock, carpenter; William Cleere, joiner; Thomas Aldworth, plumber; Thomas Dobbins, plumber; Edward Freeman and Richard Howe, smiths; Robert Bird, coppersmith; Henry Doogood and John Grove, plasterers; John and Mary Odell, glaziers; Thomas Martyr, painter; Bartholomew Scott, labourer and carter.

FIGURE 174. St Peter Cornhill, tower, cupola and steeple. (*NMR*)

The church is brick-built, partly stuccoed and with some stone dressings. The tower, on the south-west corner, is also of brick. It was surmounted by a lead- (now copper-) covered timber cupola, lantern and spire. This is crowned by a ball and vane in the form of a key.

The east front has five round-headed windows, separated by Ionic pilasters, on a high stylobate. The three centre bays are broken forward and the windows of these are decorated with cherub-head keystones. Above the cornice is an attic story with triangular pediment containing a further round-headed window, flanked by circular windows, all without keystones.

The body of the church is in the form of a nave and aisles, separated by five arches supported on piers that have high, octagonal, wainscotted bases. Each pier has four pilasters, three of which are of the Doric order; the fourth on each pier, facing the nave, is carried high and has Corinthian capitals. The nave has an elliptical barrel-vault, ornamented with enriched bands dividing the ceiling into panels with plaster roses. The aisles have transverse barrel-vaults to each bay.

The chief glory among the fittings is the chancel screen which extends across nave and aisles, with six bays on either side of a central opening, divided by slender square and fluted Doric columns supporting round-headed arches with pierced spandrels. The central opening has fluted Corinthian pilasters and, above the cornice, the Stuart royal arms with lion and unicorn supporters.

St Sepulchre

The church of the Holy Sepulchre, or St Sepulchre, was formerly dedicated to St Edmund, suggesting a Saxon origin. It was also known as St Edmund and the Holy Sepulchre, St Sepulchre Newgate and St Sepulchre Old Bailey or by-the-Bailey. The earliest mention appears to have been in 1137. The church is on the north side of what is now Holborn Viaduct, not far from the site of the Newgate itself and of Newgate Gaol, with which the parish has gruesome associations.

The medieval church was rebuilt about the middle of the fifteenth century with the addition of a chapel on the south side of the choir and a parvis porch at the western end of the south front. The tower was rebuilt between 1630 and 1634. The church, 150 feet in length, was the largest parochial church in medieval London, a position it lost to Christchurch, made parochial in 1547, but regained after the Great Fire when Christchurch was rebuilt on a smaller scale.

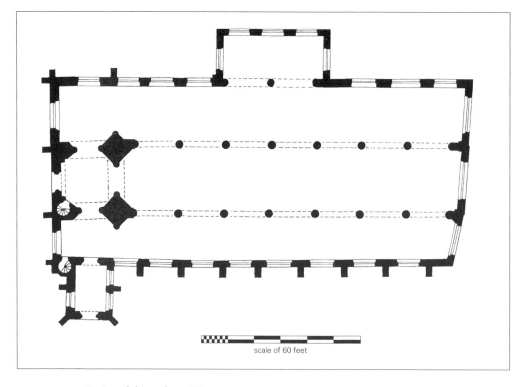

scale of 60 feet

FIGURE 175. St Sepulchre, plan. (PJ)

FIGURE 176.
St Sepulchre, tower
from the south west.
(*NMR*)

The City walls had to some extent prevented the further spread of the Great Fire, but the church had been burnt and the southern part of the parish destroyed. Nevertheless, a large part of the parish to the north of the church escaped and the parish organisation survived.

St Sepulchre was one of the first of the London parishes to restore its church. Repairs to the tower and steeple seem to have been completed by the end of 1667, or early in 1668, when the bell-founder was ordered to make a 'good and substantial Frame to hang six bells'. Whereas the vestry was able to undertake this much restoration from its own resources, the rebuilding of the body of the church was a different matter. Nevertheless, the vestry lost little time in attending to this too. In May 1667 it ordered that workmen should be employed to make an estimate 'to the end the Parish may take it into consideration what course they may take concerning the same'. Work on the church appears to have started in 1667 and by March 1668 there were discussions with a Mr Marshall concerning the twelve columns required. The churchwardens' accounts for 1668–69 include a payment for measuring the mason's work. By 1670 the vestry had exhausted its available resources and approval was given to take up a loan of £500 at interest towards the finishing of the church.

However, in June 1670 the responsibility for the rebuilding was assumed by the Commissioners, who then allocated £1700 to the church, being about half of what was then estimated would be required. A further sum was allocated in October. The accounts for the rebuilding were examined by Richard Ford, Lord Mayor (as one of the Commissioners), and Robert Hooke in June 1671, by which time the church must have been completed, at a cost of £5276 15s. 8d., including £283 11s. 8d. judged to be the responsibility of the churchwardens. There is no suggestion that Sir Christopher Wren had any part in the designing of the church.

In the rebuilding, the surviving walls, porch and tower were used to reconstruct the church in the form that it had before the Great Fire. The piers supporting the roof were replaced by Doric columns with round arches, but much of the perpendicular character of the building was retained, notably the windows of the church and the fan-vaulting of the porch.

As with other churches repaired or restored soon after the Fire, problems with the fabric began to be apparent long before the end of the century. In 1680 the vestry ordered that the steeple should be repaired. By 1695 they had agreed to petition the House of Commons for a further repair or rebuilding of the steeple from the revenues of the coal tax. Responsibility was again taken by the Commissioners, with the top part of tower rebuilt by their surveyor, William Dickinson, in 1667–71.

Reconstruction of the Church and Tower, 1667–71, £4993 4s. 0d.

Of the craftsmen, only Bates (carpenter) and Marshall (mason, presumably Joshua Marshall) were named.

Repairs to the Tower, 1712–14, £2933 6s. 3½d.

Craftsmen: Samuel Fulkes, mason; Matthew Fortnam, bricklayer; Richard Jennings, carpenter; Joseph Roberts, plumber; Thomas Robinson, smith; Andrew

Niblett, coppersmith; Chrysostom Wilkins, plasterer; Matthew Jarman, glazier; Joseph Thompson, painter.

Total cost £7926 10s. 3½ d.

The perpendicular windows of the church were replaced by round-headed ones in 1790 and most of them converted back to gothic in the restoration of 1878 – one of a number of restorations of the nineteenth century. The tower was refashioned, buttresses added to the south front of the church, the roof renewed and the interior much remodelled. The present layout of the church dates from 1875, with a remodelling of the interior by Sir Charles Nicholson in 1932.

St Stephen Coleman Street

The church was named after Stephen, the Proto-Martyr, who was stoned to death outside Jerusalem. It was on the west side of Coleman Street, not far from its junction with what is now Gresham (formerly Cateaton) Street, in the district known as Jewry or Old Jewry. Its early history is confused, but the earliest record seems to be from between 1171 and 1181. According to Stow, the late medieval church was carefully repaired and 'fairly and commendably beautified' by the parishioners in 1622, further enriched with a 'very fair' gallery in the south aisle in 1627.

The determination of the parish to rebuild their church after its destruction in 1666 can be seen in a vestry decision, of 22 October 1667, 'to draw a Petition to the Common Counsell for their approbation about the Building or Repairing of our Parish Church'. What they expected is not clear. Little seems to have been done until 1674, when the vestry petitioned the Commissioners, who ordered it to be put in hand 'upon the extraordinary'. Building seems to have started later that year.

Thomas Horton, carpenter, was paid for work including the roof, ceiling, vestry floor and floors to the tower, measured on 15 June 1676, indicating that by then the walls and the tower had been completed. Apart from the mason's bills, some of which were outstanding until 1681, all work on the church had been paid for by 1677. The accounts record only a small sum spent in digging new foundations at the west end. It may therefore be concluded that, with this exception, the church was rebuilt on its old foundations and, moreover, followed its old, late medieval plan.

In 1686 the vestry voted to have a gallery built, the cost to be defrayed by subscription. In 1691, however, the Commissioners agreed

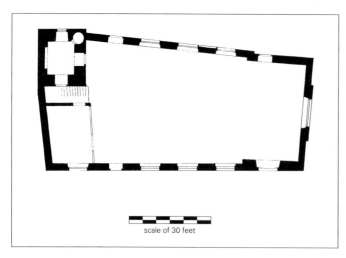

scale of 30 feet

FIGURE 177. St Stephen Coleman Street, plan. (*PJ*)

to provide 'some additional workes' for the church, which included a gallery as well as a new vault.

Construction of the Church, Tower and Steeple, 1674–77, £3938 19s. 10d.

Craftsmen: Joshua Marshall, mason; Joseph Lemm, bricklayer; Abraham Williams, bricklayer; Robert Horton, carpenter; William Cleere, joiner; Thomas Balland, plumber; Richard Howes, smith; George Bower, coppersmith; Thomas Burton and Robert Horton, plasterers; Joseph Panton, glazier; Isaac Fuller and Thomas Martyr, painters.

Construction of the Gallery and Vault, 1691–92, £496 4s. 2½d.

Craftsmen: Samuel Fulkes, mason; Richard Billingshurst, bricklayer; John Longland, carpenter; Jonathan Maine, carver; Richard Howes, smith; Henry Doogood, plasterer; Widow Panton, glazier; William Thompson, painter; James Hurst, labourer.

Total cost, £4517 0s. 9½d.

FIGURE 178. St Stephen Coleman Street, interior looking east. (*NMR*)

The church of St Stephen was constructed of rubble and brick, later largely covered with stucco, but with Portland stone dressings. The roof was originally covered with lead; at some later date this was replaced by slate. Only the south and east fronts were generally visible. The east front, faced with stone, was described, in 1708, as adorned with a 'cornish' (cornice) and circular pediment between two pineapples and, under the pediment, the figure of a cock between two large festoons. Later descriptions record a somewhat different design.

The interior of the church was an auditorium of irregular shape, undivided by columns or pillars. The ceiling was flat, coved to the sides and groined to the windows. The church had galleries on three sides, together with a children's gallery erected in 1827 above the original gallery at the west end. The church was subject to much change and alteration in the course of its history before it was again destroyed by fire, this time by incendiary bombing in 1940. The ruins were demolished and the site redeveloped.

St Stephen Walbrook

The church takes the name Walbrook from the small stream or river which, although now covered over, still drains much of the area in the centre of the City and discharges to the Thames at Dowgate. The church was founded at some time prior to 1100 on the west bank of the Walbrook. In 1429–36 it was rebuilt on the east bank, largely at the expense of Sir Richard Chicheley, twice Lord Mayor of London, who also gave ground for a churchyard and a rectory. It was a large church, roughly rectangular in shape but with the east wall at an angle. There were doors from the church to the churchyard on the north-east corner and in the west wall to Walbrook. The church was divided into nave and aisles with a clerestory. The tower intruded into the body of the church on the north-west corner. By the Act of 1670 the parish was united with that of St Benet Sherehog.

In its design and complexity, St Stephen Walbrook is quite unlike all the other City parish churches; yet it was seemingly no more than just another of the parish churches to be rebuilt. What was so special about St Stephen Walbrook? The answer seems to lie partly with Sir Robert Hanson, Lord Mayor 1672–73 and a member (later Master) of the Grocers's Company, the patron of the living. It is not, however, to Hanson that the major credit is due: this is due to Adrian Quiney and John Simpson, the churchwardens who were the

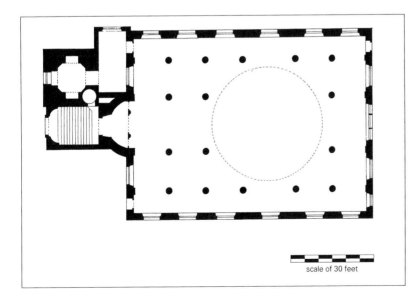

scale of 30 feet

FIGURE 179.
St Stephen
Walbrook, plan.
(PJ)

driving force behind the enterprise, the men who waited on Sir Christopher Wren for the grand design, and who enlisted the Lord Mayor and the near-bankrupt Grocers' Company in its support.

This is one of the few City parish churches where there is a record of a foundation stone. This too was a grand affair, with stones being laid in the foundation at the east end of the church on 17 December 1672 by Sir Robert Hanson, Lord Mayor, Sir Thomas Chicheley, a Privy Counsellor, and Sir John Robinson ('of His Majesty's Tower'), individuals representing the Crown and both civil and military power. Six members of the Court of Assistants of the Grocers' Company were also present.

Work on the new building began in 1672, with a contract to Thomas Strong dated 16 September to pull down the tower and the west wall adjoining; also the east wall and the pillars and arches of the north side. What remained of the north and south walls may have been left. The new church was to be as wide as the old and some of the old fabric may therefore survive in these walls. Construction must have started soon after and seems to have continued without interruption. The dome and lantern were covered with lead by 1677 and the church glazed by early in 1678. The body of the church was probably complete by 1679, but work at the west end continued to 1680 with the tower raised to 127 steps at which height it was covered over. The western porch between the church and Walbrook was also completed at this time.

The tower was built at the west end upon the site of the pre-Fire tower and probably also on its foundations. This new tower seems not to have been a part of Wren's original design for the church, as there is a petition from the parishioners recording that 'the steeple was . . . to be made fronting the Stocks Market'. In 1675 the vestry were considering how to get a grant of land on the north side of the church from the City in order to build the steeple. This location must have been abandoned soon after, when the idea of having a north porch was conceived. A drawing for the north side of the church, showing the porch opening to the Stocks Market, probably dates from this period. Discussion about how to add the porch continued for a few years. The Commissioners were said to be willing to build, but the land was owned by the City and was in use as part of the market. What seems to have been an agreement between all the parties is recorded in 1682. Designs were obtained but the scheme came to nothing. Wren's original intention for the north front is not known. The exterior of this front now shows the remains of a doorway as evidence of an entrance of some sort.

FIGURE 180. St Stephen Walbrook, undated engraving of the interior looking west, drawn by Samuel Wale and dedicated to Christopher Wren junior. (*NMR*)

In the course of building the church a Mr Pollixifen, who owned the house on the south-east corner, complained that the new building was reducing the light available to his property. The matter was referred to Wren for arbitration. The details of the settlement are not given, but the building accounts record the construction of a small vault for Pollixifen in the south aisle 'upon an agreement in lieu of some lights'.

The rebuilding of St Stephen Walbrook is recorded in greater detail than that of most of the City churches. This is in direct contrast to the building of the steeple in 1713–14, which is poorly documented although the building accounts survive. It was built by Edward Strong junior, to a contract price of £1150, but with additional work in providing vases and other ornaments 'about the spire and parapet wall'.

Construction of the Church and Tower, 1672–80, £7652 13s. 8d.

Craftsmen: Christopher Kempster, mason; Thomas Strong, mason; Edward Strong, senior, mason; Thomas Horn, bricklayer; John Longland, carpenter; Roger Davis, joiner; Thomas Aldworth, plumber; Matthew Roberts, plumber; Stephen Leaver, smith; Robert Bird, coppersmith; Henry Doogood and John Grove, plasterers; George Peowrie, glazier; Richard Pinder, glazier; Edward Bird, painter; William Davis, painter; Thomas Laine, painter.

Construction of the Steeple, 1713–14, £1838 0s. 0d.

Craftsmen: Edward Strong, junior, mason; Richard Jennings, carpenter; Joseph Roberts, plumber; Thomas Robinson, smith; Andrew Niblett, coppersmith; Joseph Thompson, painter.

Total cost, £9490 12s. 8d.

The building is constructed largely of stone rubble. It is in the form of a regular rectangle – appreciably shorter than its predecessor. The body is divided by sixteen columns with Corinthian capitals into a nave and both inner and outer aisles. It has a shallow dome over the central area, lit by a lantern. The principal entrance is via a flight of steps from Walbrook and through a semi-circular vestibule into the centre of the west side of the church.

This is the most complex of all the City churches. At first entry it is seen as a nave and aisles building – or at least it was originally, when the body of the church was filled with box pews. The present arrangement, with its central altar, gives an entirely different impression. This view of the church derives not only from the pewing but from the architectural setting, in which the Corinthian columns with their entablatures leads the eye towards the altar and the reredos against the east wall.

Advancing into the church one became aware of the central space beneath the dome, with a cross-axis, in which there were no pews, towards the door originally in the north wall. At the higher level this axis is marked by transepts with Diocletian windows. The clerestory, of which the transepts form a part, forms a cross with the projecting bays marking the angles of the square central area, the focus of the church when viewed from the centre. This space is square, not circular. It is marked by twelve of the columns and by the entablature. The ingenuity of the architect is shown in the way the dome is carried on arches that bridge the corners of this space, converting the square to octagonal only at the higher level, before transforming to the circular base of the shallow dome.

FIGURE 181. St Stephen Walbrook, interior. (*A. F. Kersting*)

The corners are groin-vaulted, as also is the chancel, but the transepts are tunnel-vaulted. The central planning is inconsistent and the longitudinal emphasis incomplete. It is left to the viewer to interpret the ambiguity.

The determination with which the churchwardens set about the rebuilding of their church can be seen also in their resolution to equip the building with the best and finest fittings and furnishings. In February 1677 they visited other churches – St Nicholas Cole Abbey, St Edmund the King, St Mary-at-Hill, St Stephen Coleman Street and St Bride Fleet Street – before choosing the pattern for their pews. The reredos, pulpit and sounding-board were to be based ('in some measure agreeable to') upon the examples in St Lawrence Jewry, the pewing upon that in St Nicholas.

The church was damaged by bombing in 1941, which destroyed the upper part of the dome. It was repaired in 1951–54 by Godfrey Allen and the church was rededicated on 29 March 1954. It was restored and rearranged in 1978–87 by Peter Potter. The church is now dominated by a large circular altar of travertine, designed by Henry Moore, and the furniture arranged around it.

St Swithin London Stone

The church of St Swithin London Stone was to the north of Cannon Street, known earlier as Candlewick Street. The London Stone, supposedly Roman, from which distances were measured, was at one time incorporated in the south wall of the church. Not surprisingly, the church is also widely referred to as St Swithin Cannon Street. Swithin, a Bishop of Winchester, died in 862. His veneration dates from about a century later and the dedication of a church to him suggests a Saxon origin, although archaeological excavations do not support this. The earliest reference to the church is in 1236. This may have been the building described by Stow, who recorded that in 1420 a one-time Lord Mayor, Sir John Hinde, procured a licence to rebuild the church and to add a steeple to it. The parish was united, by the Act of 1670, with that of St Mary Bothaw.

In November 1670 a committee was appointed to organise repairs to the steeple, but the walls of the church, tower and steeple were pulled down in 1675. The rebuilding of the church seems to have started in 1678, with Joshua Marshall's contract for the mason's work signed in 1677. The church was built upon the 'extraordinary'. The fabric was completed by 1683, with the spire added in 1685–86. The new church was erected upon the old foundations, but with the north wall placed further north. This wall is at an angle to the main part of the building, probably marking the limit of the earlier vestry.

Construction of the Church, Tower and Steeple, 1677–83, 1685–86, £4687 4s. 6d.

Craftsmen: Joshua Marshall, mason; Samuel Fulkes, mason; John Longland, carpenter; William Cleere, joiner; John George, plumber; Samuel Colbourn, smith; Stephen Leaver, smith; Edmund Smith, smith; Robert Bird, coppersmith; Henry Doogood and John Grove, plasterers; Richard Bowler, glazier; Edward Bird, painter; William Thompson, painter; John Veare, painter.

St Swithin was built largely of stone rubble, faced with Portland stone. It was not large, the

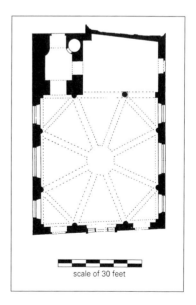

scale of 30 feet

FIGURE 182. St Swithin London Stone, plan. (*PJ*)

main space being roughly square in shape. Its principal feature within is, or was until its destruction, the octagonal dome resting upon an entablature supported by seven half columns and one full column of the Composite order. In the centre of the dome was an octagonal panel containing a plaster rose. The ceiling of the church was richly decorated with plaster work.

The tower of the church was on the north-west corner, providing an entrance from the north. The top part of the tower was cut back with concave surfaces on each of the four corners to reach the octagonal cornice and balustraded parapet. The spire, timber with lead covering, rose to a height of 150 feet, terminating with a ball and vane in the form of a phoenix.

The church was destroyed by bombing in 1941 and, with the decision not to rebuild, the site was cleared for development.

FIGURE 183.
St Swithin London
Stone, south front.
(*NMR*)

St Vedast Foster Lane

St Vedast was a sixth-century Bishop of Arras in Flanders who died in 540; the church may well have been founded by a Flemish community settled in London. The earliest known reference to it is in 1249 when land in Westchepe, now Cheapside, was granted to the parish. The present irregular outline shows how it has grown by accretion. It may have been rebuilt, completely or in part, more than once. Prior to the Great Fire it had a nave with both north and south aisles, separated by arches supported on columns. By the Act of 1670 the parish was united with that of St Michael-le-Quern.

The contract for the restoration, signed by the churchwardens of St Vedast, is dated 10 August 1669. In 1670 this contract was taken over by the Commissioners, who paid the contractors the outstanding sum for the work and reimbursed the churchwardens the sums already paid. The contract price was £1800. This sum had all been paid by 8 February 1672, indicating that by then the work was essentially complete. It seems unlikely that either Hooke or Sir Christopher Wren was consulted about the repairs, or involved in other than passing the accounts.

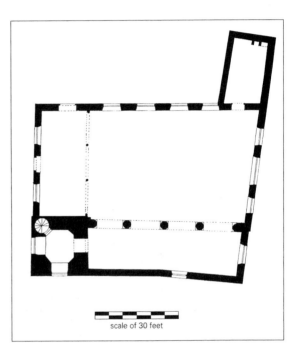

FIGURE 184. St Vedast Foster Lane, plan. (*PJ*)

scale of 30 feet

The restoration seems to have been unsatisfactory. From 1689 onwards the churchwardens' accounts of St Michael's (which for this period survive, whereas those for St Vedast do not) show continuing expenditure in maintaining the fabric. After a visit from Hooke, the decision was made to rebuild the church once more. The first bill was that of Edward Strong senior, mason, of 7 November 1695. He pulled down the old steeple, the roof and the wall between the nave and the north aisle with its supporting arches and columns.

Some, but not all, of the exterior walls were also pulled down. The church was finished in 1699.

In this new reconstruction the church was once again built upon the old foundations, retaining its old irregular plan, but with the tower reerected on the south-west corner on entirely new foundations. The north wall, with new windows, was raised to the height of the old nave and the nave and north aisle replaced with a box-shaped auditorium having a flat ceiling, suitably decorated with an oval of festoons. The windows of the east front were realigned to suit the new church, to which the south aisle remained attached. The plan thus resembled that of St Margaret Lothbury and St Clement Eastcheap, where the towers were similarly located at the south-west corners.

The tower was completed to a height of ninety feet and must have resembled those of All Hallows-the-Great, St Clement East Cheap and St Andrew-by-the-Wardrobe, all with a plain parapet or balustrade. The steeple for the church was added by Edward Strong junior in 1709–12, built under the surveillance of William Dickinson. It rises by stages to a height of seventy feet above the Doric frieze of the tower. At the lowest stage its four principal faces are concave with complex corner pilasters, each with three complete and three broken faces of the Composite order, twenty-four faces in all. This stage is completed by a further grand cornice on which rises the second, convex stage, again with complex but unadorned pilasters. A further cornice provides the platform for two steps upon which is mounted the panelled obelisk or spire, square in cross-section but with diagonal corner faces to answer the pilasters of the lower stages, and buttressed with scrolls.

Restoration of the Church and Tower, 1669–72, £1845 3s. 6d.

Craftsmen: John Thompson, mason; Christopher Russell, bricklayer; Jonathan Wilcox, carpenter.

Reconstruction of the Church and Tower, 1695–99, £5435 14s. 7d.

Craftsmen: Edward Strong senior, mason; John Longland, carpenter; Phillip Rogerson, carpenter; John Smallwell, joiner; Matthew Roberts, plumber; Richard Flowes (Flowers?), smith; Thomas Colbourn, smith; Henry Doogood, plasterer; Francis Moore, glazier; William Thompson, painter.

Construction of the Steeple, 1709–12, £2958 1s. 3d.

Craftsmen: Edward Strong junior, mason; Matthew Fortnam, bricklayer; Richard Jennings, carpenter; Joseph Roberts, plumber; Thomas Robinson, smith; Andrew Niblett, coppersmith; Matthew Jarman, glazier; Joseph Thompson, painter.

Total cost, £10,238 19s. 4d.

The church was badly damaged by incendiary bombing on 29 December 1940. The roof was destroyed and the furniture and fittings lost, leaving the church as a burnt-out shell. As in the Great Fire of 1666, the fire-scarred walls, tower and steeple survived. The church was restored by Dykes Bower in 1953–62. The replacement fittings came from other City churches.

'St Mary-in-the-Fields', Lincoln's Inn Fields

The first documented reference to the church proposed for a site in Lincoln's Inn Fields is an engraving by Gribelin, signed by Christopher Weedon, describing it as a 'singing chapel'. This proposed use may have been no more than a preliminary to establishing a new parish in the area. A design for the chapel was secured from Sir Christopher Wren and a model of it constructed. The design was engraved by Sturt and an appeal opened. The project is known also from an original drawing, now in the City of Westminster Archive; and two engravings, showing the identical model, said to have been 'drawne by Sr Christopher Wren', by Sturt and Gribelin. Although none of these are dated, the engraving by Gribelin carries the arms of William III and cannot therefore be earlier than 1688 and most probably is from after the death of Mary II in 1694. A note of expenditure in the churchwardens' accounts of St Bride Fleet Street records a meeting of 'the Gentlemen that were erecting of a Church in Lincoln's Inn Fields', dated 2 June 1696, confirming a date of 1695–96 for the project. The dedication to St Marie (St Mary) on both engravings would have been rare at that time.

All three designs, the drawing and the two engravings of the model, show a square building, appropriate for the situation in the centre of the great square of Lincoln's Inn Fields, with approaches from the north, south and west. The body of the building was to be raised above an open-vaulted basement story resembling that of Lincoln's Inn Chapel. The chapel would have had five bays to each front, the centre three being broken forward or marked with engaged half-columns of a giant order forming an applied portico. All four corners of the building were capped with small cupolas and at least two of them had spiral stairs giving access to galleries. The auditorium would have consisted of a cross-within-a-square, with the central area of the church positioned beneath the dome.

Although Wren's St Mary was not built, the need for a new church and parish in this area remained and the site continued to attract proposals for new churches, notably for the 1711 Act Commissioners by Archer, Campbell, Gibbs, Hawksmoor and possibly others. Opposition from the Benchers of Lincoln's Inn ensured that none of them was built.

The French Protestant Church in the Savoy

French Protestant refugees were, from about 1653, allowed to worship in the chapel of Somerset House but, with the return of Charles II in 1660, the house was given to his mother, Queen Henrietta Maria, and the chapel converted to Roman use. The refugees petitioned the King for permission to worship in the Savoy Hospital, which was granted on 10 March 1661, subject to their attachment to the Church of England and the use of the Book of Common Prayer in French. The chapel was too small for the congregation and in 1685 they petitioned the new King, James II, for approval to rebuild their chapel on ground which they leased from the Master of the Savoy to a design provided by Sir Christopher Wren. (As Surveyor General of His Majesty's Works, he was responsible for the Savoy.) The design has some resemblance to Wren's 'St Mary-in-the-Fields', especially in the floor plans and elevations. Both are cross-in-a-square designs of five bays, the centre three being broken forward. In each case the corners have lower ceilings than the remainder of the church and both are galleried. There the similarity ends. The Savoy church had four columns supporting a simple structure of intersecting pitched roofs and, unlike St Mary, the church in the Savoy was not raised over a vaulted basement.

Neither building accounts nor the craftsmen's names have been traced. Such records as were kept by the congregation have disappeared. The church cannot have been well built. In the early 1730s it was closed 'on account of the danger whereunto the congregation was continually exposed of being suddenly crushed by the falling in of the roof'. The congregation moved to the French Protestant churches in Spring Gardens and Soho.

St Paul's Cathedral

The conversion of Britain to Christianity and the appointment of a Bishop of London in the fourth century is likely to have been accompanied by the building of a cathedral church in the City. No record of any such a building has survived and the earliest known cathedral was that founded in 604 by Mellitus, Bishop of London. It was dedicated to St Paul. This building, probably enlarged and possibly rebuilt in whole or in part, was destroyed in a fire of 1087 which, like that of 1666, also destroyed much of the City of London. The work of rebuilding was slow and occupied several centuries, with a serious fire in 1135 delaying the work. The romanesque design was complete by early in the thirteenth century, but gave way to the gothic style with more rebuilding, notably of the eastern choir, in the thirteenth to fourteenth centuries.

On 4 June 1561 the lead-covered timber spire of the cathedral was struck by lightning. It was never to be rebuilt, although plans for a new stone steeple were prepared. By the end of the Commonwealth, the building was in poor condition and, in 1661, Dr Christopher Wren was called in to advise on the problem of its repair. He recommended a rebuilding of the nave crossing and proposed to replace the lost spire with a dome supported on the crossing piers. Nothing was done between his proposals of the summer of 1666 and the Great Fire later that year, when the cathedral was so badly damaged that its replacement become inevitable. The crypt beneath the choir had been was used as the parish church of St Faith, and a second parish church, dedicated to St Gregory, adjoined the south wall of the cathedral at its western end. Neither was rebuilt, the parishes being united with those of St Augustine Old Change and St Mary Magdalen Old Fish Street respectively.

Wren was not officially appointed architect to the cathedral until 1673, but as Surveyor to the King's Works from 1670 he had already been engaged in providing designs for it. These include the Greek Cross design of 1672, which gave rise to the Great Model completed in 1674. Further developments include the so-called Warrant design, attached to a royal warrant dated 14 May 1675; what Summerson has called the Penultimate design; and the Definitive design to which work began with the laying of the first stone in the foundation on 21 June 1675.

In the course of designing for the cathedral Wren became more secretive about his ideas and intentions, tending to keep his own counsel: 'the Surveyor

FIGURE 185.
St Paul's Cathedral,
west front, 1957.
(*NMR*)

resolved to make no more models or publically expose his drawings, which . . . did but lose time and subject his business many times, to incompetent judges'. As a direct consequence of this, little is known of the design process, or of the developments and changes to the design as the building proceeded.

Detailed planning continued as the building rose throughout the rest of the seventeenth and into the eighteenth century, with the cathedral nominally completed in 1710. The construction had by then lasted for thirty-five years, all under the direction of Sir Christopher Wren; contrasting with 145 years for the rebuilding of St Peter's Rome under twelve architects. Inevitably not all the detail approved by the Commissioners was to Wren's liking, notably the addition of a balustrade above the roof line, with Wren commenting 'Ladies think nothing well without an edging'.

Although the inspiration for the design and much of its detailing were by Wren himself, in some of the later stages, notably the west towers and the dome, may have been completed with assistance from Nicholas Hawksmoor. Hawksmoor's contribution has been much debated, but documentary evidence for and against is lacking and stylistic evidence is inconclusive.

In the years in which the cathedral was built, a large number of master craftsmen, journeymen, apprentices, labourers, suppliers and others were employed. At one time six teams of masons were at work and in all a total of thirteen master masons were awarded contracts. These included Joshua Marshall, Thomas Strong, Edward Strong senior and junior, Edward Pearce, Thomas Wise senior and junior, Jaspar Latham, John Thompson, Samuel Fulkes, Nathaniel Rawlins, Christopher Kempster and William Kempster. Carvers included Grinling Gibbons, Caius Cibber, Edward Bird and Jonathan Maine. Joiners included William Cleere, Charles and John Hopson, Roger Davis, Hugh Webb and John Smallwell. Jean Tijou supplied iron work.

The cost of rebuilding St Paul's Cathedral has been calculated from the building accounts as £722,779 3s. 3¼d. in the period October 1675 to Midsummer 1712. The total cost including the clearing of the site and the provision of further fittings and furnishings would have added to this figure.

St Thomas the Apostle, Southwark

The church of St Thomas, Southwark, is on the north side of St Thomas Street. It was formerly a part of St Thomas' Hospital, which traces its origin on this site to a rebuilding of the 'spital' of St Mary Overy, following a fire about 1212. The dedication was to St Thomas the Martyr, i.e. St Thomas Becket. Since the refounding of the hospital by Edward VI in 1551 it has been known as St Thomas the Apostle, or more simply St Thomas, Southwark.

In 1697 the President, Treasurer and Governors of the hospital petitioned Parliament for an allowance from the imposition on coals coming into the Port of London to rebuild its church, which was said to be so decayed that people were afraid to go into it. The House of Commons was then considering an extension of the coal tax and agreed a sum of £3000 for St Thomas's, to be paid from the tax receipts 'as the Archbishop of Canterbury, Bishop of London and Lord Mayor of London for the time being [the Lords Commissioners for rebuilding the parish churches] shall approve and allow'. There was no further involvement of the Commissioners and none has been traced of Wren, Hooke or Hawkesmoor.

The Commissioners' approval is indicated as an inscription on a plan of the hospital dating from 1693, which is probably the work of Thomas Cartwright, mason. His design for the church was modified as the building proceeded, notably by 'Mr Cooper's freind [sic]', who was paid two guineas for drawing up a new scheme for the roof in 1701. Cartwright seems to have died at about this time and payments for the mason's work were made to his son, also a mason, who took over the contract.

The old church was pulled down in 1698–99. The foundations were cleared, new ones laid where necessary and the walls raised to a height of twelve feet before boarding over for the winter in 1700. Construction of the walls of the church and tower was resumed in 1701 and the church roofed

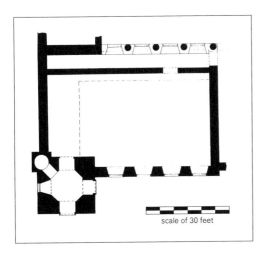

scale of 30 feet

FIGURE 186. St Thomas Southwark, plan. (PJ)

and covered with lead later that year. It was plastered and painted in 1702 and fitted out in 1703. The tower of the late medieval church was located to the west of the nave but in the rebuilding it was moved to the south. The curious shape of the stairwell suggests that it survives from the late medieval church and was incorporated in the new building.

Craftsmen: Thomas Cartwright, mason; Christopher Johns and James Mason, bricklayers; Robert Calcutt, carpenter; William Jeffs, carpenter; William Abbott, joiner; Jonathan Maine, carver; Samuel Hutton, plumber; Samuel Keimer, smith; Zachery Gisburn, ironmonger; David Ellis, plasterer; Matthew Whittaker, glazier; James Wilson, glazier; Zachery Clarke, painter; William Wright, painter.

The total cost of £3718 15s. 6d. was partly offset by the sale of lead, tiles, timber and iron from the old church. It included the new pewing; possibly also

FIGURE 187.
St Thomas South-
wark, south front
and tower. (*NMR*)

the new pulpit, dated 1702; and the reredos, which has the royal Stuart coat of arms.

The church was closed in 1898 when the parish of St Thomas was united with that of St Saviour, Southwark. It was used as the cathedral chapter house from 1905 to 1988. It is now used for secular purposes, with the tower giving access to the roof space containing an old operating theatre, now a museum.

APPENDIX A

Costs of the City Churches

These costs are indicative only. They relate principally to the sums paid from the coal tax revenue. The total for each church has been calculated taking into account the craftsmen's bills as given in the building accounts; sums discounted for the sale of the tabernacles; and the cost of other miscellaneous items, such as the stone and stone rubble from Old St Paul's which was used in some of the parish churches.

No account has been taken of private contributions towards the cost of rebuilding. In a few cases these were considerable, amounting to £3000 to St Dunstan-in-the-East and £5000 to St Mary Aldermary. Other churches are known to have received smaller sums, but the true extent of this source of revenue remains unknown.

The costs of rebuilding St Andrew Holborn and St Clement Danes was met by parish levies. The cost of St James Piccadilly was met from private sources. St Thomas the Apostle, Southwark, received £3000 from the coal trax revenue.

	£	s.	d.
All Hallows Bread Street	4881	3	6
All Hallows Lombard Street	8058	15	6
All Hallows-the-Great	5930	5	6
Christchurch Newgate	13741	17	10¼
St Alban Wood Street	4418	11	7
St Andrew Holborn	9530	1	4
St Andrew-by-the-Wardrobe	7062	14	10¼
St Anne and St Agnes	2348	0	10
St Antholin Budge Row	5702	10	1¾
St Augustine Old Change	4175	0	7
St Bartholomew-by-the-Exchange	5077	1	1
St Benet Fink	4129	16	11
St Benet Gracechurch	4599	9	5¾
St Benet Paul's Wharf	3472	1	11¼
St Bride Fleet Street	15163	1	10¼
St Christopher-le-Stocks	6240	2	7¼
St Clement Eastcheap	4365	3	5
St Clement Danes	9568	13	0

St Dionis Backchurch	5737	9	10
St Dunstan-in-the-East	8286	17	11½
St Edmund the King	6424	2	7½
St George Botolph Lane	4466	7	11
St James Garlickhithe	7230	6	6
St James Piccadilly	7000	0	0
St Lawrence Jewry	11870	1	9
St Magnus the Martyr	12125	10	11½
St Margaret Lothbury	6399	8	8
St Margaret Pattens	7748	7	1¾
St Martin Ludgate	5378	10	3
St Mary Abchurch	4974	2	5½
St Mary Aldermanbury	5237	3	6
St Mary Aldermary	6352	13	8
St Mary-le-Bow	15645	18	2¾
St Mary-at-Hill	5137	2	8
St Mary Magdalen Old Fish Street	4315	12	10
St Mary Somerset	6579	18	1¼
St Mary Woolnoth	3202	7	2
St Matthew Friday Street	2309	8	2
St Michael Bassishaw	5703	9	4¾
St Michael Cornhill	12861	10	8
St Michael Crooked Lane	8086	4	5
St Michael Paternoster Royal	8937	1	0¼
St Michael Queenhithe	4375	10	0¾
St Michael Wood Street	2554	12	10½
St Mildred Bread Street	3705	13	6
St Mildred Poultry	4654	0	4¾
St Nicholas Cole Abbey	5042	6	11
St Olave Jewry	5580	4	10
St Peter Cornhill	5647	8	2
St Sepulchre	7926	10	3½
St Stephen Coleman Street	4517	0	9½
St Stephen Walbrook	9490	12	8
St Swithin London Stone	4687	4	6
St Vedast Foster Lane	10238	19	4
St Thomas the Apostle, Southwark	3718	15	6
Total	362793	7	10
St Paul's Cathedral	722779	3	3¾

APPENDIX B

Parish Churches of the City of London
Destroyed in the Great Fire and not then Rebuilt

All Hallows Honey Lane
All Hallows-the-Less
Holy Trinity-the-Less
St Andrew Hubbard
St Anne Blackfriars
St Benet Sherehog
St Botolph Billingsgate
St Faith-under-St Paul's
St Gabriel Fenchurch
St Gregory-by-St-Paul's
St John the Baptist Walbrook
St John the Evangelist
St John Zachary
St Lawrence Pountney
St Leonard Eastcheap
St Leonard Foster
St Margaret Moses
St Margaret New Fish Street
St Martin Orgar*
St Martin Pomary
St Martin Vintry
St Mary Bothaw
St Mary Colechurch
St Mary Magdalen Milk Street
St Mary Mounthaw
St Mary Staining
St Mary Woolchurch Haw
St Michael-le-Quern
St Nicholas Acons
St Nicholas Olave

St Olave Silver Street
St Pancras Soper Lane
St Peter Paul's Wharf
St Peter Cheap
St Thomas the Apostle

* This parish was united with St Clement Eastcheap, both parishes then using the rebuilt church of St Clement. St Martin's church was patched up and used by a French Protestant Congregation until 1820.

APPENDIX C

Parish Churches of the City of London
Which Survived the Great Fire

All Hallows-by-the-Tower (All Hallows Barking)	Rebuilt following destruction by bombing in 1940
All Hallows London Wall	Rebuilt by George Dance the Younger, 1785
All Hallows Staining	Demolished
St Alphege	Demolished
St Andrew Holborn	Rebuilt by Wren 1684–86; tower recased and heightened, probably by Hawksmoor, 1704
St Andrew Undershaft	
St Bartholomew-the-Great	
St Bartholomew-the-Less	Rebuilt by George Dance the Younger, 1789; then by Thomas Hardwick, 1823
St Botolph Aldersgate	Rebuilt *c.* 1788
St Botolph Aldgate	Rebuilt by George Dance the Elder, 1741–44
St Botolph Bishopsgate	Rebuilt by James Gold, 1725–29
St Dunstan-in-the-West	Rebuilt by John Shaw the Elder, 1831
St Ethelburga	Destroyed by bombing, 1993; proposals have been submitted for rebuilding
St Giles Cripplegate	
St Helen Bishopsgate	
St Katharine Coleman	Demolished
St Katharine Cree	
St Martin Outwich	Demolished
St Olave Hart Street	
St Peter-le-Poer	Demolished

Notes

Notes to Chapter 1, Sir Christopher Wren

1. BL, MS Add. 25071.
2. The construction of the cathedral can be assumed to have started soon after 19 May 1675, when the Commissioners for rebuilding the cathedral ordered that Wren 'with his Assistants and Officers should immediately sett out the Ground and cause the Foundation to be laid . . . and pursue the Work with all Diligence . . .' (GL, MS 25622/1) but, as Kerry Downes has noted, *Sir Christopher Wren: The Design of St Paul's Cathedral* (London, 1988), p. 35 n. 8, there is no record of the laying of a foundation stone for the new cathedral. In the absence of a formal ceremony it seems that at St Paul's it was left to the mason, Thomas Strong, and the carpenter, John Longland, to mark the laying of the first stone in a position on the south-east corner, Edward Hatton, *A New View of London* (2 vols, London, 1708), ii, p. 456; see also Kerry Downes, 'Sir Christopher Wren, Edward Woodroffe, J. H. Mansart and Architectural History', *Architectural History*, 37 (1994) pp. 37–67. Formal stone-laying ceremonies are known to have taken place in the rebuilding of some of the parish churches, the most notable being that for St Stephen Walbrook.
3. Colvin, *Dictionary*, pp. 1083–97.
4. The earlier biographies and studies of Wren, such as those by Elmes, Phillimore, Milman and Weaver, are now largely obsolete. For a perceptive view of the mind of Wren, see Sir John Summerson's essay reprinted in *RIBA Journal* (London, 1936).
5. Christopher Wren, *Parentalia: Memoirs of the Family of the Wrens*, edited by Stephen Wren (London, 1750), p. 309.

Notes to Chapter 2, Christian London

1. Alban was a young Romano-British official of Verulamium who, whilst still a pagan, gave shelter to a Christian priest and later refused to sacrifice to Roman gods. AD 209 has been suggested for his martyrdom, but some time in the persecutions of Decius (250–51) or Valerian (257–59) is more likely. See Charles Thomas, *Christianity in Roman Britain to AD 500* (London, 1981); Eileen Roberts, *The Hill of the Martyr* (Dunstable, 1993). However, the traditional version of the story, dating the martyrdom to the early fourth century, has in no way been disproved.
2. Ralph Merrifield, *The Roman City of London* (London, 1965), p. 62 n. 60.
3. Alan Vince, *Saxon London: An Archaeological Investigation* (London, 1990), p. 59.
4. The extent of such invasions and the numbers involved remains a matter of debate between those who envisage large-scale migration and those who argue for a British population dominated, politically and culturally, by a small warrior elite from the north German plain.

See Helena Hamerow, *Building on the Past*, Royal Archaeological Institute (London, 1994), pp. 164–77.

5. Martin Biddle, Daphne Hudson and Carolyn Heighway, *The Future of London's Past: A Survey of the Archaeological Implications of Planning and Development in the Nation's Capital*, Rescue Publication, 4 (1973), p. 19.

6. Alan Vince, in *Aspects of Saxo-Norman London* (London, 1991), ii, p. 427.

7. Also known as All Hallows Barking. It has been suggested by Montague Fowler, *History of All Hallows Church* (London 1909), p. 25, that the church was probably rebuilt by Erkenwald, Bishop of London (d. *c.* 693). There is no confirmation of this, although the discovery of a blocked arch composed of tile fragments and other details lend support: see Vince, *Aspects of Saxo-Norman London*, ii, pp. 427–29.

8. St Vedast was a sixth-century Bishop of Arras who died on 6 February 640, credited with the conversion of Clovis to Christianity as well as a number of miracles and cures. Gertrude Sparrow Simpson and W. Sparrow Simpson, *The Life and Legend of St Vedast* (London, 1896).

9. William Jenkinson, *London Churches before the Great Fire* (London, 1927), pp. 299–300.

10. FitzStephen's euphoric description of the City of London is known from an early transcript by John Leyland and its publication by Stow. A number of editions were printed in the eighteenth century.

11. Caroline Barron, *The Late Middle Ages, 1270–1520*, in *The British Atlas of Historic Towns*, iii, *The City of London* (Oxford, 1989), p. 48.

12. Paul Jeffery, 'The Later History of St Martin Outwich, City of London', *London Journal*, 14, pp. 160–69.

13. James P. Malcolm, *Londinium Redivivum* (London, 1807), iv, p. 73.

14. The spread of the fire and the destruction of the parish churches is described in greater detail by Walter Bell, *The Great Fire of London in 1666* (London and New York, 1920).

15. An unnamed nonconformist parson, preaching on the anniversary of the Fire of London, asserted that 'the calamity could not be occasioned by the sin of blasphemy for in that case it would have begun at Billingsgate; nor lewdness, for then Drury Lane would have been first in fire; nor lying, for then the flames had reached them from Westminster Hall; no, my beloved, it was occasioned by the sin of gluttony; for it began at Pudding Lane and ended at Pie Corner', Jacob Burn, *Tradesmen's Tokens* (2nd edn, London, 1855), p. 192.

16. T. F. Reddaway, *The Rebuilding of London after the Great Fire* (London, 1940); P. E. Jones and T. F. Reddaway, *The Survey of the Building Sites in the City of London after the Great Fire of 1666* (London, 1967), i, p. ix.

Notes to Chapter 3, Rebuilding the City

1. 18 and 19 Charles II, cap. 7; Philip E. Jones, *The Fire Court: Calendar to the Judgments and Decrees* (London, 1966).

2. The figure most frequently given is eighty-seven, but this does not tally with the names of the churches listed in the Act of 1670. The eighty-six include both St Gregory-by-St Paul's and St Faith-under-St Paul's.

3. These include the churches of All Hallows, Barking (All Hallows-by-the-Tower), St Alphage, St Botolph Aldersgate and St Peter-le-Poer. Leake's post-Fire map of the City

shows St Alphage within the devastated area, but there does not seem to be any evidence for this or for fire damage to St Peter-le-Poer. Some damage may have been inflicted on all of the remainder. On 5 September 1666 Pepys reported: '[The Fire] having only burned the dyall of Barking Church [All Hallows-by-the-Tower], and part of the porch and was there quenched.'

4. ASC, Wren I, 7.

5. Christopher Wren junior, *Parentalia*, edited by Stephen Wren (London, 1750), p. 269.

6. T. F. Reddaway, 'The Rebuilding of London after the Fire', *Town Planning Review*, 97 (1937), pp. 205–11.

7. GL, Prints and Maps, Pr. Gr. 2, e.g. engraving by Cole.

8. GL, Prints and Maps, Pr. Gr. 2, engraving of mid eighteenth century.

9. John Evelyn, *Londinum Redivivum or London Restored*, GL, MS 94; see also Sydney Perks, 'London Town Planning in 1666', *Royal Institution of British Architects Journal*, 3rd series, 27 (1920), pp. 467–70.

10. GL, MS 3441; Reddaway, 'The Rebuilding of London after the Fire', *Town Planning Review*, 18 (1939), pp. 155–61; 10, 18 and 19 Charles II, cap. 8; 22 Charles II, cap. 11.

11. James Ralph, *A Critical Review of the Buildings of London* (London, 1734), p. 2.

12. 18 and 19 Charles II, cap. 8; 22 Charles II, cap. 11.

13. 3 James I, 1605, 12 James I, 1614. See also Martin Nail, *The Coal Duties of the City of London and their Boundary Marks* (privately published, London, 1972).

14. Bodleian Library, Oxford, Tanner MS 142, fol. 118.

15. An agreed list of churches to be united, Tanner MS 142, fos 38, 42.

16. Bodleian Library, Oxford, Tanner MS 142, fol. 42, 17 July 1667/8.

17. Pepys, *Diary*, 5 April 1667.

18. The earliest so far found is in a minute of 13 July 1670, 'the Lords Commissioners have directed fifteen churches to be first built . . .', GL, MS 25540/1, fol. 7.

19. These were parish churches where the patronage was in the hands of the Archbishop. The parishes owed their allegiance to him rather than to the Bishop. They were abolished by Order in Council of 1845, *London Gazette*, 20 August 1845.

20. GL, MS 25540/1, fol. 1, 17 May 1670.

21. 1 James II, cap. 15.

22. 8 and 9 William III, cap. 14.

23. *VCH, London*, i (London, 1909), pp. 346–48.

24. *DNB*, 50, pp. 244–50.

25. E.g., 'For Bags and Coach hire to bring home ye remainder of monies in the Chamber in Specie, 7s. 6d.', GL, MS 25543, fol. 34.

26. Three payments were made to Hawksmoor for copying the accounts: £10 'for transcribing and engrossing all the books that contain all the bills and workmanship of the Parochial churches to bring to one generall account' (GL, MS 25543, fol. 55); £35 for more extensive work in 'abstracting the states of accounts' to midsummer 1693; and £9 10s. 0d. for 'transcribing the Books of the Churches and Tabernacles for the Great and General Account for the Exchequer', GL, MS 25543, fol. 57.

27. Bodleian Library, Oxford, MS Rawlinson B. 387–89.

28. GL, MS 25539/1 to 12.

Notes to Chapter 4, Architects and Surveyors

1. GL, MS 25540, p. 3.
2. GL, MS 25548.
3. E.g. a proposal was made to make the site available for rebuilding of St Anne and St Agnes more regular by including ground formerly occupied by a house on the south-east corner. Sir Thomas Bludworth and Sir Thomas Exton were asked to advise what would be an appropriate recompense to make, GL, MS 25540, 9 March 1677.
4. Kerry Downes, *The Architecture of Wren* (London, Toronto, Sydney and New York, 1982), p. 24.
5. T. F. Reddaway, *The Rebuilding of London* (London, 1940), p. 58.
6. *The Diary of Robert Hooke*, ed. H. W. Robinson and W. Adams (London, 1935).
7. BL, MS Add. 5238.
8. Wouter Kuyper, *Dutch Classicist Architecture* (Leyden, 1980), p. 115–16.
9. In addition to the published diary for 1672–80, an unpublished manuscript for the period December 1692 to August 1693 has also survived, BL, MS Sloane 4024.
10. *The Diary of Robert Hooke*, 22 June 1674; 14 October 1673.
11. *The Survey of Building Sites in the City of London after the Great Fire of 1666*, i, London Topographical Society, 103 (London, 1967), p. xvii.
12. Colvin, *Dictionary*, p. 1078.
13. PRO, PCC Prob 11/349.
14. Kerry Downes, *Sir Christopher Wren*, exhibition catalogue, Whitechapel Art Gallery (London, 1982), pp. 73–74; John Bold, *John Webb* (Oxford, 1989), p. 10.
15. John Summerson in *The History of the King's Works* (London, 1975), iii, p. 67; Kerry Downes, *Sir Christopher Wren: The Design of St Paul's Cathedral* (London, 1988), p. 6 n. 25.
16. ASC, Wren II, 47.
17. *DNB*, 27, p. 399.
18. Colvin, *Dictionary*, p. 714.
19. He succeeded Thomas Wise as the King's Master Mason in 1686, holding the post until his death in 1701, *The History of the King's Works*, gen. ed. H. M. Colvin (London, 1976), v, p. 471.
20. Howard Colvin, 'The Church of St Mary Aldermary and its Rebuilding after the Great Fire of London', *Architectural History*, 24 (1981), pp. 24–31.

Notes to Chapter 5, The Commission at Work

1. GL, MS 25540, 17 June 1670.
2. GL, MS 25540, 13 July 1670; 7 October 1670.
3. GLRO, MS 222.11.
4. GL, MS 25547.
5. A carpenter, Thomas Piggott, offered to supply such a tabernacle which the Commissioners agreed to accept for the sum of £50, which was to include: 'table, pulpit and reading desk . . . [it was] agreed that after Mich[ael]mas day 1674 he shall take away the said tabernacle at his own charges and to his own benefit', GL, MS 25542/2.
6. GL, MS 25540, 7 February 1671; 15 June 1671.

7. GL, MS 25540, 26 November 1670.

8. GL, MS 25540, 6 September 1671; Chamber of London copy GLRO, MS 157.14.9 GL, MS 25540, 28 June 1672.

10. 'In the Finances of the Office of Works there was a basic distinction between regular maintenance on the one hand and new works ordered by the king or his ministers on the other. The former constituted the "ordinary" expenditure for which a fixed annual allowance was made, while for any "extraordinary" expenditure appropriate provision was in theory made by the Treasury Lords who authorised it. It was in the nature of things that the "Extraordinary" of today should become the "Ordinary" of tomorrow.' Colvin, *History of the King's Works*, v, p. 39.

11. GL, MS 25542, p. 53.

12. GL, MS 25540, p. 48, 25 October 1677.

13. Strictly speaking this claim can be made for Edward Jerman's (or Jarman's) tower of the rebuilt Royal Exchange, although this was neither ecclesiastical nor influential.

14. GL, MS 25539/4.

15. *Commons Journal*, 1667–87, ix, p. 718; 1 James II, cap. 15.

16. GL, MS 25539/4; MS 25539/10.

17. GL, MS 25539/7.

18. GL, MS 25539/1.

19. GL, MS 25539/5.

20. GL, MS 25539/8.

21. GL, MS 25540, 20 December 1671.

22. *Commons Journal*, 1685, ix, p. 744.

23. 8 and 9 William III, cap. 14.

24. Including All Hallows London Wall, St Andrew Holborn (for assistance in the rebuilding of its tower), St Botolph Aldersgate, St Botolph Bishopsgate, St George the Martyr Southwark, St John Wapping, St Helen Bishopsgate, St Margaret Westminster, St Martin-in-the-Fields, St Olave Southwark and St Thomas the Apostle, Southwark.

25. The church of St Thomas the Apostle, Southwark, was rebuilt in 1700–3, seemingly to the design of Thomas Cartwright, Paul Jeffery, 'The Parish Church of St Thomas the Apostle', *Ecclesiological Society Newsletter*, January 1993.

26. E.g., John Bedford, *London's Burning* (London, 1966), p. 291, 'availability of materials was the controlling factor in the rate of rebuilding of churches. Where stone was being used it had to be brought from distant quarries, which could not rapidly increase their outputs . . .'

Notes to Chapter 6, Parish Records, Patronage and Influence

1. Hawksmoor claimed to have built the tower of St Michael Cornhill for the 1711 Act Commissioners, see *WS*, 11 (1932), p. 33.

2. *Parentalia*, p. 309.

3. *WS*, 9 (1932), p. 17.

4. Ibid., p. 33.

5. GL, MS 593/4.

6. GL, MS 594/2.

7. GL, MS 5006/1.

8. *Parentalia*, p. 314.

9. Ibid.

10. GL, MS 25540, 11 August 1671.

11. *SL*, 33(1966), pp. 256–74.

12. GL, MS 3892/1.

13. GL, MS 25540A.

14. GL, MS 4256.

15. GL, MS 6554/1.

16. GL, MS 6554/1, 15 August 1671.

17. GL, MS 25539/2.

18. GL, MS 25542/1, p. 92.

19. GL, MS 25540, p. 61.

20. GL, MSS 6554/1; 6554/2.

21. *Parentalia*, p. 311.

22. CWA, VL, MS B1058; WS, 19 (1942), p. 109.

23. CWA, VL, B1058.

24. CWA, VL, B1057; BL, MS Chart 1605.

25. Bute, nos 27 and 28.

Notes to Chapter 7, Architectural Drawings, Illustrations and Models

1. Sir John Soane's Museum, Sales Catalogue 19 and AL 36a; BL, 603. c.4; BM (Medal Room), a.37.1. The text of *WS*, 20 (1943), p. 78, duplicates that of *WS*, 3 (1926), p. 3, but the table contains information which does not appear in any of these four copies. Did Bolton have access to a fifth? Sir John Summerson, 'Drawings for London Churches in the Bute Collection: A Catalogue', *Architectural History*, 13 (1970), p. 30, does not enlighten.

2. Oxford, Bodleian Library, Mus. Bibl. III, 8°.53.

3. This portfolio may have contained the drawings for the Hôtel des Invalides, Paris, sent at the request of the Duke of Monmouth, to Charles II by Francois Michel le Tellier, Marquis de Louvois in 1678. They were likely to have been handed to Wren, who was then considering the design for the Royal Hospital, Chelsea. Alternatively, these drawings may have been those sent by Sir William Trumbull, Envoy Extraordinary to the French Court, to William Blathwayt, Secretary at War in 1686, *HMC, Downshire*, i (1924), p. 140.

4. W. R. McKay, *Clerks in the House of Commons, 1363–1989*, House of Lords Record Office, Occasional Paper, 3 (London, 1989), p. 52; Paul Jeffery, 'Originals or Apprentice Copies? Some Recently Found Drawings for St Paul's Cathedral, All Saints, Oxford, and the City Churches', *Architectural History*, 35 (1992) p. 133 n. 3.

5. Kerry Downes, *Sir Christopher Wren: The Design of St Paul's Cathedral* (London, 1988), p. 11.

6. Dr Thomas Stack, MD FRS (d. 1756); *Musgrave's Obituary*, new series (1901), p. 48.

7. Oxford, Bodleian Library, 2593 e 2 (1752).

8. J. S. G. Simmonds, 'The Wren Drawings at All Souls: Notes for Members of the National Art Collections Fund, Oxford, 28 May 1977'.

9. *WS*, 20 (1943), p. 80.

10. Paul Jeffery, 'Where Are They Now? Wren Drawings from the Bute Collection', *Society*

of *Architectural Historians of Great Britain Newsletter*, 50 (1993), pp. 4–5. Tim Knox, ibid., 51 (1994), 5–6; ibid., 52 (1995), p. 5.

11. BL, K. Top.

12. Arthur T. Bolton, *WS*, 20 (1943) p. x.

13. Ibid., 3 (1926), p. 6.

14. Viktor Fuerst, *The Architecture of Sir Christopher Wren* (London, 1956), p. 229.

15. Including seven Hawksmoor drawings and twenty-eight topographical sketches, some signed by N. T. Dall (d. 1777), see n. 8 above.

16. GL, MS 25543.

17. John Summerson, 'Drawings for London Churches in the Bute Collection: A Catalogue', *Architectural History*, 13 (1970), pp. 41–42.

18. Paul Jeffery, 'Originals or Apprentice Copies?', pp. 118–39.

19. John Summerson, 'Drawings for the London City Churches', *Royal Institute of British Architects Journal*, 59 (1952), pp. 126–29.

20. *WS*, 10 (1933), p. 6.

21. Catalogue of Pepys Library, Magdalene College, Cambridge, 2972 (London and Westminster).

22. Paul Jeffery, '"The Lost Crace": Frederick Crace's Plans, Elevations and Sections of the Churches of London', *London Topographical Record*, 27 (1995), pp. 119–34.

23. In George H. Birch, *London Churches of the Seventeenth and Eighteenth Centuries* (London, 1896).

24. GL, MS 25543.

Notes to Chapter 8, Design, Classification and Style

1. *Parentalia*, pp. 318–21; WS, 9 (1932), pp. 15–18.

2. Ibid.

3. Ibid.

4. Kerry Downes, *The Architecture of Wren* (London, New York, Sydney and Toronto, 1982), p. 34.

5. Cecil A. Hewett, *English Cathedral and Monastic Carpentry* (Chichester, 1985), p. 68.

6. David Yeomans, *The Trussed Roof: Its History and Development* (1992), p. 57; *The Architect and the Carpenter*, exhibition catalogue, Heinz Gallery, RIBA (1992).

7. There is little information concerning the roof structures of these Wren churches. The dimensions and descriptions given here are based the drawings published by John Clayton, *WS*, 9 (1932).

8. The medieval church of St Clement Danes in the Strand was irregular in shape and on a restricted site. The apse designed for it made a virtue of the narrowing at the east end. It is the only apsidal parish church designed by Wren.

9. These small rooms foreshadow the requirements of the 1711 Act Commissioners, 'one for vestments, another for vessels or other consecrated things' (LPL, MS 2690, p. 42, 16 July 1712).

Notes to Chapter 9, Who Did What?

1. BL, MS Add. Sloane 5238, no. 58; WS, 9 (1932), pl. 21.
2. SL, 29 (1960), p. 33.
3. ASC, Wren II, 44; WS, 9 (1932), pl. 15.
4. GL, MS 4165/1, 31 December 1672; 16 June 1673.
5. ASC, Wren I. 77; WS, 9 (1932), pl. 29.
6. GL, MS 3570/2, 10 April 1673.
7. GL, MS 25542/2, p. 127, 18 November 1680.
8. GL, MS 25540/1, 4 July 1681.
9. GL, MS 1257/1, 1681–83.
10. GL, MS 1257/1, 28 December 1682.
11. Howard Colvin, 'The Church of St Mary Aldermary and its Rebuilding after the Great Fire of London', *Architectural History*, 24 (1981), pp. 24–81.
12. A report on Westminster Abbey, 1713, WS, 11 (1943), p. 20.
13. The church was known by a variety of names including St Audoen, St Edwin, St Ewan, St Ewin, St Iweyne, St Ouen, St Owan, St Owen and St Owyn, see H. A. Harben, *Dictionary of London* (London, 1918), p. 139.
14. Ernest Harold Pearce, *Annals of Christ's Hospital* (London, 1901), p. 196.
15. Keeping the children in order was a problem. It was agreed that 'the Steward of this Hospital shall sit in the gallery of Christ Church on the North side and the Matron on the South side, that soe between them they may view and observe their respective charges'. Ibid., p. 201.
16. GL, MS 12811/5; WS, 11 (1943), p. 72.
17. Thomas Allen, *History and Antiquities of London* (London, 1828), iii, p. 529.
18. 'It is impossible to tell exactly to what extent the great church suffered in the Fire, but Wren has been accused of unnecessary destruction of the ancient fabric. The school chronicle speaks of "the glazed windows of the church on that [south cloister] side being very little damnified". Money spent by the churchwardens in clearing the church floor, removing stones, and making doorways also suggests that the main part of the fabric was left secure.' W. G. Bell, *The Great Fire of London* (London and New York, 1920), p. 143.
19. RIBA, Drawings Collection, Wren [1]1 and 2 (2 copies).
20. GL, MS 25540, 23 December 1676.
21. If, as seems likely, Hooke's original plan covers the entire area of pre-Fire parish church, then the post-Fire church occupied only a part of the site. The new church extended 120 feet east of the tower, rather than 150 feet of the earlier design attributed to Hooke. Part of the old church, amounting to some thirty feet in length, was demolished, necessitating a new east wall, which was then buttressed, possibly because of the poor quality of the made-up ground or to limit the effect of any consolidation in the new masonry. The west wall, similarly buttressed, was presumably also newly constructed.

   Excavations in the eastern part of the Wren period church, made prior to road widening were not entirely satisfactory, Tony Johnson, 'Excavations at Christchurch, Newgate Street, 1973', *London and Middlesex Archaeological Society Transactions*, 25 (1974), pp. 220–34. No trace was found of the tomb of Queen Margaret, second wife of Edward I, nor of the pavement given by her. Furthermore, excavated graves do not correspond with recorded information about them. Could it be that her grave, the remains of the pavement and the high altar lay beyond the east wall of the seventeenth century church, and perhaps still do, some feet below the surface of King Edward Street?

22. *State Papers Domestic, 1668–69*, p. 369, edited by Mary Green.
23. RIBA, Drawings Collection, Wren [12]1.
24. Collection of Mrs Tweet Kimball.
25. GL, MS 25540, 6 June 1671.
26. GL, MS 25540, 6 June 1671.
27. GL, MS 2590/2, 3 April 1679.
28. GL, MS 977/1, 1684/85.
29. GL, MS 25540, 1684.

Notes to Chapter 10, Elements of Central Planning

1. A sketch of the intended roof structure attached to the contract shows beams laid across the columns, GL, MS 25542/1, 2 December 1670.
2. Any ceremonial use made of these entrances on the cross-axis is unrecorded. It is known that they were reserved for the residents of St Mary's parish, whereas the residents of St Andrew Hubbard, united with it, used the entrance beneath the tower.
3. Drawing purchased at the Bute Sale, present whereabouts unknown.
4. GL, MS 25540, 9 March 1677.
5. Robert Somerville, *The Savoy* (London, 1960), p. 229; PRO, MPA 41; *The Quiet Conquest: The Huguenots, 1685–1985*, Museum of London catalogue (London, 1985), p. 62.
6. A convenient name for a cross-in-a-square design is badly needed. The word quincunx, sometimes used, refers specifically to a design with five similar elements, four of which occupy the corners of a square and the fifth the centre. Thus 'St Mary-in-the-Fields', which has domes in these positions, is a quincunx whereas the church in the Savoy is not.
7. John Summerson, 'Drawings for the London City Churches', *Royal Institute of British Architects Journal*, 59 (1952), pp. 126–29.
8. RIBA, WREN [6], 1, 2 and 3.
9. GL, MS 2791/1, 11 December 1671.
10. GL, MS 25539/2.
11. GL, MS 25540, 12 March 1671/2.
12. Bridget Cherry, 'John Pollexfen's House in Walbrook', in *English Architecture: Public and Private. Essays for Kerry Downes*, ed. John Bold and Edward Chaney (London and Rio Grande, OH, 1993), pp. 89–105.
13. GL, MS 25539/1.
14. Paul Jeffery, 'The Church that Never Was: Wren's St Mary and Other Projects for Lincoln's Inn Fields', *Architectural History*, 31 (1988), pp. 136–47.
15. CWA, extra-illustrated Pennant; WS, 18 (1941), pl. VIII.
16. Pepys Library, Magdalene College, Cambridge.

Notes to Chapter 11, Towers and Steeples

1. GL, MS 25542/1, p. 30, 28 March 1671.
2. GL, MS 594/2, 19 February 1674/75 and 3 May 1675.
3. Gerald Cobb, *London City Churches*, revised by Nicholas Redman (London, 1989), pp. 38–39.
4. H. Gerson and E. H. ter Kuile, *Art and Architecture in Belgium, 1600–1800* (Harmondsworth, Baltimore, Maryland, and Mitcham, Australia, 1960), pp. 18–25.

   Charles Borromeo was canonised in 1610. The Jesuit church in Antwerp was therefore one of the earliest to be dedicated to him. Pieter Huyssens is generally credited with the church as it was built, probably from about 1615, with the tower from 1620. It was decorated by Rubens and he, too, is credited with a contribution to the design, see J. H. Plantenga, *L'architecture religieuse dans l'ancien duché du Brabant, 1598–1713* (The Hague, 1926). The church was gutted by fire in 1718, but the choir, two chapels, the portal and the tower all survived. The church was reconstructed in the following year by Jan Baurscheit the Elder.
5. Sir John Soane's Museum, 'Wren-Inigo Jones Volume', fol. 2.
6. Frans Baudouin, 'De toren van de Sint-Carolus-Borromeuskerk te Antwerpen, *Academiae Analecta: Mededelingen van de Koninklijke Academie voor Wetenschappen, Letteren en Schone Kunsten van Belgie*, 44 (1983), pp. 15–56.
7. Sir John Soane's Museum, 'Wren-Inigo Jones Volume', fol. 1.
8. GL, MS 1176/2.
9. Cobb, *London City Churches*, p. 176.
10. Parish vestry minutes for the period are missing. The information is from a transcript in *WS*, 19 (1942), pp. 18–19.
11. GL, MS 4882/3.
12. Bute, no. 16; RIBA, Wren [5], 1.
13. Bute, no. 18; ASC, Wren IV, 88; there are two very similar drawings.
14. ASC, Wren II, 6.
15. GL, MS 5038/1.
16. ASC, Wren II, 46.
17. ASC, Wren IV, 85, and Bute, no. 26.
18. Paul Jeffery, 'Originals or Apprentice Copies? Some Recently Found Drawings for St Paul's Cathedral, All Saints, Oxford, and the City Churches', *Architectural History*, 35 (1992), pp. 118–39.
19. GL, MS 4266/1.
20. Bute, no. 32.
21. GL, MS 4863.
22. Howard Colvin, 'The Church of St Mary Aldermary and its Rebuilding after the Great Fire of London', *Architectural History*, 24 (1981), pp. 24–31.
23. For a review of the events, see Paul Jeffery, 'Originals or Apprentice Copies? A Postscript', *Architectural History*, 36 (1993), pp. 46–48.
24. GL, MS 4072/2, p. 111.
25. BL, K. Top., XXIII, 29a.

Notes to Chapter 12, Christian Worship: The Liturgy, Fittings and Furnishings

1. Worcester College, Oxford, Cat. 146A-D; John Harris and A. A. Tait, *Catalogue of Drawings by Inigo Jones, John Webb and Isaac de Caus at Worcester College, Oxford* (Oxford, 1979).

2. Peter Guillery, 'The Broadway Chapel, Westminster: A Forgotten Exemplar', *London Topographical Record*, 26 (1990), pp. 97–133.

3. E.g., at St Stephen Walbrook, see A. W. Pugin and Thomas Rowlandson in Rudolph Ackermann's *Microcosm of London* (London, 1808).

4. Throughout the Wren period and for long after the decorated screen behind the altar was referred to as an altar-piece. This practice has been followed here. The word reredos, commonly used in early times, disappeared about 1550 to be reintroduced in the nineteenth century.

5. Except for the period from the death of Mary II to that of William III, when the Stuart arms were, as shown here, surcharged with William's paternal arms of Nassau (St James Piccadilly: St Michael Paternoster Royal). In 1707 the royal arms were remarshalled as a result of the Act of Union with Scotland. St Sepulchre has a Hanoverian coat of arms.

6. Gerald Cobb, *London City Churches*, revised by Nicholas Redman (London, 1989), p. 107.

7. E. H. Freshfield, 'Sword Stands in the Churches of the City of London', *Archaeologia*, 54 (1894), pp. 41–58.

8. Most of the plaques were painted. One of the six at St Mary-at-Hill has enamelled plaques. Frequently the arms of one Lord Mayor would be overpainted with those of the next Lord Mayor to make a visit.

9. Paul Jeffery, 'The Great Screen of All Hallows-the-Great', *Transactions of the Ancient Monuments Society*, 37 (1993), pp. 157–64.

10. E. Tyrrell-Green, *Baptismal Fonts Classified and Illustrated* (London, 1928), p. 38.

11. Francis Bond, *Fonts and Font Covers* (London, 1985).

12. The finely-carved font cover at St Sepulchre, the gift of a parishioner, is also dated 1670.

13. G. K. Brandwood, *Archaeological Journal*, 147 (1990), pp. 420–36.

Notes to Chapter 13, Past Destructive, Future Uncertain

1. 21 George III, cap. 71; John Deacon, *The Old Lady of Threadneedle Street* (London, 1982), pp. 76–78.

2. The church was surrendered on 22 March 1831 and pulled down shortly after: see GL, MS 10968.

3. Michael Jerome Peel, *Bishop Tait and the City Churches, 1856–69* (London, 1992).

4. Report to Court of Common Council, Corporation of London, 1834, GL, FoPam 3523.

5. 23 and 24 Victoria, cap. 142.

6. 'The Proposed Demolition of Nineteen City Churches', Report to Council, LCC (1920); GL, SL 11.

7. Lord Phillimore, *City of London Churches Commission* (London, 1919); GL, FoPam 3072.

8. Passed by the Church Assembly on 18 November 1924 but rejected by Parliament in 1926. The Corporation petitioned for its rejection, GL, FoPam 69.

9. Lord Merriman, *The City Churches: Report of the Bishop of London's Commission*, September 1946.

10. Sir Denys Buckley, *Report of the Commission of Churches in the City of London, October 1970* (1971) GL, Pam 11656.

11. Lord Templeman, *City Churches Commission: Report to the Bishop* (London, 1994).

12. Paul Jeffery and Bruce Watson, 'The Templeman Report on London's Churches: Can Wren's Legacy Survive?', *London Archaeologist* (1994), pp. 184–88.

13. *A More Excellent Way*, Submission to the Bishop of London, St Andrew-by-the-Wardrobe and St James Garlickhythe, 17 November 1994.

Note to Chapter 14, Sir Christopher Wren: By Hooke and by Hawksmoor

1. Sir John Summerson, *Architecture in Britain, 1530–1830* (7th edn, London, 1983), p. 355.

Bibliography

Bernard Adams, *London Illustrated, 1604–1851* (London, 1983).

G. W. O. Addleshaw and Frederick Etchells, *The Architectural Setting of Anglican Worship* (London, 1948).

Thomas Allen, *The History and Antiquities of London, Westminster, Southwark and Parts Adjoining* (4 vols, London, 1828).

Colin Amery, *Wren's London* (Luton, 1988).

Frances Arnold-Foster, *Studies in Church Dedications, or England's Patron Saints* (London, 1899).

Walter G. Bell, *The Great Fire of London in 1666* (London, 1920).

——, *The Great Plague in London* (London, 1924).

John Betjeman, *The City of London Churches* (London, 1974).

Martin Biddle, *Daphne Hudson and Carolyn Heighway: The Future of London's Past*, Rescue Publication, 4 (London, 1973).

G. H. Birch, *London Churches of the XVII and XVIII Centuries* (London, 1896).

Francis Bond, *Fonts and Font Covers* (London, 1908).

Geoffrey K. Brandwood, 'Immersion Baptisteries in Anglican Churches', *Archaeological Journal*, 147 (1990), pp. 420–36.

Christopher N. L. Brooke and Gillian Keir, *London, 800–1216: The Shaping of the City* (London, 1975).

T. F. Bumpus, *Ancient London Churches* (London, 1923); a revised edition of *London Churches* (2 vols, London, 1908).

Bridget Cherry, 'John Pollexfen's House in Walbrook', in *English Architecture: Public and Private. Essays for Kerry Downes*, edited by John Bold and Edward Chaney (London and Rio Grande, OH, 1993), pp. 89–105.

B. F. L. Clarke, *Parish Churches of London* (London, 1966).

Charles Clarke, *Architectura Ecclesiastica Londini* (London, 1819).

John Clarke, *Saxon and Norman London* (London, 1989).

Gerald Cobb, *London City Churches* (London, 1977), revised edition by Nicholas Redman of Gerald Cobb, *The Old Churches of London* (London, 1941 and 1948).

Howard M. Colvin, *A Biographical Dictionary of British Architects, 1660–1840* (3rd edn, London and New Haven, 1995).

——, 'The Church of St Mary Aldermary and its Rebuilding after the Great Fire of London', *Architectural History*, 24 (1981), pp. 24–31.

J. Charles Cox and Alfred Harvey, *English Church Furniture* (London, 1907).

A. E. Daniell, *London City Churches* (London, 1895 and 1907).

John Deacon, 'The Story of St Christopher-le-Stocks', *The Old Lady of Threadneedle Street*, 52 (1982), pp. 76–78.

Kerry Downes, *Hawksmoor* (2nd edn, London, 1979).

——, *Sir Christopher Wren* [catalogue], The Whitechapel Art Gallery (London, 1982).

——, 'Sir Christopher Wren, Edward Woodroffe, J. H. Mansart and Architectural History', *Architectural History*, 37 (1994), pp. 37–67.

——, *Sir Christopher Wren: The Design of St Paul's Cathedral* (London, 1988)

——, *The Architecture of Wren* (London, New York, Toronto and Sydney, 1982).

Margaret Epinasse, *Robert Hooke* (London, 1956).

William FitzStephen, *Norman London, Including an Essay by Sir Frank Stenton* (London, 1990).

Edwin Freshfield, [published parochial records of] *St Margaret, Lothbury with St Christopher-le-Stocks and St Bartholomew-by-the-Exchange* (London, 1876); *St Stephen, Coleman Street* (London, 1887).

——, 'Sword Stands in the Churches of the City of London', *Archaeologia*, 54 (1984), pp. 41–58.

Viktor Fuerst, *The Architecture of Sir Christopher Wren* (London, 1956).

Walter H. Godfrey, *St Bride Fleet Street*, Survey of London Monograph, 15 (London, 1944).

George Godwin and John Britton, *The Churches of London* (2 vols, London, 1838).

William F. Grimes, *The Excavation of Roman and Mediaeval London* (London, 1968).

Peter Guillery, 'The Broadway Chapel, Westminster: A Forgotten Exemplar', *London Topographical Record*, 26 (1990), pp. 97–133.

Henry A. Harben, *A Dictionary of London* (London, 1918).

Robert H. Harrison, *St Edmund King and Martyr*, Ecclesiological Society (London, 1960).

Edward Hatton, *A New View of London* (2 vols, London, 1708).

William Herbert, *Londina Illustrata* (London, 1819–34).

——, *The History of St Michael Crooked Lane* (London, 1831).

Gordon Huelin, *The Pre-Fire City Churches* (London, 1968).

Paul Jeffery, 'Originals or Apprentice Copies? Some Recently Found Drawings for St Paul's Cathedral, All Saints, Oxford, and the City Churches', *Architectural History*, 35 (1992), pp. 118–39.

——, 'Originals or Apprentice Copies? A Postscript', *Architectural History*, 36 (1993), pp. 46–48.

——, *St Mary-at-Hill*, Ecclesiological Society (London, 1996).

——, *The Church of St Vedast Foster Lane*, Ecclesiological Society (London, 1989).

——, 'The Church That Never Was: Wren's St Mary and Other Projects for Lincoln's Inn Fields', *Architectural History*, 31 (1988), pp. 136–47.

——, 'The Great Screen of All Hallows-the-Great', *Transactions of the Ancient Monuments Society*, 37 (1993), pp. 157–64.

——, 'The Later History of St Martin Outwich, City of London', *London Journal*, 14 (1989), pp. 160–69.

——, '"The Lost Crace": Frederick Crace's Plans, Elevations and Sections of the Churches of London', *London Topographical Record*, 27 (1995), pp. 119–34.

——, 'The Parish Church of St Thomas the Apostle', *Ecclesiological Society Newsletter*, 38 (1993), not paginated.

——, 'Where Are They Now? Wren Drawings from the Bute Collection', *Society of Architectural Historians of Great Britain Newsletter*, 50 (1993), pp. 4–5.

Paul Jeffery and Bruce Watson, 'The Templeman Report on London's Churches: Can Wren's Legacy Survive?', *London Archaeologist* (1994), pp. 184–88.

Wilberforce Jenkinson, *London Churches before the Great Fire* (London, 1917).

Tony Johnson, 'Excavations at Christchurch, Newgate Street, 1973', *Transactions of the London and Middlesex Archaeological Society*, 25 (1974), pp. 220–34.

Tim Knox, 'Wren Drawings for London Churches in the British Architectural Library Drawings Collection', *Society of Architectural Historians of Great Britain Newsletter*, 51 (1994), pp. 5–6; 52 (1994), p. 5.

Jane Lang, *Rebuilding of St Paul's after the Great Fire of London* (London, New York, Oxford and Toronto, 1956).

James Leasor, *The Plague and the Fire* (London, 1962).

Henry Littlehales, *The Mediaeval Records of a London City Church* (St Mary-at-Hill) (London, 1904).

A. H. Mackmurdo, *Wren's City Churches* (Orpington, 1883).

William McMurray, *Records of Two City Parishes* (St Anne and St Agnes; and St John Zachary) (London, 1925).

William Maitland, *History of London* (London, 1739 and 1756).

James P. Malcolm, *Londinium Redivivum* (4 vols, London, 1803–7).

P. R. V. Marsden, *Roman London* (London, 1980).

——, *The Roman Forum Site in London* (London, 1987).

Ralph Merrifield, *The Roman City of London* (London, 1965).

Merriman, Lord, *The City Churches: Report of the Bishop of London's Commission* (London, 1946).

Thomas Milbourn, *The Church of St Mildred Poultry* (London, 1872).

Gustav Milne, *The Great Fire of London* (New Barnet, 1986).

Dewi Morgan, *The Phoenix of Fleet Street: 2000 Years of St Bride's* (London, 1973).

John Morris, *Londinium* (London, 1982).

T. B. Murray, *Chronicles of a City Church* (St Dunstan-in-the-East) (London, 1859).

W. Niven, *London City Churches Destroyed since AD 1800, or Now Threatened* (London, 1887).

Philip Norman, 'St Mary Aldermary', *St Paul's Ecclesiological Society*, 8 (1919), p. 148.

Sydney Perks, 'London Planning Schemes in 1666', *Royal Institution of British Architects Journal*, 27 (1920), pp. 467–70.

Nikolaus Pevsner, *The Buildings of England: London*, i, *The Cities of London and Westminster* (3rd edn, revised by Bridget Cherry, London, 1973).

Phillimore, Lord, *City of London Churches Commission* (London, 1919).

Samuel Pogge, *Fitz Stephen's Description of the City of London* (London, 1772).

James Ralph, *A Critical Review of the Public Buildings, Statues and Ornaments in and about London and Westminster* (London, 1736).

T. F. Reddaway, 'The Rebuilding of London after the Fire', *Town Planning Review*, 17 (1937), pp. 205–11, 271–79; 18 (1939), pp. 155–61.

——, *The Rebuilding of London after the Great Fire* (London, 1940; reprinted, 1951).

Herbert Reynolds, *The Churches of the City of London* (London, 1922).

Royal Commision on Historical Monuments, *London*, iv, *The City* (1929).

G. H. Salter, *A Watcher at the City Gate for Thirty-Eight Reigns* (St Sepulchre) (London, 1931 and 1956).

Eduard F. Seckler, *Wren and his Place in European Architecture* (New York, 1954).

Alastair Service, *The Architects of London* (London, 1979).

E. B. S. Shepherd, 'History of the Church of the Franciscans', *Archaeological Journal*, 59 (102), pp. 238–87.

E. E. F. Smith, *The Church of St Mary Abchurch*, Ecclesiological Society (London, 1959).

John Stow, *Survey of London* (London, 1598, 1603, 1633 and 1754). Stow's *Survey of London* was updated and adapted by a number of authors and book publishers, issuing 'Histories', 'Surveys' and similar compilations under a variety of names, some fictitious. These include John Strype, 1720; 'Robert Seymour' (John Mottley), 1734–35; Henry Chamberlain, 1770; John Noorthouck, 1773; Walter Harrison, 1775; William Thornton, 1784; W. J. Thoms, 1842; C. L. Kingsford, 1908; Henry Benjamin Wheatley, 1912, 1970.

John Summerson, 'Drawings for London Churches in the Bute Collection: A Catalogue', *Architectural History*, 13 (1970), pp. 41–42.

——, 'Drawings for the London City Churches', *Royal Institute of British Architects Journal*, 59 (1952), pp. 126–29.

——, *Sir Christopher Wren* (London, 1953).

Templeman, Lord, *City Churches Commission: Report to the Bishop* (London, 1994).

E. Tyrrell-Green, *Baptismal Fonts Classified and Illustrated* (London and Toronto, 1928).

Victoria County History, London, i (London, 1909), pp. 171–406.

Alan Vince, *Saxon London: An Archaeological Investigation* (London, 1990).

H. B. Walters, *London Churches at the Reformation* (London and New York, 1939).

A. J. B. West, *The Church and Parish of St Dunstan in the East* (London, 1930).

Margaret Whinney, *Wren* (London, 1971).

J. G. White, *Churches and Chapels of Old London* (London, 1901).

——, *History of the Ward of Walbrook* (St Stephen Walbrook) (London, 1904).

Christopher Wren, *Parentalia: Memoirs of the Family of the Wrens*, edited by Stephen Wren (London, 1750).

Wren Society, edited by A. T. Bolton and H. D. Hendry (20 vols, Oxford, 1924–43).

Nigel Yates, *Buildings, Faith and Worship: The Liturgical Arrangement of Anglican Churches, 1600–1900* (Oxford, 1991).

Elizabeth and Wayland Young, *London's Churches* (London, 1986)

Index

Illustrations are shown in bold type